D0977131

Cracking the Japanese Market

Cracking THE Japanese Market

Strategies for Success IN THE *New Global Economy*

JAMES C. MORGAN
J. JEFFREY MORGAN

THE FREE PRESS
A Division of Macmillan, Inc.
NEW YORK

Collier Macmillan Canada
TORONTO

Maxwell Macmillan International
NEW YORK OXFORD SINGAPORE SYDNEY

The Free Press
A Division of Macmillan, Inc.
866 Third Avenue, New York, N.Y. 10022

Collier Macmillan Canada, Inc.
1200 Eglinton Avenue East
Suite 200
Don Mills, Ontario M3C 3N1

Printed in the United States of America

printing number

1 2 3 4 5 6 7 8 9 10

Library of Congress Cataloging-in-Publication Data

Morgan, James C.
Cracking the Japanese market: strategies for success in the new global economy / James C. Morgan, J. Jeffrey Morgan.
p. cm.
Includes bibliographical references and index.
ISBN 0-02-921691-5
1. Marketing—Japan. 2. Industrial management—Japan. 3. Corporate culture—Japan. 4. Corporations, American—Japan. 5. Competition—Japan. 6. Competition—United States. 7. Japan—Economic conditions —1989- 8. Japan—Economic policy—1989- I. Morgan, J. Jeffrey. II. Title.
HF5415.12.J3M66 1991
658.8'0952—dc20 90-43895
CIP

To Becky Morgan, wife and Mother,
and all Applied Materials employees
who made this story possible

Contents

PART III
Succeeding in Japan

Acknowledgments

Cracking the Japanese Market was written with the goal of making you and your organization more successful in the Japanese market and, as a result, more successful in your domestic and global business. The book was developed to include critical information that we ourselves would have liked to have known as we made our original journeys and developed our businesses in the Japanese market.

Many deserve a thank you for their direct contribution or influence. This book was Jeff's idea, and he developed some of the initial manuscript based on his research while working at Mitsui & Co. in Japan and international sales in California. Encouragement for our collaboration came from Becky Morgan, wife and mother, who saw the potential of our joint effort. Credit should go to Dennis Hunter, who has worked to provide the mediums to illustrate many of the ideas that are being shared with you about Applied Materials. Tom Hayes knows Applied Materials well, and his writing greatly improved the communication of our ideas and the understandability of the material for those without extensive experience in Japan. Betty Moyles' detailed editing improved and expedited the authors' work. Thanks go to Applied Materials' many customers plus the Applied Materials' Japan employees and their president, Tetsuo Iwasaki, who provided the company the opportunity to build a Japanese business.

The following people also deserve thanks for their extensive reflections, review, and suggestions: Takeshi Uchida, Gary Robertson, Stephen Clayton, Bill Davidow, Ted Iwasaki, Jim Bagley, Valerie Disle, and, at The Free Press, Robert Wallace.

JAMES C. MORGAN J. JEFFREY MORGAN

Introduction

In one of San Francisco's many fine restaurants facing the bay, we sat and enjoyed lunch. Off in the distance, the bay waters glistened. It was a clear afternoon and the fog had yet to settle in. Between the city and Alcatraz Island, we saw a magnificant ship slowly slicing through the current heading west to the Pacific. The enormous grey superstructure proudly flew the colors of the United States Navy. Beyond the Golden Gate Bridge, we watched as another massive freighter gradually came into view. It was coming from the other direction, heading into port. This ship showed the Toyota Company colors and the Hinomaru flag of Japan. Instead of armaments, its cargo hold was stacked high with automobiles. Hundreds of cars to be sold to hundreds of American consumers. Just past the bridge, where the bay waters confront the tide, the two ships silently passed each other.

The scene is replayed every day in ports across the United States and provides an ironic metaphor for the relationship between the United States and Japan; both countries may share an ocean, but they are two different types of ships. And for the last half century, the two ships have headed in different directions with differing agendas, differing cargoes. And then the seas changed.

THE GROWING CHASM

It's a new world. Tensions between the United States and the Soviet Union have eased, Western Europe is unifying, and Eastern Europe is unwalling. A new era of global opportunity and prosperity is dawning. Yet America, at least economically, appears to be out of synch. Even amid the longest peace time economic boom in U.S. history, things seem awry. America is less certain about itself. It is a frame of mind that the nation is unaccustomed to, and it engenders confusion and, in some cases, anger. As a result, the hostilities and mistrust that were once aimed at ideological foes are now being directed to a friend, Japan. At issue is Japan's economic "miracle" measured against America's economic muddle. At the root of the debate is a disparity in the way the two countries have ordered national priorities and in the way national will and creative *geist* have been harnessed.

Since World War II, the United States and Japan have played distinctly different roles on the world's stage; the United States as policeman of the West to Japan's itinerant peddler from the East. And to those roles vast national resources have been dedicated. In the past decade alone, the United States spent trillions of dollars on strengthening its military. At the same time, the Japanese government and industrial complex invested heavily on business and wealth building. The United States has been a leader in global political affairs; Japan has been all but silent. While the United States provided Japan (and the rest of the world) with open sea lanes and an open market, Japan used those seas for trade while constructing structural impediments to its own markets. Throughout the immediate postwar years, Japan's barriers were tolerated (if even realized), principally because American businesses failed to take much interest in this marketplace. The United States market was more than enough to contend with, and besides, America reasoned, Japan needed some degree of latitude in order to rebuild itself.

It was not until the mid-1970s that America took serious notice of Japan's rise—when its economy began to explode and America's began to slide. And now, less than ten years from the close of the twentieth century, many Americans fear that the era of American leadership, politically, militarily, and particularly economically, also may be coming to a close. And some believe Japan's gain has come at America's expense. Looking at some of the raw facts, this sentiment is understandable.

- In five years, between 1981 and 1986, the United States reversed positions from the world's largest creditor nation to its largest debtor nation. Japan is now the largest creditor nation, and in the past ten years has built over a $400 billion trade surplus with the United States which continues to grow at a rate of about $50 billion per year.
- Today, no American bank is in the world's Top 10—a listing which has been dominated by Japan for many years (Citicorp ranks number twelve). Many bankers say they would not be surprised if Japan's aggressive moves in the United States captured 25 percent of the U.S. commercial loan market by the mid-1990s.[1]
- Presently, the total value of land in Japan is worth $14 trillion, twice the value of that in the United States, for a country only one-twenty-fifth the size.
- The world's largest securities brokerage firm is now Nomura Securities Co. Ltd., with over $430 billion in assets. Its 1988 net income of $1.7 billion on revenues of $8 billion was more than the profits of Merrill Lynch, Morgan Stanley, Paine Webber and Salomon Brothers combined.
- Machinery, which amounts to 25 percent of American exports to Japan, comprises 80 percent of Japanese exports to the United States. In electronics, Americans exported $5 billion to Japan in 1987, but imported $26 billion from it. Roughly nineteen of every twenty "memory chips" in American computers sold today are from Japan.[2]
- While devaluation of the U.S. dollar turned a deficit of $30 billion with Europe into a surplus, it had almost no effect on the balance of trade with Japan.
- David C. Lund, an economist with the U.S. Department of Commerce, estimates that the import share of what Americans buy has soared from 12.8 percent in 1970 to 22 percent in 1989. Import volume has doubled since 1982 from $244 billion to an estimated $475 billion in 1989.[3]

A disturbing indicator points to America's loss of control over its own economic destiny. In 1989, the U.S. Commerce Department reported that Japanese government agencies, corporations, and individuals held almost $400 billion in American assets—$200 billion in direct investment and $195.8 billion in bank loans, U.S. Treasury notes, and other securities. Doubling its direct investment from $98 billion the year before, Japan leapfrogged Britain as the largest foreign investor in the United States.[4] By some estimates Japanese-owned banks, with over 275 branches in California alone, now hold 25 percent of the state's banking assets, up from 10 percent seven years ago. If combined, their $93.4 billion in assets outweigh even the Bank of America's $83 billion. The U.S. government now relies on Japanese investors, mainly large insurance and savings companies, to finance as much as 30 percent of the annual budget deficit.[5] Japanese financial institutions have become such a powerful force in the United States today that some pundits wonder how long it will be before they seek to translate this clout into political influence. There is growing concern that the Japanese lobby in Washington may be enjoying an undue and growing influence on Congress. Others even argue that Japan's influence on the actions of the U.S. Treasury and Federal Reserve Board is already evident.

If today's statistics seem alarming, they are nothing compared to the implications of current trends. The long-term direction of key technologies and investment by American manufacturers point to a continued decline in the United States' competitive position. While Japanese industry's investment in research and development rose by nearly 20 percent in 1989, U.S. R&D investment on the aggregate declined. This trend alone indicates an erosion in the fundamental prospects for American competitiveness. Combined with high capital costs (the cost of raising investment money at a rate two to four times that of Japan) and a low rate of savings and investments, America's relative position will clearly worsen over time.

At its core, we believe the problem is not that Japanese companies have forged such a major presence in America, but that Americans and American companies do not have corresponding presence in Japan, either in direct holdings and operations or in the ability to generate real revenues from exports to the Japanese market. This failing has already had wide ramifications, impacting American competitiveness throughout the global arena. The popular mythology regarding America's relative absence in Japan is that the market is "closed," that pervasive trade barriers created by a conspiracy of government and big business have kept American companies out. The problem is not that simple. The solutions will not be either. Yes, Japan has historically thrown up ramparts to outside competitors. Yes, at various times these obstacles have been institutional as well as informal. But today most of the formal restrictions have been legislated away. Even before they were, many American businesses failed to succeed in Japan not because the markets were inaccessible, but because most American companies were inattentive. America simply failed to compete. Now, as America begins soul-searching for a cure to its economic ills, it is easy to deal in recriminations and complaints about the structure of Japan's market and the inequitable trade policies the Japanese have pursued. But this debate skirts the real issues at hand. The Japanese know it, and deep down most American business people know it as well. It is not only a macro-economic problem of savings and budget deficits. Its roots are microeconomic in education, in industrial companies, in our financial institutions and in our legal system. Japan and what it represents can no longer be ignored. Changes in American definitions of competitiveness will have to be made.

We are positive about the prospects for an America committed to renewal. Japan's journey to economic stardom began forty-five years ago in the rubble of destruction following World War II. America begins its journey to economic renaissance in far better shape. However, American business and the American people must recognize the new realities. It must recognize what it takes to compete against Japan, and execute its course based on this knowledge. We believe this journey begins with the will to compete, a will borne of a commitment to survival no less intense than that mustered by the Japanese in the late 1940s and 1950s—a time when Japan's very survival was in no way assured.

WHY AMERICA MUST COMPETE IN JAPAN

Thirty years ago, "Made in Japan" meant cheaply made. Even a decade ago, the Japanese were widely perceived as copycats, capable only of using their cheaper labor and lower cost of capital to produce inexpensive knock-offs of American products. Even more recently, American industry viewed Japan as too small a market to dedicate the enormous time and energy that was required to make headway. All that has changed. On an absolute basis, Japan now has the second largest and fastest growing economy in the world. At $2.85 trillion, its economy constitutes over 10 percent of the world's combined GNP. Japan has become extremely rich, owing to its success in exports, skyrocketing domestic real estate and stock prices, and the artificially strong yen.

More important than today's figures, at an unrelenting growth rate of 5 to 6 percent a year, Japan promises to become an even larger economic force in the future. For many companies, that means that even a relatively small marketshare in Japan can translate into a very large sales volume. For instance, a 4 percent share in a segment of the computer market in Japan could be equivalent in dollar terms to a marketshare of over 20 percent in West Germany, 30 percent in France, and more than 40 percent in Switzerland. Every American company must consider Japan a genuine market opportunity.

The Japanese no longer need to copy anybody. Many of the most important industrial developments and competitive forces are now originating in Japan—in telecommunications, semiconductors, consumer electronics, automobiles and surface transportation equipment, robotics, and manufacturing and process industries, and even finance and fashion design. If for no other reason, American companies must compete in Japan as a means of sourcing new ideas and technologies. And when one considers the dramatic changes taking place within Japan itself, the reasons to compete inside the market become even more compelling.

With the death of Emperor Hirohito in early 1989, the war-scarred *Showa* period of "everlasting peace" came to a close in Japan. The new *Heisei* era of "enduring peace and opportunity" may well prove to be a major turning point in Japanese history and in Japan's relations with the world. Historically, the Japanese regard the beginning of a new emperor's reign as an opportunity for serious, society-wide introspection and a commitment to renewal. This promises to result in many changes in Japanese society, politics, and commerce. The year 1989 was also a watershed of change in other ways. With the fall of prime ministers Takeshita and Uno, and a sharp decline in the popularity of the ruling Liberal Democratic Party (LDP), a new generation of younger, postwar leaders, including women, is gaining power. In 1989 the "father" of the Japanese electronics industry, Shinsuke Matsushita, founder of Matsushita Corporation, passed away. With him was lost the symbol of an era of Japanese commerce based on discipline, sacrifice, manufacturing excellence, adaptation of foreign technology, and an export-led economy. The new political leaders and industrialists may not be as conservative and doctrinaire as their predecessors and may be more prone to reach out and join the rest of the world.

In some ways, Japan is opening up to the rest of the world. U.S. and European pressure on Japan is starting to pay off. If for no other reason than to expand the markets for its goods and services, Japan is slowly realizing it also must take in its share of manufactured products, bear a responsibility for supporting other economies, and open its doors to its trading partners. Almost every formal tariff or quota restriction has come down, and major changes are taking place in the distribution structure, opening the door for more imports. Liberalization is taking place in almost every industry, from telecommunications and finance, to the railroads and agriculture. Japanese consumers themselves are pushing for many of the market reforms, having grown weary and impatient with the limitations on personal freedom and choice caused by the domination of conglomerates and entrenched distribution systems. Its *nouveau riche* consumers are now demanding the same benefits, products, and lifestyles available in other industrialized countries. More and more, the tastes of Japanese consumers are becoming internationalized. Japanese companies also want change. Like consumers, fewer companies are willing to pay a premium for products simply because they are Japanese-made. More than ever, Japanese companies realize they need global partners to broaden their sales networks and give them greater inroads into new markets in the Americas, Europe, and throughout Asia. The opportunities for American business to succeed with Japan have never been greater.

Owing to this growing promise, American companies not participating as insiders in Japan today are losing an opportunity to get in on the ground floor of a stunning metamorphosis. There are big opportunities in numerous untapped sectors of the Japanese economy, especially in services, advanced technologies like biotechnology and leading-edge pharmaceuticals, leisure and resort businesses, specialty foods, and new modes of distribution. In these and scores of other industries, Japan has far less experience than its Western counterparts. And while some markets may be small today, the potential is enormous.

We see genuine change also taking place in America, with an increased emphasis on quality, manufacturing excellence, customer service, vendor partnering, and a new orientation to overseas markets, especially Japan and all of Asia. There is increasing emphasis on Japan as an integral factor in American companies' corporate strategies, and growing consensus that success in Japan will be critical to success elsewhere in the world. While many companies continue to bemoan the impediments to Japan's markets—or worse, deny Japan ascendency—those companies that have made the effort and invested the time in Japan are today making headway and profits.

THE TOOLS TO COMPETE

Many books have been published about Japan, its history, people, and markets. Numerous recently published books have focused upon the

Japanese threat, and chronicled how and why the United States has lost its edge to Japan. This book is different. Its emphasis is on the role of the individual company in the new global economy, an economy created largely by Japan. Certainly, global trade is more complex than ever, but in our view business still boils down to a head-to-head contest between individual companies and products. Squaring off against a giant Japanese competitor—in Japan—is not easy, but it can be done. The Japanese market is not impenetrable. We know American companies can succeed by building the right products and by employing the right strategies for Japan's unique market. Our goal is to show why *now* is the best time to do business in Japan, and by extension, the rest of the world.

It is our hope that through this book the reader will come to understand the Japanese market and its business practices, and will begin the process of becoming more expert in the strategies of building a Japanese business. The lessons we provide are based largely upon our actual experiences with sales and marketing in Japan. Jim Morgan is chairman of Applied Materials, a half-billion dollar semiconductor equipment company which does about 40 percent of its business in Japan. Jeff Morgan has worked in Tokyo on "the inside" at Mitsui & Co., Japan's oldest trading conglomerate, and in international business development for Sun Microsystems, a rising star in Japan's advanced computer market, and today is president of RAD Technologies, a developer and distributor of computer software for the international marketplace, particularly Japan and the Far East.

In the first section of this book, we examine traditional and potential obstacles in Japan—cultural influences on the Japanese people, their companies, the nuances in these markets and the unique marketing strategies the Japanese employ. In the second section, we look at ways to navigate the obstacles and penetrate Japan's lucrative markets. We explore some of the proven strategies used by successful global companies to meet the Japanese challenge at home and abroad. The third section provides an action plan for cracking the Japanese market; a framework for structural and attitudinal change within a company or organization and a guide for execution.

We believe American businesses can and must compete and succeed in Japan. First, because the market is much too large and opportunity-filled to ignore any longer. And secondly, because, by doing business with the Japanese in Japan, companies simply become better organizations, better marketeers and better able to meet the requirements of the new global markets. We believe participation and success in Japan will permit American businesses to gain new strengths—in management, in technological development, in quality control and production, in product design, and in new ways to satisfy customer needs. These strengths will lead to global success for corporations and an economic renaissance which will benefit all nations and peoples of the world.

PART

I

Islands in the Mist

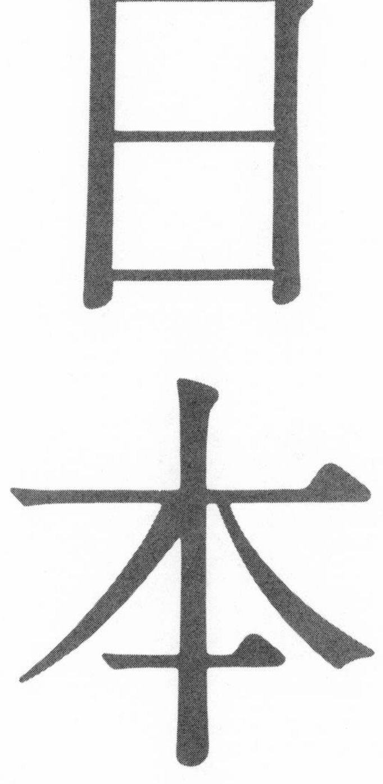

1

Sunrise over the Pacific

The Japanese Challenge

When two cultures collide is the only time true suffering exists.

HERMAN HESSE

You can pick up a newspaper in virtually any community in America today and read the same story. American business is in crisis: a major company retreats from a competitive industry, another lays off thousands of employees, still another is acquired by a foreign conglomerate. Nearby, other articles tell a different story: a new electronic product from Japan hits American shores, a Japanese company now dominates a critical market, another has passed its U.S. competitors in the development of a new technology. The disparity between the two economies is no longer the stuff of drab journals; it makes headlines from Wall Street to Main Street. And Americans have grown understandably concerned. It can be argued that at no time in its history has the United States faced any greater challenge than that now being posed by Japan. More potent than any military threat or contrary political ideology, Japan's economic juggernaut casts a long shadow over America's capability to remain a global leader in the next century.

That they now pose a threat to the United States is not to say that the Japanese are doing anything sinister, or even fundamentally wrong. The Japanese industrial machine is working; its greatest "sin" is that it is successful. And its success tells us something about how global business must be conducted today. In this sense, the Japanese should no more be faulted for their ability to read the shifting tides of world trade than the Phoenicians or the Dutch could be faulted for the advancements they precipitated in their time. In the long run, the Japanese have discovered new global trade routes and strategies that history will look back upon favorably. In the short run, the fallout of these discoveries is painful to the United States. If fault is to be meted out, it is likely that America would take the lion's share. A steady diet of hubris over the last four decades kept American business and government from seeing the changes taking place in the world. During the immediate post-World War II years, America's home markets were large, and growing. And those American businesses that bothered to look beyond home shores virtually had the world to themselves. Few other countries in the then-industrialized world had escaped the ravages of the war. For American businesses, selling to the global marketplace was like "shooting fish in a barrel." It was not a very competitive world, and Americans learned how *not* to compete.

The Japanese have taught us that everything has changed. Industrialization is worldwide and trade is now a matter of national priority in most countries. Competition is now intense in every market, with the toughest competitors of all coming from Asia. Yet, despite these changes, America has been late in developing an appropriate response. The Japanese, on the other hand, have been quick to seize the opportunities of change.

THE JAPANESE MONEY MACHINE

How did one nation no larger than the state of California and endowed with few natural resources accumulate so much wealth in such a short period of time? While the answer is complex, hard work and dedication should not be discounted. And as we discuss in Chapter 3, these attributes were contributing factors. In its simplest terms, the Japanese economic miracle came about by way of a coordinated effort between government and industry to forge a national strategy of economic growth. World trade was the linchpin of this program, advantageous trade was its hallmark. What do we mean by advantageous trade? Using 1989 as an example, Japan shipped $80 billion worth of goods to the United States, while the United States exported only $35 billion to Japan. This is analogous to the United States spending three American dollars on Japanese goods for every one dollar spent by Japan on American goods. That delta, $45 billion, benefits the entire Japanese society by improving the standard of living, and providing the means

Figure 1.1. United States and Japan: Debtor and Creditor Nations

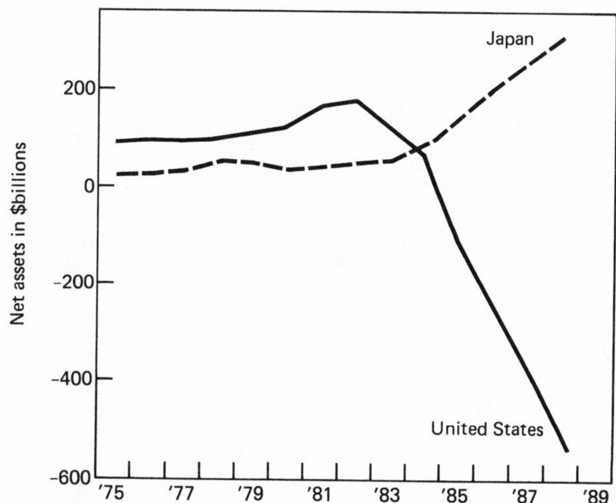

SOURCES: U.S. Department of Commerce and Japanese Ministry of Finance.

to invest for greater economic growth. As a result of trade deficits, poor U.S. fiscal policy, and a low savings rate, we are in the weak position so clearly shown in Figure 1.1.

A policy of aggressive trade by Japan has been accompanied by a real effort to limit the need for imports—a sort of economic self-sufficiency doctrine. In general, the Japanese have succeeded in limiting imports to only necessary items, items they either could not or would not produce for themselves. This strategy was based on two considerations. The first was a lack of currency after the war. Japan looked to husband its limited currency by making as many repeatable items as possible themselves, selling them to the world, then using the cash it received to purchase commodities essential to the commonwealth, like timber, fuel, and technology. The second motive was a need to build the domestic economy by developing the skill level of the people and the manufacturing capability of the nation generally. By focusing on the rudiments of manufacturing, by producing initially simple, yet progressively more complex products, Japan was preparing for the day when it could take on the best the world had to offer. Today, Japan imports fewer manufactured goods per capita than any other industrialized nation. While manufactured goods comprise about 75 percent of U.S. and European nations' imports, they only constitute 50 percent of Japan's imports. In 1988, Japan imported $750 worth of goods per cap-

Figure 1.2. U.S. Declining Worldwide Market Shares in Key Industry Segments, 1978 to 1988

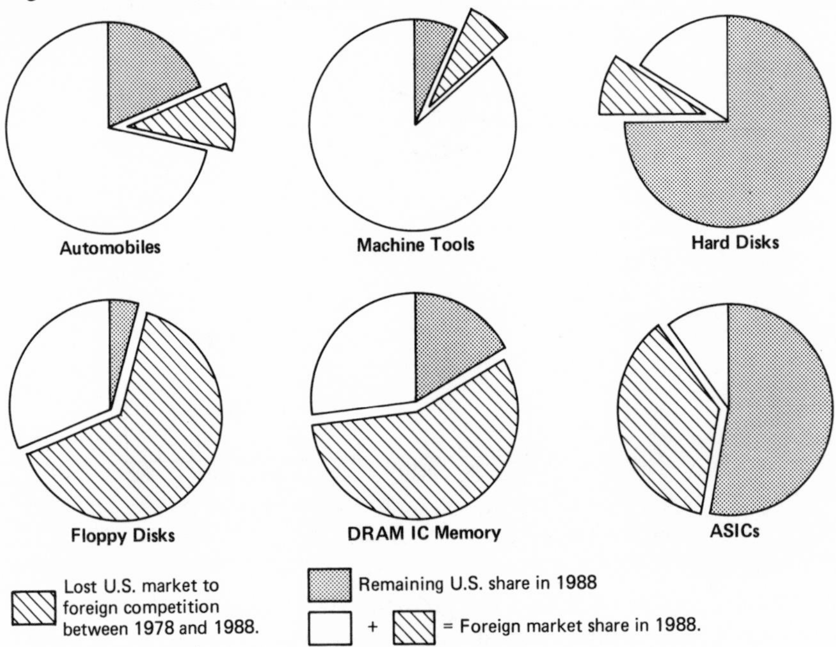

SOURCE: Joel Dreyfuss, "Getting High-Tech Back on Track," *Fortune* (January 1, 1990), p. 74. © 1990 The Time Inc. Magazine Company. All rights reserved.

ita, exactly half the corresponding figure for the United States and far lower than Britain's $2,700 and West Germany's $3,000.[1] As a rule, the Japanese only import manufactured goods until they develop a capability to satisfy the need themselves.

In four key industrial areas, the United States has accrued dramatic trade deficits in just the past five years. Looking at Figure 1.2, one can't help but notice the steep decline in America's positions, in a number of critical growth markets. In automobiles, consumer electronics, machine tools, and electronics, the United States is mounting multibillion dollar trade deficits which continue to grow only bigger. The rate of change is what is most frightening. Through dogged determination and coordinated industrial policies and by limiting competition from foreign companies (particularly in young industries), Japan has successfully built the basis for self-sustaining economic growth. Funds generated through exports are reinvested in plants and equipment, in training, in research and development, and in building a distribution infrastructure. With the proceeds from their export imbalance and the high yen, the Japanese are pioneering new technologies and setting the stage for a new era of growth in the twenty-first century.

INNOVATORS, NOT IMITATORS

For years, American business wrote off the Japanese challenge as inconsequential. To its industrialists, the Japanese were merely capable of reverse engineering American technology and producing cheap copies. In early stages of its economic rebirth, this may have been true. Now, Japan is leading the way in improving existing technologies and pioneering new ones. Even in America's strong-suit industries, electronics and computers, the Japanese are steadily gaining ground and likely will soon pass the United States in a number of key technology fields. A Ministry of International Trade and Industry (MITI) study concluded in 1989 year that Japan is now at least on par with the United States in ten high technology areas: computer-aided design and computer-aided manufacturing (CAD/CAM), communication satellites, mid-range computers, copiers, laser printers, microprocessors, optomagnetic disks, IC memories, and superconductive materials.[2] The U.S. Department of Defense estimates that America is now lagging behind Japan in a number of technologies critical to its national security, including biotechnology, development of applications for gallium arsenide, high-powered microwaves, integrated optics, machine intelligence and robotics, microchips, pulsed power and superconductors. In new technology development, Japan is now becoming the world leader.

This is because Japan is out in front in funding new technology development, in preparing its workforce for business in these and other new technologies, and in developing its capability to compete across the globe. The United States spent 1.9 percent of its gross national product on civilian R&D in 1985, compared with Germany's 2.4 percent and Japan's 2.5 percent. Japan spent $34 billion on basic research in 1984, the same sum per capita as the United States, but while America spent $96 billion on R&D, nearly one-third of that money was going toward defense.

Japan's primary and secondary educational system is probably the most comprehensive and most disciplined in the world. While American children attend school an average of 175 days per year, Japanese students have a 240-day school year. In the area of higher education, while lacking the strong university system which exists in the United

States, the curriculum is equally rigorous, and Japan is graduating 75,000 engineers per year, 3,000 more than the United States, from a university population one-fifth the size. And the Japanese hunger for knowledge is not limited to its shores. Japan sends over 24,000 students to the United States, more than the total of all foreign students in Japan, while under 1,000 American students attended Japanese universities last year.[3]

In 1989, 56,000 Japanese researchers went overseas, half of those to the United States, while only 3,633 American researchers went to Japan. At the U.S. National Institutes of Health alone, there are nearly 400 Japanese scientists as health sciences is a key field for the future of Japan's aging population. This is the case throughout America's research establishment. The largest Japanese companies are sponsoring Japanese scholars in America and American professors in Japan in order to gain access to the most advanced technologies in their early stages of development. Quoted in a *Wall Street Journal* article appropriately titled, "Harvesting the American Mind," Shoji Kumagai, general manager of technology development at Sumitomo Corporation, said, "Ten years ago, it was enough to latch onto something 100 percent proven; today we have to grab it at the idea stage."[4] And whether it is through grants for university professors or by funding small companies eager to make technology deals for cash, Japanese companies with deep pockets are taking advantage of America's open system of education and idea exchange.

In 1988, Japanese individuals and companies received 16,158 or 21 percent of the patents issued in the United States, in the process flooding the U.S. Patent Office with tens of thousands of applications. Of the top five companies filing for American patents, a good barometer of creative renewal, only one is an American company (there are only two U.S. firms in the top ten). The Japanese patent process, by comparison, limits the issuance of patents to foreigners. There, only 10 percent of all patents are foreign, versus 48 percent in the United States, 56 percent in West Germany, 71 percent in Britain, and 78 percent in France. Only this year did the Japanese government acquiesce and accept a 1960 patent request made by Texas Instruments for invention of the integrated circuit.

In Japan, the issuance of patents has increased 350 percent in the last twenty years; in the same time period they have fallen in the United States by 10 percent (see Table 1.1). In 1988, foreign investors received 48 percent of the 77,924 patents issued in this country, a proportion that has been rising steadily for 25 years. In 1963, the share was only

Table 1.1
Top Recipients of U.S. Patents in 1978 and 1988

1978			*1988*		
1. General Electric	U.S.	820	1. Hitachi	Japan	907
2. Westinghouse	U.S.	488	2. Toshiba	Japan	750
3. IBM	U.S.	449	3. Canon	Japan	723
4. Bayer	W.G.	434	4. General Electric	U.S.	690
5. RCA	U.S.	423	5. Fuji Photo Film	Japan	589

SOURCE: Intellectual Property Owners, Inc.; reprinted from *New York Times*, "Foreign Push for U.S. Patents" (June 4, 1989). Copyright © 1989 by The New York Times Company. Reprinted by permission.

18.6 percent and in 1974, some 25 percent. The U.S. Patent and Trademark Office reported that Japanese applicants received 16,158 American patents in 1988, or 21 percent of the total, more than double the 6,352 or 9 percent in 1975.[5]

LOSING THE BUILDING BLOCKS

For all intents and purposes, Japan is now equal in electronics production with the United States. According to electronics industry analyst Dataquest, in 1988 Japan produced $250 billion worth of electronic goods—everything from computers to copiers, facsimile machines to mobile phones. The United States, with twice as large an economy, produced $262.8 billion. At the beginning of the 1980s, the United States exported $27 billion more in computers than it imported. By 1988, the United States imported $4 billion more in computers than it exported. And because Japan's computer industry is dominated by the same companies that control the semiconductor and component (disk drives, monitors, ICs) markets, American and European computer manufacturers have become dangerously dependent on components from their Japanese competitors.

But Japanese gains in electronics technology are more significant than the loss of just another industry by the United States. America is in danger of losing its component base and foundation for competing in the so-called Information Age. For every great leap forward made in technology, there exist fundamental building blocks. In today's economy, these building blocks of technology and manufacturing skill provide the basic electronic and mechanical components, and the production equipment used to build more complex systems. Without the capability to competitively manufacture these components at home,

America's long-term tax base and job-creation capabilities are being gradually diminished and its defense capabilities compromised. In semiconductors, the tiny electronic miracles that provide the heartbeat and brains for tens of thousands of products, America has perilously lost market share to the Japanese. Today, over half the world's merchant semiconductor production is controlled by Japan.

In areas where the United States continues to lead Japan, such as engineering workstations, the picture is murky. While Hewlett-Packard, Apple Computer, Sun Microsystems, Digital Equipment Corporation, and IBM compete for the title "market leader," (see Figure 1.3) almost all get their system components from Japan. Color monitors come from Sony, dynamic random access memory chips (DRAMs) from Toshiba, high-capacity disk drives from Fujitsu, and even the central processing chips themselves are coming from Japan. In laptop or portable computers, Toshiba, NEC, and Sanyo (sold by Zenith) led the hottest growing market segment in 1988. Only one American company, GRID Systems, a small start-up which was acquired by Tandy Corporation, has a position in the race against Japan's largest companies. And the majority of GRID's own components are sourced from Japan—flat panel displays, VLSI, and memory. For many of these systems, half their value is made up of Japanese components. The net result is that American companies are not technology developers in their own right,

Figure 1.3. U.S. Computer Company Dependence on Japanese Components

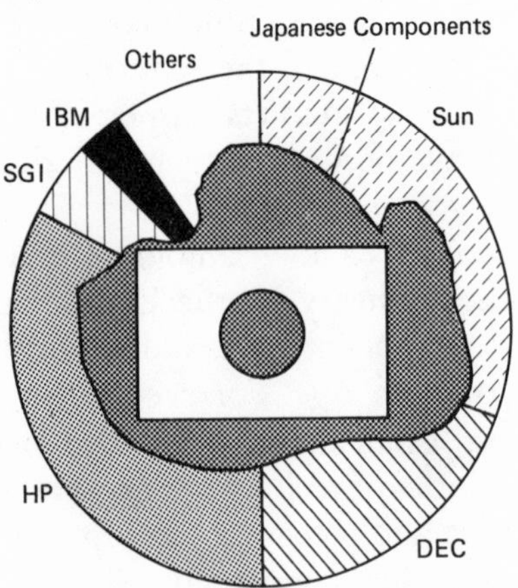

but systems integrators and distributors of Japanese components and systems.

Some economists argue that it makes no difference where products are developed and manufactured. The consumer benefits, they say, from purchasing from the lowest cost source regardless of the nation of origin. But we see some technologies as a different matter. High-technology production provides benefits to society far beyond the end products themselves. Participating in the development and manufacturing of technology goods builds skills and capabilities that can, in turn, lead to new products to serve new markets in a self-perpetuating, regenerative cycle. In the way that U.S. investment in defense and the space program in the 1960s stimulated private-sector industry growth in semiconductors, lasers, satellites, telecommunications, and miniaturization, the commercial electronics industry now leads the way in advancing technology. These advancements broaden the U.S. economy, provide tax revenue, create jobs, produce new products and services, and raise the nation's overall capability to meet the needs of the twenty-first century.

Japan's strategy in electronics is not new, and can be seen in scores of other industries. After gaining leadership in the component base, the Japanese methodically move from this platform to build entire systems. In the easily differentiated stages of market growth, once the standards have been set and the market becomes large and begins to mature, Japan's huge, vertically integrated manufacturers can begin to ramp up for supplying the second part of the growth curve having never borne the R&D and market education costs of the pacesetters. In VCRs, copiers, and supercomputers, the Japanese government and industry have targeted and succeeded. New areas, like data bases, telecommunications, biotechnology, and engineering workstations, now constitute Japan's strategic industries for the 1990s.

It is a dilemma American companies have created for themselves. On one hand, without the Japanese as sources of high-quality components, the hottest American companies could not have grown so fast. Highly successful American companies like Compaq, Sun Microsystems, and Apple Computer would not have been able to provide the necessary range of technology or cost-effective components and subsystems they needed to fuel rapid growth without the help of Japan's mammoth partners. Yet, this Faustian drama means that American companies may well be making a pact with self-destruction. The almost wanton substitution of Japanese, Taiwanese, and other foreign components is hollowing out the very core of the U.S. electronics industry, and its ability to research, design, develop, and continuously improve manufacturing skills. With no domestic subcontractors, American businesses will be forced to look overseas for its advanced products' essential parts. From this position of vulnerability, there will be little defense as foreign suppliers move to higher levels of value-added manufacturing based on what they have learned from supplying components to their U.S. customers.

And what about American defense considerations? The loss of a viable component base is a clear and present danger to America's ability to protect itself in the age of advanced military systems. In the book *The Japan That Can Say 'No'*, leading Japanese politician Shintaro Ishihara sounds a warning that America's dependence on Japanese memory chips may come back to haunt us: "If Japan sold chips to the Soviet Union and stopped selling them to the United States, this would upset the entire military balance."[6] Clearly, the implications of reliance on foreign semiconductors in a world where semiconductors have become so fundamental to national defense and commerce are numerous and foreboding. Owing to this growing value—both in revenue-generated terms and as a precursor to more value-added manufacturing—virtually every industrialized country today is working hard to develop and maintain a domestic semiconductor capability. Only the United States seems to be retreating from this critical technology.

SYMPTOMS OF A LARGER MALAISE

As substantial as they are, statistics understate the enormity of the real challenge facing America. A huge federal deficit, coupled with an enormous trade deficit, threatens the very core of the American economy. The impact can be seen in areas of production, employment, and other key economic indices. In numerous areas of investment and finance, industry, research and education, America and Europe now trail Japan. Every hour of every working day, American businesses are being challenged by corporations that are not only the biggest and the best in the world, but which are learning, improving and globalizing at a faster rate, creating still wider gaps in competitiveness. These realities make old ways of doing business outmoded. The American government's regulator stance for a free market economy is not shared by other countries of the world which are increasingly viewing trade as a national priority and resource. It is time for America to understand that the world has changed and that, if it does not respond to these changes, it risks losing the very economic foundation which made it a world leader. Americans who consider a national industrial strategy as anathema fail to see that America already has an industrial strategy. Everything the government influences in some way, from the tax structure to the cost of capital to the infrastructure and transportation system, to the education and legal system, constitutes an industrial policy. The problem is, the American industrial policy is not working. It needs to be fixed.

The correlation between competitiveness, investment in plant and equipment, production capability, and standard of living has not yet hit home for most Americans. It must be more widely understood that America's economic future depends on its competitiveness in international trade. Today, almost one-fifth of American industrial production is exported and fully 70 percent of the goods produced compete with merchandise from abroad. America is no longer a domestic economy, and the post-industrial age will be dominated by the demands of overseas trade. If drastic changes are not made with respect to America's ability to trade overseas—to deal effectively with the new global realities posed by Japan and other nations of Asia and Europe—the future will not be benign. As economist Lester Thurow has written, if changes are not made, by the end of the twentieth century Americans "will have become the workers for the rest of the world, while the rest of the world will have become the owners of America."[7]

And the battle is not just over economic supremacy. Owing to its enormous deficits in trade and government accounts, the United States is rapidly ceding worldwide political leadership to Japan. Declining contributions to foreign assistance programs and financing for the Import-Export Bank have raised Japan's potency as a political force in the world. While the United States funds a war machine for military leverage in global political affairs, the Japanese are proving that diplomatic power is increasingly a function of spending power. America's relegation to the world's largest creditor nation will have grave long-term impacts on its influence in Southeast Asia and other corners of the Third World which are highly dependent on foreign aid—aid America may no longer be able to afford. Japan now leads the world in giving foreign aid and plans to cycle $60 billion back into developing countries during the next five years. This investment—which is focused on economic rather than political objectives—should guarantee future business for Japanese companies in these regions in construction, large infrastructure projects, and natural resource development. And with these strengthened ties comes growing influence.

The fact is, global competition is only going to become more intense, particularly as American and Japanese business begin to square off in

Europe and other emerging markets. Japanese companies are ready to succeed. They are now running at peak efficiency at home and building strong local bases of operations in most U.S. and European markets, and even more aggressively in Asia. These new overseas bases include consolidated headquarters, sprawling manufacturing complexes, world-class, globally aware management, and thousands of local employees in each country. Building capability as a local player will bring even stronger and more sustainable growth over the remote, export-based economy that got Japan this far.

The shape of today's global economy is a study in contrasts; the world's two leading economic powers reached their positions from two entirely different routes. Americans have historically been makers, the Japanese traders. The Japanese have, however, learned to manufacture and continue to improve. The Americans have not, on the other hand, learned to trade competitively with the world. The Japanese challenge notwithstanding, the trade problem is an American problem. The United States has no one else to blame for its declining fortunes, nor should it. It is only now, with Japan's growing dominance becoming apparent, that Americans have come to see the changes which have taken place, and continue to take place, in the world. What makes the Japanese challenge all the more troubling is the growing realization that it cannot be adequately answered without making profound changes in the national sensibilities that have always been uniquely American. The broad scope of the Japanese challenge is testing principles that are deeply woven into the American character and way of life. Called into question are America's values, the organization of its economy, and even its system of governance. Yet, in some ways, Japan's ascendency is fortunate. As John Young, president and CEO of Hewlett-Packard, has noted, America has needed "another Sputnik" to galvanize our national will. We don't have to look far to see that the Japanese challenge is off the launching pad. The key to America's response must begin with greater awareness and understanding of the similarities and differences between the two nations and, indeed, the two worlds. That's where we begin.

2

The Japanese Way

Origins of a Merchant Nation

It is impossible to fully understand the Japanese economic machine without first understanding the society that spawned it. The birth of modern Japan has deep-seeded cultural origins. Dating back some two thousand years, the ways of the Japanese provide a foundation of continuity that is the basis for their resiliency and adaptability in modern times. Over the millennium, the roots that cleave the Japanese people to their tiny island nation have evolved much, but changed little. Many of the traditions and business values have changed only slightly since the feudal days of the Tokugawa Shogunate. Japan is a culture where human relations and preservation of harmony are the most important elements of society. A combination of history and customs, geography and climate, religion and philosophy, and what some refer to as the "atmospheric pressure" of everyday living have each come together to make the people of this small archipelago unique. And it is their unique sense of identity and destiny which gives their industrial machine its potency. Gaining an insight into these influences is a key first step to succeeding in the Japanese market.

NIHONJINRON

If Japanese society is an unbending stream, there are many tributaries. Japanese life represents an accretion of thousands of years of history and customs which define how one treats peers, inferiors and superiors, children and elders, and in the business arena, customers, suppliers, and co-workers. Among the Japanese, there exists an inherent respect for institutions and government, for the rules of etiquette and service, for social functions and their rituals of business. The Japanese believe they are, indeed, on a "different wavelength." If so, it is a frequency which springs from their unique sense of self, history, and culture and their need for harmony and balance in a crowded, busy world. As one Japanese executive puts it, "Because Japan has been traditionally crowded and the inhabitants of the little islands have been unable to claim a vast territory of individual freedom, Japanese are forced to share most of the limited space with each other to live peacefully, thereby developing common but unseen criteria of behavior, which become the "air" for everybody to breathe. This air has an atmospheric pressure under which people are homogenized by internal frictions of daily activities, precipitated and crystallized into the tradition of society."[1]

The Japanese Way, as a set of cultural touchstones, has long eluded foreigners. And for good reason. The Japanese are very protective of their culture, very conservative with respect to outside encroachment. The Japanese are as fascinated as anyone with their own uniqueness and offer a set of theories on their national origin called *Nihonjinron,* which attempt to define why they are different from other people. A key is community. *Ningen kankei,* human relations, is at the heart of the society which is Japan. Commonality is a large component of ningen kankei. It is therefore not surprising that the history of common experiences or associations is also the foundation of business dealings in Japan: a shared childhood, high school or college classmates, growing up in the same neighborhood, hometown or prefecture, working in the same company or group, or being in the same sports club are all bonding elements. These ties are essential in building business relationships in Japan, and few foreigners can share them. Due to its distinctive ways and emphasis on homogeneity, the Japanese do not suffer *gaijin,* or foreigners, gladly. Their distinctive ways are a source of pride and a font of national strength, and form a wall of exclusivity and segregation. Hegemony is vital to holding the center firm. For instance, interracial marriages are frowned upon and are rare. Westernization is not seen as a positive trend; it is a threat to the age-old fibers that bind the society. This is not to say that Japan today is not influenced by Western ways. It is, but outside ideas are processed and amended by Japanese society to work within the existing boundaries.

This national pride in a pure, self-perceived superior race is in obvious conflict with the American "melting pot." Japan's striving for purity is at the opposite pole from the U.S. idea of open doors and diversity as strength. To this day, Japan remains relatively closed to immigration from outside countries. And while it is possible for an immigrant to become a citizen, the point is why would anyone want to. As the saying goes, you can gain Japanese citizenship but you will never be Japanese. The underlying feeling that you as a foreigner can never become "one of us," and therefore trusted and loyal, has a negative impact on the ability of foreigners to build strong business and personal relations with the Japanese.

POOR ISLAND MENTALITY

With all their emphasis on superiority and uniqueness, the Japanese paradoxically have an inferiority complex. This is probably because the Japanese know their economic house is forever on shaky ground—literally. Japan is eternally at nature's mercy, vulnerable to the sea that surrounds it, to earthquakes of the soil beneath it, and a real shortage of raw materials, particularly food and fuel. Surrounded by politically unfriendly oceans, and not nearly as broad-based economically as the United States and Canada, or the European Community of nations, a period of extended isolation could easily be Japan's undoing. It has been predicted that in the event Japan was cut off from the world trading system, the country would be without food or fuel within only two months. Therefore, the Japanese hedge their bets against the future every day. A book entitled *Nihon Chibotsu* (The Sinking of Japan) by Sakyo Komatsu was a best-seller offering a frightening scenario of the last days of the island nation. The Japanese are ever mindful of their precarious position. As a result of these dynamics, making and trading goods is a near compulsion for the Japanese people, representing a collective way to meet the nation's needs. Japan's trade surplus is its only generator of wealth. This is a fact of life that is instilled through the media and taught constantly to Japanese throughout their lives, in school, from parents, and when they enter the working world. The message is: Japan is always vulnerable, we must protect her.

Despite its wealth and high per-capita income, the people of Japan, particularly those who live in cities, face a difficult life. Cramped housing, expensive food, crowded trains, and gridlocked roads challenge the citizenry daily. Housing prices have soared far beyond the reach of most salaried workers. In this crowded crucible, competition for everything is fierce. Social status is crucial, as is success through education in order to gain the stability of lifetime employment which, contrary to common opinion, is derived only from employment by a major corporation. To the employees of vendor companies, small firms, and foreign companies little prestige or security is accorded.

Obsessed with national character, the Japanese are proud and ambitious, constantly measuring themselves against the world's best and biggest. For forty-five years, Japan has had a single, unifying goal: "*Oitsuke, Oikose,*" "to catch and pass" the West. Accordingly, one of the main sources of Japan's strength is its people's willingness to sacrifice, to be regimented and homogenized, and to subordinate personal desires to the harmony of the working group.

"The Japanese tend to divide the world into two types: resource-rich countries, like Brazil or China, that promise to alleviate Japan's mineral poverty; and consumer countries, like America, that provide markets for manufactured products," said Kenichi Ohmae. Early on, Japan realized that its only resources are its people, and those who don't work don't eat. As he stated in his book, *Beyond National Borders,* "Perhaps at no other time in history (as in postwar Japan) have so many people embraced such a clear definition of the economic underpinnings of their society."

A GROUP-ORIENTED SOCIETY

In stark contrast to Western ways, Japan is a group-oriented society. While in the United States and Europe individuality and independence are highly valued, Japanese society emphasizes group activity and organizations. In such a society, the individual has little identity but that which is derived from the groups to which he or she belongs. Prior to World War II, the central group around which the society thrived was the *ie,* or extended family clan. Of course, all Japanese were members of the Emperor's family, and therefore part of this large *ie.* While the *ie* structure waned after the war, today such tight groups still dominate the Japanese landscape. From birth, a Japanese is part of several *habatsu,* or clique, and a group orientation will follow throughout life. In a company or other organization in Japan, there are many subgroups, including such cliques as *kyodobatsu,* or regional, prefecture, or hometown affiliations; *gakubatsu,* or school and college associations; and *keibatsu,* family and marriage ties. The Japanese form of the "old boy network" is based on the use of group memberships to conduct business, and, to a much greater degree than is true in America, is of central importance in determining one's ability to succeed and reach the upper ranks.

THE QUEST FOR WA

Japanese learn endurance and stoicism from childhood—patience with life, with traffic, with slow decision making. They accept that they will belong to one social group and work for one company for life. They complain little. *Sho ga nai* ("there is no way"), one of the most common Japanese expressions, is used so often because in so many cases there is no other way for them. They can't just pack it up and move West to get away from their problems back home. This is very much a part of why "saving face" is so important. In Japan, you know you will be with the same people all your life.

Japan's crowded island conditions have driven society to value conformity. The highest priority is placed on *Wa*, or harmony. In a small, crowded pond, one can't make too many waves. Without smooth relationships and an established code for business and social life, 120 million people could not function efficiently and without internal strife on such a small landmass. Conflict in such a crowded society would be chaotic. Thus, the nationwide uniform education system, in which all grades of students countrywide study the same material at the same time (and wear basically the same uniform), is a key shaper of the Japanese value of belonging to a group and blending into the crowd. From the earliest school years, Japanese teachers promote and reward group achievement, not individual distinction. "The nail that sticks up gets hammered down" is an age-old expression that poignantly summarizes daily life in Japan.

Japan's history as a nation of farmers contrasts quite drastically with America's roaming cowboy heritage. In Japan, you can't just fence off your own space and claim a big territory, as was done in the American West of days past. The Japanese have learned to share their limited space and value the precious distance between themselves and others. "We all have to live together," they say, whether they like it or not. This lack of space has resulted in the development of small gardens and special places within the home, such as the *tokonoma*, an alcove containing a special possession or flower arrangement. The Japanese retreat here as a means of relieving the pressure of daily life. Another relaxing tradition is the *ofuro* where a Japanese unwinds from the day by soaking in a tub of steaming water.

Conformity is a survival tactic and helps explain the orderliness of Japan's society. Years of early training provide the grounding required to operate successfully in this milieu. Politeness and deference abound, and the Japanese make every effort not to stand out in a crowd. Although on the trains you may see signs of modest rebellion by some youth—odd hair styles and Western "punk" fashions—these rebels rarely display raucous or disrespectful behavior publicly. Passive, clean, and quiet, even the restless young are keenly aware of the "atmospheric pressure" and social norms that guide every Japanese throughout his life. Often there is no need to speak; situations can be sized up from feeling, past history, and a knowledge of the tacit Japanese Way to handle things. When two strangers meet, they have a common database of proper behavior; each can be confident that the other will act accordingly. This may seem overly ritualistic and confining by American standards. However, there is a certain degree of liberation in knowing that there are established ways to handle any situation. When there are givens, one need not worry about appearing awkward or inappropriate in a social setting.

This ideal of harmony goes hand-in-hand with the concepts of "saving face," minimizing embarrassment, and karma—the idea that doing good for others will come back to you in the end. Japanese rarely show outward aggressive displays of emotion in public—because somebody is always watching. Since people will know you for most of your life in your neighborhood, in your company, and in your social group—high school, university, or sports club—one must always strive to save face, for others and oneself, and maintain harmonious relationships over a long period of time. No one wants to cause disunity or friction. Life based on Wa demands a stability in personal affairs, in striking contrast to life in the United States, where people may change jobs, communities, and social levels many times in a lifetime. Rugged individualism is dissuaded since it can undermine the network of obligations. Since the preservation of harmony is paramount, it often results in Japanese taking ambiguous or noncommittal postures to avoid direct confrontation in a negotiating situation. The Japanese tendency to show agreement, while actually not agreeing, can be quite confusing to an American businessman sitting across a negotiating table. Outward humility and emotional calmness will be the facade, but often behind this *tatemae* (superficial appearance) is the *honne* (underlying reality) and the fierceness and loyalty of *Bushido* (the Way of the Samurai). Even today, the Bushido ethic lingers in the background of Japanese behavior.

THE STATUS HIERARCHY

Japan is a vertical society; everything is in its hierarchical place. To a Japanese, hierarchy is orderliness. A group is not considered organized unless its members are ranked. Being largely a middle-class country where income differentials are not as extreme as in the United States, Japanese use these rankings to determine one's place in the society. Social ranking determines the amount of respect given and the amount of effort made in maintaining relationships, in greeting and bowing, even in framing everyday speech, which reflect rank through honorifics and the conjugation of verbs. This is the reason the ritual of giving business cards, or *meishi,* is so important, since a great deal of importance is placed on one's position. One's ranking in the society is arrived at through a number of considerations, including one's company, the division of the company one works in, length of employment, and position. Other factors, such as the status of one's university, the *senmon* (university major), family pedigree, and hometown, are also contributors. *Senpai-kohai* relationships, which are bonds formed between elder and junior people in school, company, government, or other groups, provide structure to an individual's role in this vertical society. These mentor-student relationships last for life. Most Japanese businessmen have had one or more mentors to guide and champion their careers. In turn, most also mentor others.

THE POWER OF OBLIGATION

Japanese human relationships might be compared to *natto,* a favorite Japanese dish of fermented soybeans which is very sticky, stringy, and gooey. One has many ties to one's relations and, like *natto,* the more one pulls away, the stringier and messier the ties become. Most Japanese feel this web of obligations continuously. One can spend an entire lifetime in Japan just maintaining relationships—of school, family, and work. Japanese spend a great deal of time attending weddings, funerals, new member parties, going-away parties, supplier parties, end-of-the-year parties, and New Year's parties. The number of work-related affairs seems almost endless. A senior director or general manager of a large Japanese firm may spend three out of four weekends at company weddings in the spring and fall, the peak seasons.

This recognition of obligation and the ensuing time commitment explains why many Japanese tend to shy away from making new relationships, especially with those outside their groups, like *gaijin.* Such relationships are simply not worth the personal energy they entail. Besides, most non-Japanese do not appreciate and reciprocate the proper and full extent of the obligation a relationship requires. This is why many Westerners find it difficult to develop close friendships with a Japanese. Before Westerners may finally begin to receive uninitated social calls from a Japanese associate, it may take months or years of continuously trying to build a relationship. But after these friendships are established, they will tend to be strong for life. It is important for foreigners going to Japan to understand this exclusionary tendency and to have patience to work continually to overcome the initial disappointments.

Obligations serve a business purpose as well, and Japanese businessmen deftly use obligations to their advantage by building interdependencies between companies that transcend the strict supplier-buyer relationships. Through gift-giving, cross-equity investment, joint development and marketing programs, exchange of information (even the arranging of introductions and marriages), obligations are cultivated so that they may then be used at an opportune time to leverage critical business decisions or to gain favor on a project.

EDUCATION: THE ACID TEST

Japanese are constantly reminded of their duties *(giri)* and obligations *(on)* to friends, company, neighborhood, ancestors, and Japanese society. In 1988, when thousands of new college graduates attended Nippon Telephone and Telegraph's (NTT) new hire employee ceremony, Chairman Shinto reminded the graduates from Japan's top universities, "You have received much from society; now is your time to pay back your debt through work."[2]

After family ties, schooling is the most important determinant of social class (and employment opportunities) for Japanese. The education system itself is a unifying force. It molds children into group-oriented beings by demanding uniformity and conformity from the earliest ages. The attainment of excellence within this complex environment, and the importance it holds for one's future is stressed early. "The road to Todai begins in kindergarten" is a popular expression. Todai, or Tokyo University, is Japan's most elite university and a symbol of ultimate success. This emphasis places a great burden on the young to perform well in school and to earn admittance to high status universities.

The public school system regimen not only produces good, obedient citizens, it produces good workers. A willingness to give of oneself to the corporation's best interest, to arrive early and stay late, and to produce good work are attributes learned in school. Those who cannot learn these skills do not do well in school or do not rise in the ranks of the corporate world. Japanese students attend elementary and secondary school six days a week and for two months longer each year than American students. In addition, they have long hours of homework. The rigorous curriculum stresses math and science at the elementary levels, and chemistry, physics, biology, geology, advanced mathematics, and English language for high school students. Augmenting their regular school program, the majority of Japanese students attend *juku,* or preparatory schools, in the evening and on Sundays. These programs are aimed at preparing the students for the highly competitive entrance examinations required by the nation's universities. Despite this nationwide focus on education, Japan has very few public universities compared to the United States. Since there are relatively few public universities in relation to the United States offering a reasonably priced, quality education, only a small percentage of the college-bound high school seniors can be accepted (see Table 2.1).

Entrance competition for the best schools is fierce. Japanese universities hold entrance exams every year, and a student must take a separate exam for each university to which he or she wishes to apply. The annual testing period for students nationwide is known as "examination hell." Those who fail will usually try again (even several times), studying for an entire year until the next round of admission tests. Those who are in limbo while seeking to gain admittance are referred to as *Ronin,* or "wave men," a term that originated with samurai warriors who had lost their clan lord and were outside any recognized group.

As in other aspects of Japanese life, a key in Japan's higher education system is to get into one of the so-called "right groups" or intramural organizations while an undergraduate. The competition for spots in fast-track organizations is intense, leading to high levels of stress felt by young people (and is a contributor to the high rate of student suicides in Japan). One's ability to get into the right company after college, such as a major *sogo shosha* (trading company), a leading bank's head office, a government ministry, or a leading manufacturer, can be deter-

Table 2.1
Leading Japanese Universities

NATIONAL (PUBLIC)

FIRST-TIER	
Tokyo University	Nihon University
Kyoto University	Tokai University
Tokyo Institute of Technology	Tsukuba University
Hitotsubashi University	Meiji University
	Okayama University
Hokkaido University	plus 40+ other national and prefectural universities
Tohoku University	
Yokohama University	

PRIVATE

FIRST-TIER	
Keio University	Aoyama Gakuin
Waseda University	Sophia University
Gakushuin	plus many second- and third-tier private schools
Kansai University	
Int'l Christian University	

mined by success in the education system. It is instructive to know the tracking system related to the particular school a Japanese attended. The graduates accepted by MITI or the Foreign Ministry, and the leading first-tier companies, traditionally have been almost exclusively from Tokyo, Keio, Waseda, or other top universities.

The Japanese Way: Summary for Understanding

- Japanese respect and preserve history, and genuinely believe they are different from other societies. While they desire to take the best ideas from outside Japan, the Japanese transform foreign ideas to suit their own tastes.
- Japanese truly feel a sense of vulnerability to the elements and their geography. Since their island nation has been endowed with few natural resources, trade and commerce are the nation's only source of sustenance.
- In a crowded society that values human relations, conformity and harmony are key in Japan. Because they feel a society-wide sense of common destiny, the Japanese feel obliged to act in accordance with traditional rules of etiquette and manners. Hierarchy is highly respected and extends into all aspects of one's life.

- Japanese are group-oriented, and do not favor extravagant or "showy" behavior by individuals. They value education, both as a route to personal development and wealth, and as a source of national indoctrination and acculturation. Every Japanese wants to succeed—for self and for society in general, for associates, family, and friends and for ancestors long passed. Hardwork is expected and Japanese are under tremendous pressure to fit within the system.

Each of these influences has contributed significantly to the formation of modern Japanese society and to the making of Japan's economy. As we proceed, these influences will manifest themselves again and again. Understanding the underpinnings of Japanese society will give you the framework to understand the workings of the Japanese market and—possibly more importantly—the Japanese mind.

3

The Global Farmer

Inside the Japanese Market

One of the greatest pieces of economic wisdom is to know what you do not know

JOHN KENNETH GALBRAITH

It was a clear day on the coast of the Izu Peninsula. We awoke near the white beaches outside the small town of Shimoda, a popular summer vacation spot at the southernmost reaches of Izu. It is a quiet region, some three hours away from the crush and heat of downtown Tokyo. Shimoda holds a unique place in the history of American-Japanese relations, for it was here in 1853 that Commodore Perry first passed his black ships before going on to Tokyo to wrest the Japanese islands from isolation and open its markets to world trade. It was also in Shimoda that Townsend Harris established the first U.S. consulate in Japan, purposely distancing it from the center of Japanese business and society in Edo City, or Tokyo.

Shimoda is relatively rustic. Many of the region's farmers and villagers live much as they did fifty years ago. Its agrarian-based economy thrives on growing rice, fruit, flowers and, along terraced river valleys and stream beds, the *wasabi* root is grown for sale to sushi shops throughout Japan. Shimoda is also famous for its *shiitake* mushrooms, a large-capped, dark mushroom that is highly prized around the world. We spent our weekend in Shimoda picking shittake in the forested mountains rising inland from the surrounding ocean. During the summer season, mushrooms are the main crop on the peninsula. They are grown along the mountains, sprouting up under rows of pine logs neatly stacked on the hillsides for this purpose. Up and down these hills one can see the bobbing bonnets of the rubber-booted *Obaasans*, elderly farm women, as they harvest baskets full of the aromatic fungus.

That day our small party carried handfuls of the mushrooms down off the mountain. Coming down the long, steep trail from the hillside, we arrived in the center of the village's activities—a modern shed that seemed to have been built a century later than the blue-tile-roofed houses that ringed the inner courtyard of the town. A long line of baskets stood outside the shed, their contents waiting to be loaded onto trays for drying in the village's communal mushroom dryer. Inside the shed sat the man in charge of operating the mammoth oven, with its many racks and large steel doors. While Obaasans came and went, loading the racks, he calmly whittled sticks of wood into various shapes and monitored the progress of the thousands of mushrooms inside. After an exchange of formal greetings, we showed him our meager harvest and told him of our plans to barbecue on the beach that evening. The mushroom dryer instructed us on the best way to barbecue fresh shiitake (upside down, with the spores filled with soy sauce).

Surveying the shed, we could not help but inquire about where all the mushrooms were going; surely they were more than the small village could consume. The old man responded that they were to be shipped to Tokyo "where the city folks will pay 800 yen (about $6.00) for 200 grams of the dried shiitake." He added that the village's mushrooms often went to places like Hong Kong and Singapore, and even to the United States and Europe. We told him we had seen large burlap bags of shiitake in Hong Kong and Korea, and commented how much less expensive they were there, compared to Japan. He seemed quite aware of the differences in price, and added, "With *endaka* (the high yen exchange rate), we're going to have an even tougher time competing with the shiitake from Korea and China in the seasons to come." He seemed unconcerned, however, and said, "But those mushrooms are not the same high quality as ours, and the Japanese demand only the best. We ship the best shiitake in the world."

"What makes these mushrooms better?" we asked, wondering if there might be some mystical qualities in the soil of the mountains.

He responded by taking us to an adjoining shed, where he proudly showed us a new high-speed drying unit the village had just purchased. Made by Hitachi, the high-tech unit is capable of drying twenty times as many mushrooms in the same amount of time as sun drying. It also dries the mushrooms more thoroughly, which minimizes spoilage. And because they are dried quickly, more of the rich, musky flavor of the shiitake is captured. He proudly showed us the end product, ready to be packaged. "This is the fruit of high technology," he said with a near toothless smile.

The lesson was not lost on us. Even in their quaint corner of the world, these simple farmers knew international end-markets and competitors, and constantly monitored market variables, like foreign exchange rates. As a group, the village worked together and made cooperative, long-term investments. The villagers were not reluctant to change, but accepted it with a problem-solving attitude. They understood the advantage of applying advanced process technology to the competitive chain.

From the hills of Izu to the mills of Nippon Steel, and the DRAM factories on "Silicon Island" in Kyushu, the people of Japan are succeeding by applying the basics of business laced with a global perspective. As we have asserted, Japan is a society dedicated to economic growth through manufacturing and trade. With no significant natural resources except water, hydroelectric power, fishing, and themselves, Japanese learn early in life that commerce and trade are the only ways for their country to meet the needs of its citizenry. It is a nation with a distinct sense of destiny.

A NATION WITH A MISSION

In the years following the Second World War, the Japanese emerged from the rubble and destruction of total defeat to rebuild a nation that is now stronger than ever—a testament to an entire nation's collective will to overcome adversity. In the immediate aftermath of the war, however, there were few hints of the modern economy to emerge. In 1945, Japan's political and social fabric was worn threadbare; most of the country's factories were leveled, its currency battered by runaway inflation, its people on the brink of starvation. Japan needed a miracle. When unconditional surrender was signed, the United States Occupation Forces under General Douglas MacArthur set about creating that miracle, and in the process reorienting Japanese society and government. The goal was to expunge the strain of racism and militarism that had been manipulated prior to the war and to erase any remnants of the dangerous dictatorship that had led its citizenry astray. MacArthur's reform efforts included rewriting the Japanese constitution and using American advisors to hasten a Japanese recovery under a new economic system. But, if Japan renewal was to be constructed according to an American design, the resulting edifice was to be Japanese.

The Japanese had been threatened before and had weathered and repelled assaults by a number of outside forces. And in the Meiji Restoration Period, when Commodore Perry reopened channels to the West, Japanese society was invaded—by new and strange ideas. Throughout these assaults, Japan may have been defeated but was never conquered. This is not to say that outsiders did not have an impact. In fact, it was through its contact with others in the ancient world, particularly the Chinese and the Koreans, that Japan acquired a language, an administrative system, a religion, and a cuisine, among other societal characteristics. The Japanese have always been a people willing and able to adopt and adapt to new approaches. And when the Westerners in their massive ships pierced the silk curtain that had isolated Japan for centuries, the people coined a phrase to describe their attitude to the invading ideas: *wakon yosai*—"Japanese spirit and Western knowledge." It was in this mindset that the new prime minister, Shigeru Yoshida, formulated a plan whereby his war-torn nation would take what the United States had to offer and then mold it to fit Japan's goals. The "Yoshida Doctrine" was based on three simple premises:

- Japan's economic growth should be the prime national goal. Political and economic cooperation with the United States was necessary for this purpose.
- Japan should remain lightly armed and avoid involvement in international political-strategic issues.
- To gain a long-term guarantee for its own security, Japan would provide bases for the U.S. Army, Navy, and Air Force.

With these guiding principles, Yoshida knew he could adequately mesh Japan's strategic interests with those of the United States. The larger country would take an active role in nurturing the little islands back to health. At the very least, the Americans would keep Japan safe while it went about its business.

Beyond a new constitution, crafted by the occupational forces, the Americans brought other innovations. Teams of civilian advisers were imported by the Occupation Forces to work with representatives of Japanese government and business. One such adviser was Detroit banker Joseph Dodge, who served as economic adviser to the Occupational Forces. When Dodge arrived in Tokyo, he found a nation in economic disorder caused not only by the war itself, but by the circumstances that preceded and sustained it. Prior to the war, the Japanese had had one of the lower savings and investment rates in the modern world. The war buildup brought confiscatory taxes and an expensive, hungry military/industrial complex. With the destruction following the war, and the rampant inflation and labor strife that accompanied the peace, Japan's economic house was in shambles.

Dodge believed that a profound shift to an investment-driven economy was the only way to turn the nation's fortunes around. To this end, he made two radical proposals. The first was to establish a very high tax rate, even at the lowest ends of the income scale. This would be a short-term hardship on Japan's workers, but it was a move that would help restore the country's deficit-torn treasury. By comparison, the second proposal seemed almost paradoxical: it was to exempt from taxes all interest earned on personal savings up to three million yen, deposited in the new Postal Savings Bank program. In 1950, three million yen was equal to little more than $8,000, not a princely sum. But at the time that sum was more than twenty-five times the annual income of the average Japanese. To its critics, the plan would permit the richest of the Japanese to vouche-safe a considerable sum of much-needed national revenue. For Dodge, his experiment was not an easy sell. However, thanks to the support of the new minister of finance, Hayato Ikeda, the plan passed through the gauntlet of a hostile cabinet and Diet. The results of Dodge's scheme were felt immediately. Inflation abated within weeks of enactment, and the national savings rate grew. Counter to what the skeptics maintained, the tax base and revenues also grew. By 1980, when the Postal Service Bank interest exemption program ended, the Japanese people had squirreled away the highest per capita savings in the world. Not only did this revitalize the country in keeping with the Yoshida Doctrine, it gave the nation's economy the capital resources it needed to dominate world trade.

THE COMMAND ECONOMY

The structure of modern Japan's market reflects the society which built it; its roots reside in ancient ways characterized by an inbred need for order and harmony. In what author Karel van Wolferen refers to as the "System," the Japanese body politic and economy is organized for group welfare at the expense of individual freedom. The sociopolitical-economic arrangements of which the society is comprised are infinitely more important to the well being of the state than any one individual or, as we shall see, even groups of individuals—like consumers. This should not seem strange in a society where loyalty to the group is a defining quality.

The Japanese market comprises distinct groupings of commercial elites. Like the powerful *zaibatsu,* or big family businesses/empires that existed before World War II, or the feudal estates of past centuries, these commercial groups have the complete cooperation of the government. In fact, cooperation must be used loosely here: genuine power in Japan is diffused among these self-contained, semi-interdependent bodies and the government-created bureaucracy that serves them, none of which are accountable to an electorate. The real power in Japan lies in the boardroom, not in the Diet. The result is a potent "shadow state" which writes the rules that all participants in the Japanese market must play by. The objective of this circle of elites is to mediate power struggles and keep business entities in an ordered orbit. Rather than permitting a no-holds-barred brawl to the detriment of the nation, Japan's market is centered upon a Marquis of Queensbury-type system of gentlemanly conflict. "Our competitiveness co-exists with the willingness to work together in adjusting to change," says Masahisa Naito, a government official. "To the Japanese way of thinking, it is acceptable and natural for companies to cooperate in order to cope with common problems." This is not to say that it is a benign market; the power elites play hard. It is a world of fierce competition. But it is better, Japanese reasoning holds, to have half a bowl of rice than an empty one.

The codes of business and behavior which characterize the Japanese market mechanism stem from the nation's shared hierarchy of needs. On isolated islands with few natural resources, survival requires everyone to work together. Among the national goals which are pursued obsessively are:

Secure food and fuel
Conserve currency
Develop human resources through education
Increase the size of GNP
Full employment
Increase worldwide opportunities for Japan

These common needs are met through joint action by each of the independent components of the system: industry, finance, government, and education. The result is a command economy or, as some have called it, a national development economy, tightly controlled and regulated to utilize national resources in a strategic, purposeful manner. Within this rubric, the citizenry is highly focused on commercial issues. As manager of the peoples' treasury, the government uses national resources to impact positively the country's commercial success by encouraging business development in targeted areas. It does so by keeping the cost of capital down, encouraging a high rate of personal savings and investment and, until recently, tightly limiting outside competition in the market through import restrictions, tariffs, and licensing requirements. The government continues to promote and support a number of large companies in each strategic industry, using government-sponsored alliances and national R&D projects, tax benefits, and outright grants to develop a national mastery in key technologies. The government's broad agenda has been to:

Educate the workforce in technology and global language

Promote cooperation and competition, not confrontation in the market

Centralize in Tokyo for rapid communications

Nurture and protect industries in early phases and encourage joint projects

Provide continuous financing for exports

Support overseas development projects coordinated with foreign governments.

Keep foreign markets open.

THE BUREAUCRACY

While the Emperor is the titular head of the state, Japan is structurally a parlimentary system. It has three branches of government: executive, legislative, and judicial (see Figure 3.1). It has a popularly elected bicameral parliament, the Diet, composed of a House of Councilors and a House of Representatives. A prime minister, selected from the parliament, chooses twenty-one cabinet members or ministers. The body politic is of a varied ideological composition, represented by a handful of formal political parties. Not uncharacteristically, one formal political party dominates—the Liberal Democratic Party—which virtually has a lock on the electoral process. Through the media, the world sees and

Figure 3.1. Structure of the Japanese Government, 1989

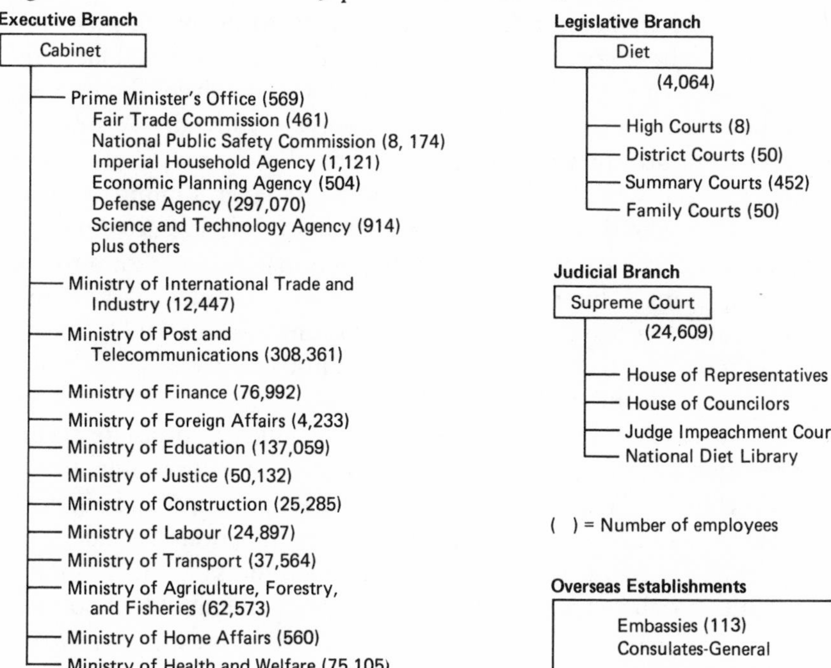

SOURCE: Adapted from Keizai Koho, "Japan 1989: An International Comparison" (1989).

hears the prime minister and thinks of him as a powerful figure, on par with the President of the United States or the Prime Minister of Great Britain. In truth, the real political power in Japan lies in the permanent government—in the bureaucracy.

The government of Japan comprises twenty-one ministries, and those wielding the most influence on Japanese business are the ministries of Finance, Post and Telecommunications, Education, and International Trade and Industry (MITI). Working closely with these and the other ministries and leading industrial corporations and business groups such as the powerful *Keidanren,* MITI has served as the coordinating body of Japan's powerful commercial machinery. In effect, MITI orchestrates the players in the economy. It is MITI's role to identify and rank national commercial pursuits and business opportunities and to guide the distribution of national resources to meet those goals. For this reason, we have chosen to focus on MITI as the single most important government entity with which foreign business people should be acquainted.

Amassing market data culled from worldwide science and business sources, MITI encourages Japanese companies to pursue targeted opportunities. These goals are predicated on the long-term viability and strategic value of the technology or product area involved, the market-share potential, and the competitive outlook worldwide. A strategic industry must also fit well into Japan's vertical economy; it must be a technology that will benefit a wide band along Japan's industrial food chain. MITI gets the required cooperation by offering government-sponsored inducements such as subsidies and market protection to the complying firms. This overall planning serves to moderate shocks to Japan's business ecosystem, like the petroleum crisis of 1973, and to ease the industrial base out of "sunset" industries, like steel and shipbuilding, without losing leadership position.

A major reason MITI has been successful in guiding corporate efforts in the nation's interest stems from the closeness of its personnel to the business elite (see Figure 3.2). Like the other ministries, MITI employs top talent. The view of bureaucrats as mere functionaries does not apply to Japan. Most MITI ministers attended the same high-ranking universities as the captains of industry, giving them old-school ties which can be used to productive purposes. Since most ministers work for the organization throughout their careers, they develop long-term relationships with business leaders, often rising in rank with their counterparts in private industry. Many times, retiring ministers will sit on the boards of Japanese corporations, or otherwise serve as advisors. When it comes to making a deal in Japan, it always helps to have commonality and a long-standing affinity for the other participants. This rapport also helps to build trust. When MITI asks a business to risk precious resources in the development of a strategic area, trust must be present. Another significant factor in bringing industry and business together is proximity. All government offices and most corporate and financial headquarters are located in a compact area within Tokyo, and encircled by the Yamanote Line of the Japan Railway. This would be something akin to clustering Washington, D.C., and New York City within city blocks of each other. The result is close communication and a feeling of joint purpose.

For almost any industry, there is a team of experts within MITI dedicated to developing an appropriate national policy for it. These ministers and staff will work with representatives from companies, universities, and banks to support a burgeoning business and to fend off foreign competition. The development of the Japanese computer industry provides an excellent example of MITI in action.

Table 3.1
The Command Economy At Work

Securing Resources

1960—IBM and MITI sign cross-licensing agreement with 13 Japanese manufacturers
1961—64 Major licensing of U.S. computer technologies by Japanese manufacturers
1968—TI licenses the Kilby IC patent to Hitachi, Mitsubishi, NEC, Sony and Toshiba.

Building the Component Base

1951—Tokyo University and Toshiba develop vacuum tube computer
1955—Computer Research Committee founded by MITI
1956—Machinery Temporary Measures Act
1957—Electronics Industry Provisional Development Act
1958—NTT introduces MUSASHINO-1 parametron computer
1975—Top five electronics companies form VLSI Research Association

Creating a Domestic Market

1961—Japan Electronics Computer Corporation (JECC) established

Promoting Internal Development/Expanding Technology Base

1961-FONTAC Computer Project starts
1971—MITI sponsored Law for Provisional Measures to Promote Electronic and Machinery Industries (Kidenho) focuses R&D on computers & ICs, magnetic disks, and facsimile
1971—MITI encourages pairing into three computer development groups:
OKI/Mitsubishi Electric (COSMOS Computer Series)
Toshiba/NEC (ACOS Computer Series)
Fujitsu/Hitachi (M Computer Series)

Results:

1988—Japan has 95% of DRAM marketshare
1989—IBM has only 30% marketshare in Japan, versus 50–60% in most other countries
TI Kilby IC patent awarded after 23 years
Japanese have 39% of the world-wide semiconductors market
Japanese have 27% of the U.S. semiconductor market vs. the 11% U.S. companies have in Japan
Heavy U.S. dependency on Japanese components and electronics technology.

Figure 3.2. MITI's Relationships in Information Technology Development

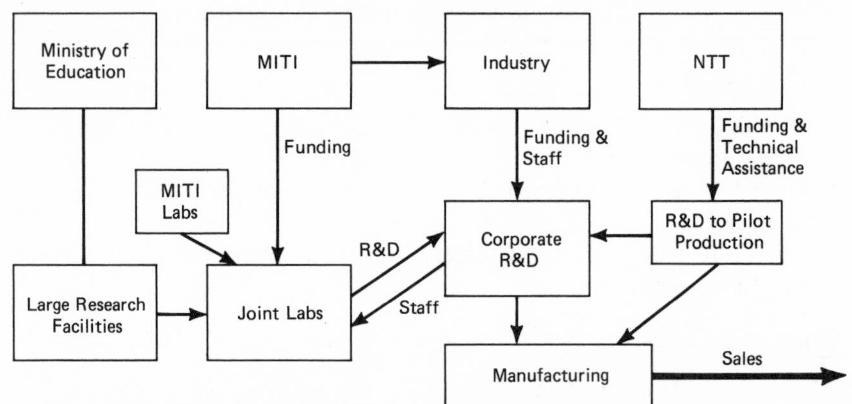

SOURCE: Adapted from Semiconductor Industry Association, "Japan Market Access Background and Source Book" (March 1, 1989).

In 1955, foreign imports accounted for 70 percent of all business machines sold in Japan. By far the largest share of imports was enjoyed by IBM. Fearing this dominance and the vulnerability it posed for the country, that year MITI recommended raising the tariffs on imported business machines from 15 to 25 percent and began work on developing a domestic capability. Since the latest trend in business machine technology was the transistor, MITI arranged technology agreements with overseas companies to allow Japanese companies to start producing transistors. Toshiba and Hitachi signed technology agreements with RCA and Western Electric; and Matsushita with Philips and Western Electric. In parallel, MITI also began sponsoring and funding university consortia to study the development of a domestic transistor business. In 1956, the Machinery Temporary Measures Act was enacted to provide the incentive and funding for transistor development at the private level. The act provided direct grants and low interest loans for R&D investment and technology licensing and purchasing. This was followed by the 1957 Electronics Industry Provisional Development Act which provided major direct subsidies, special tax depreciations and loans for capital equipment.

By 1960, Japanese companies like Fujitsu, Hitachi, Matsushita, NEC, and Toshiba were all producing transistors. American firms such as General Electric, Motorola, RCA, and Zenith had too much money tied up in existing tube radio plants to make the move at the time. This was clearly a turning point. Finally, in an outright move to undermine IBM and Univac, in 1961 the Japanese government created the

Japan Electronics Computer Corporation (JECC) to accelerate demand for domestic production. At a time, when close to 80 percent of all computers were leased, JECC bought Japanese computers and leased them—becoming immediately a major force in the computer market. MITI went a step further and required companies seeking Japan Development Bank funding to lease only Japanese technology, and at that time almost all companies were going to the JDB for money. In 1971, MITI began to encourage the strategic pairing of companies to create Japanese computers. In return for directing their energies and personnel in this cause, MITI provided them with financial assistance and grants of up to 50 percent of the cost of designing and bringing out the new models. From these arranged "marriages," NEC-Toshiba developed the ACOS system, Hitachi-Fujitsu the M-Series, and Mitsubishi-Oki the Cosmo. At the same time IBM was encouraged to make its system software and technology available to these companies. The rest, as they say, is history.

It is important to understand the power of a MITI endorsement. The significance is usually less a matter of money (although this is central) than it is the assurance given to cooperating companies that the government will help out in every way it can until the projects are successful. This greatly reduces the risk and leads to lower cost of capital since the financial institutions are assured of a long-term commitment. The risk then is limited to the capability of the individual company. A Japanese company working on a strategic product or technology will know that it has deep pocketed resources to draw upon.

Symbolic of Japan's broad focus on the future in areas of education, new technology, and advanced industrial development is the "technopolis" strategy. Conducted on a national level, MITI is coordinating multiple programs among regional governments in each prefecture, university, and industry to achieve leadership in strategic twenty-first century industries (see Table 3.2)—what they call the ABCD industries: automation, biotechnology, computers, and data processing.[1] In nineteen centers around the nation, MITI is creating technopolises—virtual communities aimed at building specific businesses. Not unlike California's Silicon Valley, Boston's Route 128, and North Carolina's Research Triangle, these technology centers will provide the infrastructure needed to incubate start-up companies in each of the targeted technologies. Each region will develop its own niche market based upon its unique skills and expertise. For example, Hokkaido is focused upon expanding marine technology; Kumamoto, applied machinery; and Okayama, biotechnology. By the early 1990s, the technopolis infra-

Table 3.2
MITI's Strategic Industries for the Year 2000

Japan Strategic R&D Directions
Advanced composite materials
Superconductors
Molecular structure design tools
Power electronics devices
Optical electronics
Neural network computing
Protein and membrane technologies
Advanced biomaterials and efficient enzymes
Animal and plant cell engineering
Software, AI, and man-machine interface
Ultra-thin films and precision molding
Sensor devices and electronic control systems

SOURCE: MITI. Adapted from "Trends and Future Tasks of Industrial Technology. Summary of White Paper on Industrial Technology" (September 1988).

structure will be complete, offering roads, industrial parks, universities, and capital equipment. In some cases, like Tsukuba Science City or Atsugi Research City, entire new cities are sprouting.

KEIRETSU—THE BUSINESS ELITE

Prior to World War II, Japan's economy was dominated by ten family-lead business giants. Known as *zaibatsu,* they included Mitsui, Mitsubishi, Yasuda, and Sumitomo—large conglomerates started at about the time of the Meiji Restoration in the late nineteenth century. After the war, the *zaibatsu* were systematically broken up by the occupation forces. The stock of the ten largest *zaibatsu* and their over 80 holding companies was handed over to a "liquidation commission" to sell to the general public. By 1949, some 69 percent of the shares in the former giant corporations were held by individuals. Since then, the original companies have bought back nearly 75 percent of those shares—approximating the closely held mass they enjoyed before the war. While no longer in name, the idea of massive, vertically integrated corporations lives on in the form of the *keiretsu* companies today, many of which bear the same names as their *zaibatsu* predecessors. There are three main types of *keiretsu:* bank or financial based-companies closely associated with a particular bank, such as Mitsui or Fuji Bank; manufacturing keiretsu of affiliated suppliers and distributors based around a certain manufacturer, like Toyota, Nippon Steel, or Matsushita; and industrial *keiretsu,* usually lead by a trading company. The *keiretsu* structure is built around close associations among companies reinforced by cross-shareholdings, cross-directorships, and long histories of joint partnerships. Not all companies within each group are closely tied, however. Many have only minor (and trivial) relations. There are six major industrial groupings which we show in Figure 3.3.

Though, in many cases, composed of independent companies, *keiretsu* groups maintain control and overall management of group activities through equity cross-holdings and directorships, intragroup financing, joint investment, and projects. All participate in a Council of Presidents whereby each group meets regularly to exchange business views, new opportunities, and help troubled member companies. Each of the top six *keiretsu* has a major trading company or bank among its ranks. Each spans a wide range of industries. The *keiretsu* structure provides a number of unique advantages:

- Keeps out corporate predators
- Lowers the cost of capital
- Ensures markets and loyal suppliers
- Lowers prices and increases information
- Gives preferential access to buying departments
- Allows early use of technology
- Provides knowledge of international opportunities from banks and *sogo shoshas*
- Gives access to group/consortium projects

The *Toyo Keizai, Kigyo Keiretsu Soran,* a survey done in 1989 estimates that 6 to 8 percent of employment by firms in Japan is by *keiretsu* group companies, and 35.4 percent of all financing in Japan is through a *keiretsu* bank or other financial institution. The average level of mutual shareholdings among *keiretsu* members ranges between 15 percent for the Sanwa Group, and as high as 26.9 percent for the traditional Mitsubishi Group. Overall, 60 percent of the shares of companies' stock on the Tokyo Stock Exchange is held by friendly companies.[2] Hitachi Ltd., one of the largest industrial groupings, makes it a policy to hold more than 50 percent of the stock of every group firm. Hitachi spends some 30 billion yen every year buying shares in these companies.[3]

SOGO SHOSHA

After the large manufacturers, the most daunting of Japan's commercial elites are the giant trading companies called *sogo shosha,* which dominate

Figure 3.3. The Japanese Keiretsu Industrial Structure

KEIRETSU GROUPS

	Mitsubishi	Fuyo	Sumitomo
Trading	Mitsubishi Corp.	Marubeni	Sumitomo
Bank	Mitsubishi Bank	Fuji Bank	Sumitomo Bank
Electric Maker	Mitsubishi Electric	Oki Electric Hitachi	NEC
Affiliated Companies	Mitsubishi Heavy Ind. Kirin Brewery Mitsubishi Motor NGK Insulators Chiyoda Chemical Honda Motor Co. Okamura Corp. Kyosan Electric Japan Electron Ajinomoto Corp. Asahi Glass Co. Ryobi, Ltd. Mitsubishi Chemical Nippon Kagaku	Showa Denko Kubota, Ltd. Yokogawa Electric Canon, Inc. Taisei Corp. Tobu Railway Sapporo Brewery Toa Nenryo Nippon Kokan Nihon Cement Nisshin Sanyo-Kokusaku Toho Rayon Nippon Seiko	Kojima Corp. Sumitomo Chemical Sumitomo Metals Sumitomo Heavy Sumitomo Cement Sumitomo Bakelite Sumitomo Precision Sumitomo Forestry Sumitomo Construction Ando Electric Anritsu Electric Sumitomo Trust Sumitomo Realty Inabata & Co. Nippon Glass

	Mitsui	Sanwa	Daiichi-Kangyo
Trading	Mitsui & Co.	Nishimen Nisho Iwai	C. Itoh & Co.
Bank	Mitsui Bank	Sanwa Bank	Dai-Ichi Kangyo
Electric Maker	Toshiba Corp.	Hitachi Sharp Corp.	Fujitsu
Affiliated Companies	Mitsukoshi, Ltd. Mitsui OSK Mitsui Engineering & Shipping Oji Paper Mitsui Trust Mitsui Real Estate Mitsui Tohatsu Mitsui Petrochemical Toray Industries Toyo Engineering Mitsui Construction Mitsui Harbor & Urban Construction Nippon Flour	Fujisawa Pharm Hitachi Shipping Kobe Steel Toyo Rubber Osaka Cement Ohbayashi-Gumi Toyo Construction Nippon Life Toyo Trust Teijin Ltd. Hankyu Corp. Ube Industries Sekisui Chemical	Kawasaki Steel Furukawa Co. Fuji Electric Nippon L. Metal Yasakawa Electric Niigata Engineering Kanematsu Gosho Shimizu Construction Iseki & Co. Meiji Milk Products Yokohama Rubber Asahi Denka Nippon Zeon Asahi Mutual

Other Groups: Tokai, IBJ; Nippon Steel, Hatachi; Nissan, Matsushita; Toshiba-IHI, Tokyu; Seibu, Toyota

SOURCE: Adapted from Dodwell, "Industrial Groupings in Japan" (1988).

Table 3.3
Japanese Sogo Shosha—1989 Rankings

Company	Trading Revenues (in $billions)	Profits (in $millions)
1. C. Itoh	$115.71	$39.0
2. Mitsui & Co.	110.00	44.0
3. Sumitomo	109.29	44.0
4. Mitsubishi	107.86	57.0
5. Marubeni	105.71	34.0
6. Nissho Iwai	85.71	23.0
7. Toyo Menka	40.71	11.0
8. Nichimen	34.64	13.0
9. Kanematsu	32.14	0.8
Total	$736.77	$262.8

SOURCE: *Japan Economic Journal* (September 30, 1989), p. 3.

trade in the country. Doing hundreds of billions of dollars in business annually, the *sogo shosha* handle nearly half of Japan's imports and exports and account for almost one-fourth of Japan's GNP. With hundreds of overseas offices trading everything from soybeans to satellites, the *sogo shosha* literally provide the lifeblood of Japanese business. More than just importers and exporters, however, the *sogo shosha* are involved in all aspects of business, from investment and finance to selling and distribution. With their worldwide networks and closely knit industrial groups, they are wired into global business trends and local market needs. With their massive resources and considerable capabilities, the *sogo shosha* tap into virtually any business in any market, regardless of the costs. The top five *sogo shosha* each handle over $100 billion in transactions annually (see Table 3.3).

A typical *sogo shosha* such as Mitsui or C. Itoh has six to eight major industry sectors, ranging in scope from steel, chemical, machinery, and electronics, with close to a hundred divisions, each handling a specific commodity, product, service, or resources development area. In addition, they have hundreds of affiliated companies throughout the world and thousands of cross investments.

No longer simply trading companies, many of the *sogo shosha* now have their own direct operations and manufacturing groups. And while they continue to dominate commodities trading—food and energy—they are continuously expanding into new areas, like resource development and telecommunications, and are expanding third-country trade.

The fact that they continue to control over 30 percent of America's exports is a strong sign of their capabilities. Their extensive outstanding obligations and powerful *Noren*, or name, and network or global affiliates will ensure they have a major role for decades to come. Cultivating its broad intelligence networks, investment areas, and partners throughout the world, the *sogo shosha* are the ideal global farmers.

THE BANKS

Japan's giant financial institutions have played an important role in the development of industrial Japan and today are overflowing with money generated by their success. Japanese companies, more than any other competitors, rely on their close banking relationships and are highly leveraged to fund rapid plant expansion and large overseas and domestic projects. This aggressive use of capital is only possible due to the close relationships among banks and individual companies reinforced through directorships and cross-shareholdings, government support, and the large, stable size of most industrial groups. The Industrial Bank of Japan (IBJ), the long-term credit bank which focuses on reconstruction of troubled industries, and the Japan Development Bank (JDB) have been instrumental in supporting the entire system of private banks financing Japanese industry. As shown in Table 3.4., Japan's banks are the largest in the world. Many are willing to help foreign companies, especially the Bank of Tokyo and JDB. For a more detailed discussion on banking relationships, see Chapter 10.

CAPTIVE AND AFFILIATED SUPPLIERS AND DISTRIBUTORS

The Japanese are masters at building webs of affiliation and joint destiny. Each of the major *keiretsu* corporations have below them a large network of affiliated suppliers and distributors splaying outward like the roots of a tree. Fujitsu's 1988 annual report listed more than fifty domestic and thirty-five overseas subsidiaries. Many of the companies were spawned by their parent and are highly dependent on the sponsor company for their livelihood. When consolidated, revenues from these affiliates can double the host company's annual revenues. The philosophy behind these offspring is to make the industrial family as self-sufficient as possible by developing a wide range of expertise and a large technology base with each group.

In Japan, it is a well-known practice for businesses to buy first from

Table 3.4
Japanese Banks Dominate the World's Top Ten

Ranked by total assets (in $billions)

Bank	*Country*	*Assets*	*Equity Capital*
1. Dai-Ichi Kangyo Bank	Japan	386.94	$10.95
2. Sumitomo Bank	Japan	376.09	10.46
3. Fuji Bank	Japan	364.04	10.73
4. Sanwa Bank	Japan	348.36	9.31
5. Mitsubishi Bank	Japan	343.59	9.68
6. Industrial Bank of Japan	Japan	257.58	8.57
7. Norinchukin Bank	Japan	241.95	1.38
8. Tokai Bank	Japan	225.12	6.16
9. Mitsui Bank	Japan	219.67	5.77
10. Mitsubishi Trust	Japan	210.47	5.13
11. Credit Agricole	France	207.99	9.03
12. Citicorp	USA	203.83	9.86
13. Sumitomo Trust	Japan	196.59	4.69
14. Banque Nationale de Paris	France	194.52	5.50
15. Barclays PLC	Britain	189.20	5.46

NOTE: All U.S. Data as of December 1988; Japanese bank data as of March 31, 1989.

SOURCE: American Banker; Robert Guenther and Michael R. Sesit, "U.S. Banks Are Losing Business to Japan at Home and Abroad," *Wall Street Journal* (October 12, 1989), p. A12, reprinted by permission of the *Wall Street Journal,* © 1989 Dow Jones & Company, Inc. All rights reserved worldwide.

within their own ranks, within their company, then from within their *keiretsu,* then from another noncompetitive Japanese company, and only as a last resort from overseas. Hitachi is the classic example of the ultimate "closed" *keiretsu* system. In 1989, even after years of prodding by MITI, the Hitachi Group plans only to import $2.1 billion which amounts to but a small fraction of its $40 billion business.

Japan's large manufacturers also have very loyal and dedicated distributors, many of which sell only that company's brand of products. Even at the retail level, large manufacturers have their own outlets. Matsushita has 25,000 shops sprinkled throughout the Japanese islands; each carries only its National and Panasonic brands. The same is true with every other major electronics manufacturer and even companies like Shiseido in the cosmetics field. Unlike the independent and large retailer networks in the United States, these exclusive channels make entire distribution structures virtually impenetrable for any outside company.

Figure 3.4. Japanese Company Specialization Within the Electronics Industry

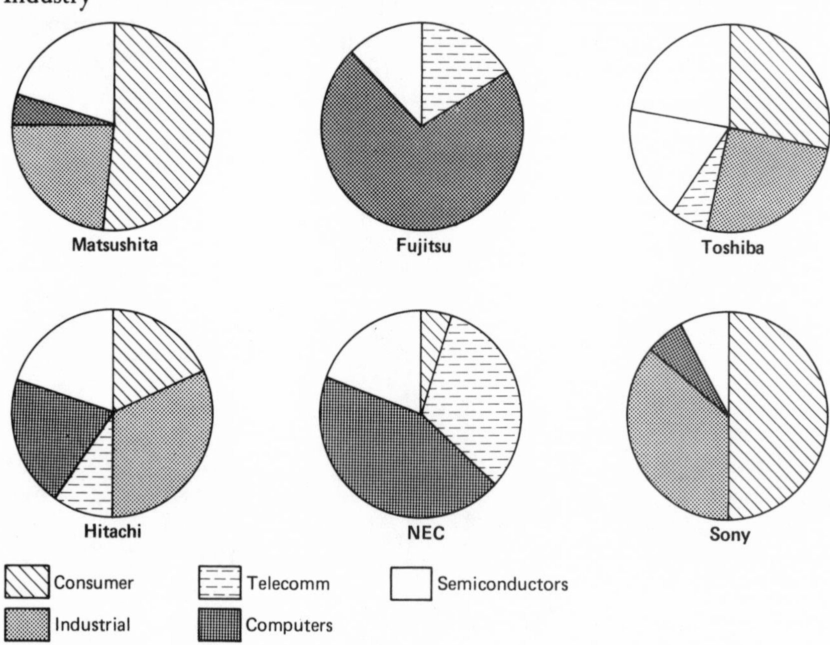

SOURCE: Adapted from data in the "Japan Company Handbook, "Toyo Keizai Shinposha (Winter 1988).

TECHNOLOGY SPECIALIZATION

While most of Japan's large conglomerates are highly diversified, each is primarily successful in a few principal areas (see Figure 3.4). Not realizing this has led many American companies down the wrong path in building partnerships with a Japanese company that turns out to be unfamiliar with the product, unwilling or unable to invest sufficient resources, or lacking in the right channels to move the goods. For instance, both Sony and Matsushita are unquestioned leaders in consumer electronics, yet both have experienced dramatic failures in attempting to enter the personal computer field. Toshiba, well regarded in specialized electronics, has been unable to wage a large-scale computer effort, while Hitachi has major business in industrial machinery and nonelectric markets. Other examples are abundant, and it is very important to understand the business mix, history, channels, and technical resources available before putting your product in the hands of a Japanese trading company. Do not rely on the Japanese to admit to shortcomings. Trading companies, especially, are masterful at portraying themselves as all things for all markets. They may make sweeping claims that they have a wide number of relationships through their industrial group, and can handle almost any business under the sun, but often each has only its own limited channels and some have very poor domestic networks. Great caution and diligent homework are required of any firm considering a trading or licensing agreement with a Japanese company. It is important to determine true sales channels, technical capabilities, and long-term commitment to your market.

HURDLES IN THE JAPANESE MARKET

The experience of most American executives going to Japan is analogous to the drive from Narita Airport to downtown Tokyo when traffic on a multilane expressway midway decelerates into a bumper-to-bumper crawl. The culture shock can, at first, be numbing. Things move differently in Japan. One needs to know this, accept it, and learn to work within this reality. There are also many differences between the Japanese market and virtually any other market in the world. These differences are the major hurdles—or structural impediments—which hinder most foreigners in Japan. Below, we examine some of the most common speed bumps on the road to profits in Japan.

Non-tariff Barriers. At one time, before American businesses paid much attention, Japan successfully blocked entry of imports into its economy through legal and administrative means, principally tariffs and content restrictions. High tariffs and strict foreign investment laws prevented foreign companies from becoming major profit-makers in the Japanese market. Moreover, by forcing technology disclosure, encouraging joint ventures, limiting foreign ownership, and excluding foreign products altogether, the Japanese government provides its companies an uncontested incubation period during which they can develop the capability to compete in world markets. To date foreign companies still cannot acquire a controlling interest in any Japanese company on the Tokyo Stock Exchange without government approval. Slowly, those programmatic barriers were lifted and, today, Japan has some of the lowest tariffs and quotas in the world. This has not resulted, however, in an open market. Informal nontariff barriers (NTBs) or structural impediments, now impede the importation of foreign goods.

In April 1989, the U.S. Trade Representative issued a report which outlined thirty barriers limiting American exports to Japan and since then has labeled Japan an "unfair trading partner." The primary barriers which are being addressed in bilateral talks with Japan are:

Pricing mechanisms—prices remain extremely high in Japan
Distribution system—liquor licensing and the Large Retail Store Law are too strict
Savings and investment—greater public investment is needed in the social infrastructure
Land use policy—tax rates on farm land in urban areas should be raised
Keiretsu relationships—these corporate groupings shut out foreign firms
Exclusionary business practices—antimonopoly law should be strengthened

One of Japan's remaining legislated barriers is the Large Retail Store Law. Passed in the 1960s, and further strengthened in the early 1980s, the law protects small store owners from the onslaught of large competitors. The law still requires that all shopkeepers within an immediate area (typically a kilometer) must approve the opening of any store with a floor area larger than 500 square meters. Today, even the largest and most powerful Japanese retailers find it can take five to ten years to open a big store.

Of course, the Japanese have found ways to deal with the law, yet efficiency is not a by-product of the solution. Due to the strictness of the law, many *yon-kyu-pa* stores, or stores of 498 square meters have been built, putting them just under the legal limit. While this satisfies the letter of the law, it makes a hodgepodge of retailing which adds to the price burden borne by the consumer. The resulting mosaic means that four separate small stores are clustered around a lot which could accommodate one larger store. Although all four may be operated by the same owner, his distribution, purchasing power, and organization are not on par with a larger outfit, and therefore his prices will be higher. There is also a correlation between a store's size and the amount of imports it carries. A MITI study concluded in 1986 that department-type stores had an overall import percentage of 12 percent and increasing, while small stores had an average import mix of only 3 to 4 percent. Again, this limits the range of choices consumers can make. But the law is not in place to protect and serve consumers. Its goal is to protect owners. Small "mom and pop" stores of four or less employees account for half of all of retail stores in Japan, versus 3 percent in United States and 5 percent in Europe.[4]

In addition, there are a large number of distribution groups which exclude foreign products out of tradition and due to established relationships. Mail order soliciting is still strictly regulated by the postal service in Japan, making the catalogue merchandising market diminutive in scope. Products must pass through many more hands and are subjected to many more markups. A distributor will not just sell your product because it is cheaper or special if it might hurt his existing relationship with his manufacturer or other distributors.

Multilayer Distribution Systems. Japan's distribution system reflects many of the dynamics we discussed in the first section. Owing to a shortage of housing, crowded living conditions, and a traditional lack of mobility, Japan's distribution system is composed of thousands of small neighborhood stores. Since it is difficult to conveniently travel any great distance (with few places to park in the inner city, relatively few city people own cars), and since small living spaces mean small refrigerators and storage areas, Japanese tend to take many short trips to nearby stores, rather than shop weekly to store up on goods. As a result, Japan has roughly twice as many small retail shops per capita as any other industrialized nation—145 per 100,000 people, compared to 83 per 100,000 people in the United States. Even though these stores are small, the space they occupy is usually quite valuable and expensive, adding to consumer costs. Since they are physically small themselves (see above) these neighborhood stores can carry only a small inventory. Without scale efficiencies, prices to the consumer naturally go up.

Serving these stores are a number of distribution levels. The wholesalers to the stores might be compared to a mobile warehousing system. Trucks from regional distribution centers may make daily deliveries to the small stores, often carrying a full stock of supplies which can be ordered right off the truck. Due to the high cost of land in the urban areas, major distribution centers are located in the outskirts, meaning trucks must often travel great distances from the main warehouse to the served routes. This extra travel again adds to the cost burden the consumer must bear.

Regional Variations. Due to its hegemony and compactness, Japan is routinely seen from afar as a singular, unified market of 120 million customers with similar tastes and habits. We have even argued here that Japan is a homogenous society. This point is only relative to a society like America. However, very different market conditions, business traditions, modes of distribution, and consumer tastes do prevail among the regions of the country. Anyone who has spent time in Osaka will tell you that the Kansai mindset is more parochial and traditional than that of the cosmopolitan world of Tokyo. Japan can generally be classified into five geographical market regions:

Hokkaido/Tohoku—the northern-most island and prefectures of the main island, Honshu

Kanto—the Tokyo area, Tama Basin, and everything north of Izu Peninsula to Tohoku

Chubu—the central area between Tokyo and Osaka centered in Nagoya

Kansai—the entire south of the main Honshu island from Osaka downward

Kyushu—the southern-most island which for many Japanese companies is thought of as a separate region all together

Each region of Japan has its own special character, and what may sell well in Tokyo may not gain market acceptance in other areas. For example, few people outside Japan know that Kansai uses a different electrical current frequency than Tokyo, which means products must be adjusted accordingly. Playing to these differences is one reason why Mister Donut opened its first test shop in Japan in a small town in the Osaka region and purposely avoided the gaudy, western-oriented Ginza strip, thereby trying to determine the reaction of a more realistic cross-section of the country to this previously untested concept in fast food. As well, each region tends to specialize in different types of industry. In electronics, Kawasaki, Yokohama and Atsugi are popular research centers, the Tama Basin around Hachijoji City is populated by consumer products manufacturers, and Kyushu island is noted for its many integrated circuit factories. Depending on your product, this means your company will need greater direct representation in some areas than others. Few Japanese companies have strong customer coverage in all regions. The majority of foreign companies usually only have have offices in Tokyo and Osaka, which means a large part of the country may not be well represented.

Licensing and Closed Bidding. Product and service licensing is also an institutional barrier. A U.S. Embassy investigation revealed that there are up to thirty-nine different licenses required by different shops—rice, liquor, gasoline, pharmaceuticals, each with its own separate law.[5] The woes of the American construction industry provide a good example of the challenge of Japanese licensing policy.

Japan is a nation in a building frenzy. The market for construction projects in Japan annually tops $250 billion. In Tokyo alone, it is projected that over $32 billion will be spent on waterfront redevelopment during the 1990s. Yet, for years, American construction and contracting firms have found it impossible to participate in this potentially lucrative building boom. While Japanese developers, major corporations, and large insurance contractors and developers have built and bought hundreds of office buildings in the United States for years, it was not until 1988 that American companies were even allowed to obtain licenses to operate in Japan. Despite America's advanced standing in many engineering and design areas, American companies picked up only $47 million in construction contracts in Japan in 1988. In the United States, Japanese companies won contracts worth $2.2 billion, many for Japanese companies relocating factories in the United States.[6] It wasn't until 1989 that Bechtel won its first contract in Japan.

The difficulty in gaining access is not due to American firms being incompetent or noncompetitive. They have simply been left out of the inner circle where contracts are divvied out. This is because the bidding system in Japan goes on behind closed doors where outsider companies have no chance of becoming a member, and where contracts only go to the established groups which have strong ties to developers and municipal authorities. This "closed-door bidding" is called the *Dango* system, in which a cartel controls the business to optimize profits and gain critical mass domestically in order to muscle up for the push into overseas markets. By not having licenses until 1988, foreign firms were precluded from participation. Even if a contract could be won, hiring workers is another problem, and so, of course, is navigating local legal and administrative procedures and building codes.

The Japanese cite foreign companies lack of commitment to the markets as the real root of the problem. They point out that only seven American companies applied for construction licenses in 1988. The International Engineering and Construction Industries Council in Washington, D.C., counters that more than 100 American companies spent $10 million that year trying to break into the market, with little success. Those companies that are succeeding in the construction business are doing so by linking up with Japanese partners. Tishman Construction teamed up with Aoki Corporation to build a $200 million hotel in Osaka, and Turner Construction has a 10 percent share in building a $77 million office building with Kumagai Gumi Company. Schall Associates has a 6 percent interest in a $138 million Yokohama hotel and conference hall with Toda Construction.[7]

The Japan Industrial Standards (JIS) Law is another example of a nontariff barrier for many overseas companies trying to export to Japan. While all industrialized countries define such standards, many find Japan's exceptionally detailed. It effectively puts unique limits on 7,800 items including construction materials, machinery parts, and chemicals. In other areas, technical specifications have stopped newcomers. Motorola was, until recently, excluded from selling its advanced, pocket-sized Micro-Tac portable telephones in the most profitable Tokyo and Nagoya areas, where a different technical system developed by Japanese competitors is used. Motorola was denied licensing just long enough for Japanese rivals working with NTT to introduce models which could compete with Motorola.

High Cost of Doing Business. The high cost of doing business in Japan has proven to be an insurmountable hurdle for many firms. Tokyo has consistently ranked as one of the most expensive cities in the world in which to live, work, or even visit. This fact has not made it an easy market for foreign firms to set up shop. And the artificially induced fluctuations of the exchange rates which occurred with the hope of making prices of American goods more attractive in Japan, have increased the price of building a Japan-based capability. With land prices increasing at 5 to 10 percent a year from already skyhigh levels, services, products, hotels, entertainment, and office space and housing for employees make Japan entry prohibitive for some firms. A square foot of residential land in Tokyo Sanbancho, Chiyoda Ward is $8,165. Commercial property in Ginza goes for about $23,000 a square foot.[8] In order to rent an office space in downtown Tokyo, upfront guarantee and deposit monies alone can be 6–10,000 yen per 3.3 square foot. John Stern, American Electronics Association vice-president in Tokyo, estimates a start-up, 1,000-square-foot office for two to three people in Japan will cost over $1 million in the first year, including a $150,000 non-refundable deposit, $82,000 a year in rent, plus salaries, office equipment, housing, and cost-of-living expenses.[9] It is little wonder that few foreign firms can sustain the necessary commitment to an operation that will not likely show a return for many years.

Lack of Protection for Intellectual Property. Japan's patent, copyright, and trademark protection laws are far different than those in the United States. And Japan has been reluctant to tighten intellectual property laws, believing that the country still needs easy access to the creative ideas of the West, particularly in the computer and entertainment software areas. One of the main problems with the Japanese system from a foreign company's perspective is the extremely long approval periods (an average of four to six years versus two in the United States) for patent applications; and such applications are open to public scrutiny after only eighteen months. Japanese patents offer narrower protection and must be filed in Japanese, and there is a dire shortage of patent attorneys to pursue the interests of foreign companies. If yours is a strategic technology, expect to wait a long time for a patent. Another concern is that domestic companies using patents pending rarely have to pay royalties for periods of use prior to patent award. In rapidly changing markets, the value of the patent protection may well have evaporated by the time the patent is issued. In 1960, John Kilby of Texas Instruments applied for a patent on the integrated circuit. The patent was not awarded by the Japanese government until 1989. In the meantime, of course, the technology had far transcended Kilby's early chip.

With large teams dedicated to the task, Japanese companies are patenting and trademarking everything that moves causing a mounting flood of thousands of very narrowly defined patents. Trademark regulations do not require that the name or mark even be in commercial use before it is registered, and rights are granted to the first applicant that files. A trademark holder has the right, by law, to sell the name. Many foreign companies come to Japan to find that some small firm, though not using the name, has already filed the trademark as an investment for the future. They then must pay royalties to buy back use of their own name or logo.

THE CAPITALIST ANIMAL

It has been suggested that the Japanese market represents the purest form of capitalism the world has known, not because it is a free and open market in the way classical economists would understand, but because virtually everything in the society is geared to support commerce first and foremost. Thus, while not a thoroughbred in textbook terms, we should consider Japan a highly developed species of capitalist animal. Japan is built for business. This is not to say it is a better model; arguments against the Japanese market model abound, and are certainly in some ways offensive to American sensibilities. But, be assured, the Japanese have elevated the phrase "we mean business" to new heights. Grasping this hard reality is a necessary precursor to winning in Japan. Go there to do business, expect to play rough, and keep your eyes on the ball.

Inside The Japanese Market: Summary For Understanding

- Japan is a nation with a mission. Its people, at all levels of society and all walks of life, think more intensely and expansively about business than possibly any other people on earth.

- Japan operates on a "heirarchy of needs" philosophy aimed at acquiring through commerce only what it cannot supply for itself, principally natural resources, fuel, and food. There is a genuine societywide bias for buying Japanese. No regulation can overcome this systemic bias.
- The Japanese market is composed of clearly identifiable elites—in government, education, banking, manufacturing, retailing, and labor—each with a specific role to play in supporting the overarching activities of commerce. While these Titans can and do clash, often with a fierce bloodlust and mortal intensity, the formal and unspoken rules of the Japanese market on the whole encourage nationalist cooperation to benefit Japanese society.
- Japan is a democracy, but the real power lies in the permanent ministries and the boardroom. Interlocking directorates and deep-rooted personal ties between members of the government and business leaders result in a close-working oligopoly of power. This power is highly concentrated in Tokyo, the seat of national government and home to all powerful corporations.

A number of hurdles continue to persist for newcomers in the Japanese market, but a great deal of progress has been made, much occurring in Structural Impediments Initiative (SII) negotiations and naturally throughout the Japanese economy. As we examined in Chapter 2, the characteristics of Japanese society are clearly visible in other areas of Japanese life, including the makeup of the market. A sense of commonality, strengthened by a threatening outside world, and a real willingness to put national interests and that of the company ahead of personal gain have resulted in an unrelenting command economy.

4

The Customer Is God

Inside the Japanese Company

Matsushita is a place where we build people. We also build electric equipment.

COMPANY SLOGAN

On a train ride back to Tokyo from Japan's northern regions, a long-time Japanese friend explained to us the Japanese approach to business. "In the United States," he observed, "you say the customer is always right. In Japan, we say "*okyakasuma wa kamisama desu*"—the customer is God. There is a big difference." To illustrate his point, he told us about an associate of his who had been a divisional president within a major Japanese conglomerate some years ago. His division made turbines for use in hydroelectric plants and, during one particularly brisk period of business, the division was running a month late in delivering a giant turbine to a regional power company. The company was building a dam and power station along Japan's northwest coast and the delivery delay was causing a major disruption. When news of the delay reached the president's office, he was mortified. The next day he traveled hundreds of miles to the remote town where the dam was being constructed. He arrived late at night, but at daybreak he was at the home of the general manager in charge of the construction project. When the general manager left for work that day, he found the distinguished division president down on his knees in the driveway. The president asked for forgiveness for the terrible loss of face his company had experienced by not meeting its customers' expectations and expressed his sorrow for the problems the delays were causing. He went on to give his solemn promise that the delivery would be made by a certain date. With the president's reputation on the line, work was conducted around the clock until the turbine was delivered as promised.

This story illustrates the impact of sociocultural influences on the Japanese way of doing business. Throughout a Japanese company, responsibility for performance is shared by all employees collectively, regardless of rank. When the company loses face, each member of the organization accepts culpability and shame. It is instructive to note that the Japanese understanding of the word *company (kaisha)* does not mean *the* company, but *my* company. The sense of individual identity and destiny, as the group is important. Not only was the president in this story not immune from blame, he took it as his role as the paternal head of the group to own up to the company's shortcomings. This code of honor is one of several key concepts Westerners must know if they are to succeed in Japan.

KAISHA: THE CORPORATE FAMILY

The Japanese corporation very much resembles Japanese society. Both are rigidly organized, hierarchical, and steeped in customs and traditions. Dating back to the "merchant houses" of the Tokugawa Era, the Japanese corporation is an extension of the family. Employees take a great deal of pride in the companies they work for and identify closely with them. Figure 4.1 shows the organizational structure of the typical Japanese corporation.

Each division in a shosha or large manufacturing company is an independent power center. In this sense, the *bucho,* or general manager, is often given the same level of respect as a president of a smaller firm. However, in most companies, the ground work is done at the level of the assistant general manager, *bucho dairi,* and the manager, *kacho.* It is important to emphasize that the highest ranking executives in Japan are rarely the drivers of a new project. Executive functions are largely to establish themes, maintain high-level relations, develop strategic direction, and above all, promote loyalty in the group. In initial meetings, higher level executives will often join in for a brief introduction, but normally will not remain as negotiators. Their role is to get an impression of the suitor company and to offer general direction on fundamental issues. With these upper managers, business people are

Figure 4.1. Japanese Company Structure

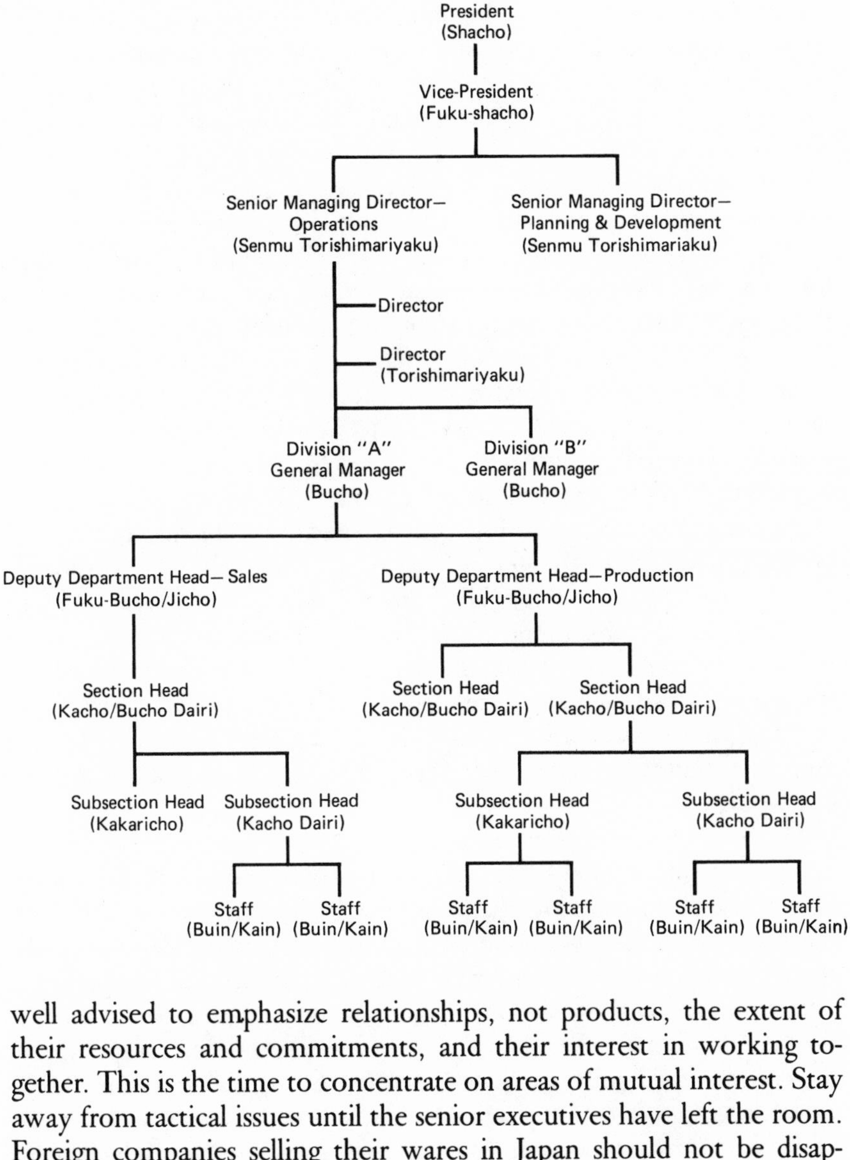

- President (Shacho)
  - Vice-President (Fuku-shacho)
    - Senior Managing Director—Operations (Senmu Torishimariyaku)
      - Director
      - Director (Torishimariyaku)
      - Division "A" General Manager (Bucho)
        - Deputy Department Head—Sales (Fuku-Bucho/Jicho)
          - Section Head (Kacho/Bucho Dairi)
            - Subsection Head (Kakaricho)
            - Subsection Head (Kacho Dairi)
              - Staff (Buin/Kain)
              - Staff (Buin/Kain)
        - Deputy Department Head—Production (Fuku-Bucho/Jicho)
          - Section Head (Kacho/Bucho Dairi)
          - Section Head (Kacho/Bucho Dairi)
            - Subsection Head (Kakaricho)
              - Staff (Buin/Kain)
              - Staff (Buin/Kain)
            - Subsection Head (Kacho Dairi)
              - Staff (Buin/Kain)
              - Staff (Buin/Kain)
      - Division "B" General Manager (Bucho)
    - Senior Managing Director—Planning & Development (Senmu Torishimariaku)

well advised to emphasize relationships, not products, the extent of their resources and commitments, and their interest in working together. This is the time to concentrate on areas of mutual interest. Stay away from tactical issues until the senior executives have left the room. Foreign companies selling their wares in Japan should not be disappointed to meet "only" with an assistant general manager, as he will likely be the key preliminary decision maker in the division.

The *kaisha* organization is typically characterized by strong "father-son" relationships between managers and their employees. After entering into a particular division or subsidiary, an employee may often serve under one *bucho* for his entire career, thereby developing a strong dependent relationship. An employee's fortune will quite often depend on the success or failure of his immediate superior. Paternal relationships between managers and subordinates, and peer networks nurtured over many years in a lifetime employment system, make the pressure for success at any cost a far more significant issue than in most American companies.

Fealty to company is a key criterion for promotion within the organization. Even the appearance of flagging loyalty—by becoming westernized or adopting modern affectations—can diminish one's chances for ascension. Non-Japanese businessmen are sometimes deceived by these appearances. Just because you feel comfortable with a certain Japanese, and he seems to be an "international" businessman, does not mean that he can be effective in his home office organization or in relations and sales with Japanese companies. It is often the case that Japanese who get along easily with Western people may actually be outside the power structure in the company. In similar fashion, Japanese who spend too much time overseas and try to blend in with local people often find when they return to Japan that they are no longer trusted, that they cannot be relied on to behave predictably. Owing to this strong social pressure at their company, Japanese will often try to overemphasize to their colleagues that they are uncomfortable around foreigners to prove their "Japaneseness." This is an important fact we will explore later when we discuss hiring challenges in Japan. Hiring a Japanese employee based on English skills and Western mannerisms can be an error.

Above all else, a feeling of loyalty to the company and a need to promote its interests pervades the Japanese's decision-making process. One caveat: Company loyalty knows few limits in the kaisha. Practices that may appear unethical and illogical by Western standards may not be out of bounds if an employee feels he is supporting the group to which he is dedicating his life. Within the context of a desire for lifetime employment, the threat of loss of face for group or company, and the concern for family status and security, questionable business practices sometimes become acceptable. Owing to the extreme verticality of Japanese corporations and the strong group loyalties which grow over time within them, decision making requires a consensus among a far-reaching group of power centers, each with a different set of goals and demands. Making one's proposal attractive to a wide number of managers throughout the organization, and building a case for each manager based on his particular interests and power center needs, will greatly improve the chances of success.

CONSENSUS MANAGEMENT

The process of a typical business decision by a Japanese company may closely parallel that of an American corporation in the initial stages, but a number of other factors come into play. If, for example, a Japanese trading company is interested in distributing a new product, here is what happens. Typically, the assistant general manager will assign a task force to evaluate the market potential of the product, and determine whether the division can be successful with the product. A great deal of effort is spent on consensus-building with upper management and related groups to foster a sense of joint destiny around the project. Thereafter, a different thought process comes into play. Over and above the potential profitability of a new joint venture or partnership, consideration will be given to the impact of the project on the entire company, and to such factors as whether the project fits with the traditions, phisolophy, and ideals of the company's founders and current management. Intense scrutiny will also be given to how other companies, both competitors and partners, the press, and the general public will perceive the project and how much face will be lost should the venture fail. This is especially so in high-risk partnerships with foreign companies. There are typically ten clearly discernible stages of the Japanese decision process, each with its own name, as shown in Table 4.1.

The *kessai* process further expands the concept of group decision making and consensus formation throughout the organization and forms the basis for cementing the funding and personnel for any project

Table 4.1
The Kessai Process: Japanese Stages of Decision Making

1. *Soodan*—discussion
2. *Johoshushu*—information gathering
3. *Nemawashi*—informal laying of the groundwork (literally, "cutting around the roots")
4. *Tatakidai*—"pounding platform," pre-proposal
5. *Yobikaigi*—preparatory meeting
6. *Totaru meritto*—"total merit"
7. *Settai*—business entertaining
8. *Honkaigi*—main or final meeting
9. *Hanko*—personal signature
10. *Kessai*—decision by top management
11. *Ringi-sho*—final approval without meeting, using circular letter

SOURCE: Brannen, Liu & Commanday, course materials for "Business Communications and the Japanese Decision-Making Process" (April 1990).

in a Japanese corporation. The *ringi-sho* is a typical business plan which outlines the details and merits of the project, its risks, resource requirements, and terms of the contract. The process of passing the ringi-sho across the desks of all the managers who may need to be involved in the decision can take several weeks—or months. A typical *ringi-sho* includes a series of boxes in which a *hanko,* or signature stamp of approval, is required from each manager. Managers not supporting the project can refrain from stamping or can place their hanko upside-down or sideways to show their nonapproval and signal to upper management the need for further evaluation or discussion. Using *ringi-sho* assures that many people in the organization are aware of the basic strategy and know who is responsible for its implementation. The *ringi-sho* builds consensus and stimulates ideas while enlisting the required *hanko* throughout the many divisions of the company, thereby guaranteeing that once the project kicks into gear, the entire group is committed to the project's success.

Not surprisingly, the *ringi-sho* process means long hours must be spent in meetings within the company and with outsiders. Meetings are not regarded negatively in Japan, and often the entire day will be taken up in conference, with ordinary daily tasks relegated to the evening hours. Because this planning and consensus-building cycle can sometimes extend for days at a time, and requires many evenings of informal dinners and drinking, non-Japanese often become discouraged or impatient. The upside to the slow decision-making process is that after the thorough planning of the project, execution becomes easier, and coordinated action can take place relatively quickly.

In negotiations held outside the corporate walls, Japanese traditionally meet in groups to guarantee conformity of corporate style and purpose. In this way, a united front is represented and decisions are shared across the group, along with the burden of possible failure. In larger corporations managers have almost no concept of "winging it." They are meticulous in their preparations for meetings and plan far ahead for every contingency in order to build a plan that can be approved by the larger group. The individual operative is almost nonexistent.

TOWARD ANSHIN

Anshin is the Japanese word for "trust from the heart," or security and comfort. Increasing the comfort level of your associates and customers in Japan goes far beyond providing quality products delivered on time and at the right price. Japanese want to feel comfortable and "in touch" with their suppliers and business partners. There is a human dimension to this desire along with the business side. Japanese want to know you can be trusted and are as interested in their success as you are in your own. The first order of *anshin* is to understand the customer's needs: response to customer demands is an obligation. This takes time and close relations. Two-way obligations between customers and suppliers are built over many years, and go far beyond traditional American expectations, extending to such nonbusiness activities as the attendance of social events and weddings. It is quite common for business associates to give jobs to each other's family members and to arrange for marriages between relatives and mutual friends.

The supplier's obligation to his customer goes beyond maintenance and service. Japanese vendors work closely with their customers. The goal of attaining anshin is to enhance satisfaction and give the customer the assurance that you will be there for him. Even more important, good communications serve to mitigate the kinds of misunderstandings that can damage long-term relations. Addressing key issues immediately reassures customers that they have a vendor that is committed to their success.

SERVICE AS RELIGION

If the universe is at ease when it is in harmony, then according to Japanese custom, the individual is at ease only when the spirit is "satisfied." In the arena of business, the spirit of a Japanese man or woman cannot be satisfied unless the customer is satisfied. *Ki ga susumanai* roughly means "my spirit is dissatisfied" and is used to describe feelings of incompleteness or angst about unfinished business. This concept is a prime motivator behind the compulsive Japanese work ethic. As we spoke of in Chapter 2, the Japanese from birth are yoked with certain inalienable responsibilities; a sense of universal obligation represented by *on* (a kind of society-wide beacon) and a personal obligation, *giri.* As a personal code, *giri* imbues Japanese employees with a deep sense of duty to fulfill their obligations to their superiors and to their customers. This is particularly so if you are a vendor. In Japan's hierarchical society, the vendor's caste is a full step below the customer. In fact, the vendor's very existence is only justified by the customer's. Any successful vendor is ever mindful of this reality. As such, they are honor bound to customer service. In Japan, no matter how unique your product or service, no matter how large and insurmountable your market share, when a customer has a problem you solve it.

At all levels of Japanese society, from equipment suppliers to airline personnel, retail clerks, cab drivers, and office workers, first-rate service is the standard upon which all Japanese are judged. First-rate in Japan is not what it is in the United States. It is a level of attentiveness and care for the customer's personal needs, as well as business needs, where Japanese surpass the usual measurements of involvement. Service is expected as part of the purchase. This extends to after-sale attention. The Japanese feel that if it is a quality product, it won't need to be repaired. If it does need service, it should be forthcoming as a matter of course. In general, the Japanese expect free after-sale service and longer warranty periods. And while this situation is starting to change (there is a reluctance in Japan to charge for service), there remains a great deal of resistance to service contracts. Whenever there is a problem at a Japanese customer site, it must first be fixed with no regard to cost. Then the customer, being a long-term partner, will tend to work to find an amenable settlement for services rendered, often without any written communications. Otherwise, charges usually must be either bundled with the parts or as upgrade packages. Admittedly, the level of customer support required in Japan does tend to require more engineering per piece of equipment or more after-sale support on products—it can seem as if service people must always be on call. But the extra effort required of doing business in Japan can be well worth the cost.

THE QUALITY OBSESSION

The Japanese are obsessed with quality. Their interest seems to be a product of a marrying of two aforementioned cultural concepts, *wa,* harmony, and *on,* obligation. To the Japanese, within everything there is an inherent state of perfection and harmony. This means that for any task, perfection is the only reasonable standard: all else falls short and is, in fact, disharmonious and therefore undesirable. This cognition then, becomes an obligation. If one knows there is a way to reach a state of harmony, one is obliged to pursue and, most hopefully, attain it. The Japanese have successfully harnessed this drive for quality into a tremendous marketing turnaround. Most of us can recall a time not too long ago when "Made in Japan" was synonymous with poor quality and poor workmanship. Few people today snicker at something bearing a Japanese label.

The American notions of "acceptable quality" and "good enough" do not work in Japan. Quality (which is more than technological superiority) is a key portal of opportunity for foreign firms seeking to penetrate the Japanese market. The quest for quality in the mind of the Japanese supersedes virtually all other considerations. The Japanese will seek out the best quality products and buy them regardless of their country of origin—until they can achieve the same level of quality on their own. This entrée for foreigners is not inconsequential. If you can "out-quality" the Japanese—if you can beat them at their own game—you can win on their home ground. Ironically, the instruments for achieving quality in the workplace are not Japanese in origin, they are American. Quality Control Circles, which have become features of virtually every corporate landscape in Japan, were first conceived of and employed in America. Since 1951, Japanese companies have competed for the most prestigious of honors, the Deming Award. Named for W. Edwards Deming, the American business professor who for many years was little known in America, the Deming Award competition is fiercely and pridefully contested by Japanese industry leaders. The awards ceremony is such a major affair that it is broadcast each year on national television the way the Academy Awards are presented in America.

The quest for quality does not, however, merely satisfy a national compulsion. It is business at its smartest. High-quality products ensure satisfied customers, which in turn results in fewer repairs, trade-ins, warrantee claims, and complaints. Unremarkably, high-quality products also result in greater sales and better market penetration. Understanding quality is a fundamental requirement for doing business in Japan. Competitive products in Japan are measured in terms of adherence to "spec," and the number one specification is perfection. If your company does not strive for product and service perfection, your company's products are in danger of being replaced by those of a Japanese company. Choosing to produce quality products must precede any entry into the Japanese market.

THE LOYAL SUPPLIER

Loyalty is the linchpin of Japanese business. This results in an approach to business grounded in reciprocity. Though they are on different rungs in the social order, the customer-vendor relationship is symbiotic; vendors are loyal to their customers and, in return, they receive loyalty back. Due to this close interdependence, Japanese customers are much more demanding in terms of what they expect in quality, service, and delivery schedules, but they are also much more cooperative than in other markets. The Japanese long ago realized that their best interests are served by being good customers.

If we examine that point for a moment, we are required to make some distinctions. A supplier or vendor is a person with whom you engage in a short-term relationship. As a customer, you shop for the best off-the-rack product that satisfies your immediate needs at the best price the market offers. You have no particular loyalties to the supplier. Communication is limited to the point of purchase and you can sever the relationship where the buck stops. On the other hand, the supplier has no real commitment to you either. His responsibility for his goods ends at the loading dock. The only phone number within your company he is likely to take an interest in is to your accounts payable department. As long as you pay your bills, he has little at stake to make sure you do well.

Now let us contrast that with the defining elements in a partnering relationship. First, there is inherently a sense of commitment, of destinies intertwined. The relationship is designed for the long term so that there is a feeling of loyalty and permanence; it is not just a series of singular transactions but an ongoing process of problem solving and opportunity-creation. Each partner accepts the required investment of time and resources to make the relationship successful. Success is measured in terms of mutual benefit. Instead of an off-the-rack approach, products and services can be customized. What Japanese companies look for in a supplier is not just the product or the price of the product, but the strength of the company that makes it, its personal history and service record. They want a partner who will be committed to make their product and their company better by his presence.

The interdependence of customer and supplier is illustrated by the practice of *hempin,* whereby manufacturers or wholesalers agree to take back unsold stock from retailers. In most cases, if goods are not sold, they are returned to the manufacturer, who accepts them as a matter of course, meaning the manufacturer will lose money as well as the wholesaler on a dead product. Also, when partner or supplier firms face difficult times in Japan, it is not uncommon for the large customer to provide financial or other assistance to help the supplier get back on its feet. Often there are cross shareholdings and it is not unusual in Japan to find business relationships stretching back over three generations.

Japanese companies are very selective in picking suppliers due to the major obligations such relationships entail. When entering into relationships with overseas companies, a potential partner will be evaluated on things such as:

1. World-class manufacturing capabilities and large automated facilities
2. Strong understanding of quality, tight process control, and data collection and analysis
3. Company-wide zero-defect campaigns and action plans in product and service
4. Stability of management and personnel
5. History of consistent growth and market-share expansion; stability of strategy and financials
6. Loyalty to long-term product and support plans for Japanese partners
7. Top-management effort and time spent proportionately in Japan
8. Survival instinct and a long-term perspective and fighting spirit

Japanese are most impressed by the supplier's people, facilities, and the production process itself, not by marketing presentations. "Even if the other party makes a good offer, I always have them show me their factory," declared one official of Honda Motor Company. "I do that to check if it's really possible for them to provide the quality, prices, and stable supplies it would take to fulfill the order. I won't sign a contract with anyone who can't do that." This view of the loyal supplier applies not just to foreign firms, but to any company. In many cases, building such relations can take a number of years, but once a trusting relationship has been established between two firms it takes a total disaster to sever business ties.

THE IMPORTANCE OF COMMITMENT

Japan's business style, and the time and technical commitments it requires, can take its toll on a manager accustomed to the American way of doing business. Daily meetings, late nights drinking with and entertaining, and weekends spent playing golf with customers are indicators that business is the center around which life revolves in Japan. This attitude is reflected in customers' elevated expectations regarding their suppliers. Some things the Japanese may take for granted would be considered "beyond the call of duty" in the United States:

- No customer inventory and very short notice on delivery-schedule adjustments
- Six-to-eight month engineering evaluation cycles and extensive and on-going modification of vendor's product capabilities prior to any major purchases
- In-person delivery of product by top management and formal apologies, in-person, for any difficulties which might impact the customer
- Arranging marriages, employment, and financial assistance for family members and associates
- Swift resignation by the company president as atonement for events that publicly embarrass the company
- Demands for 100 percent quality in all aspects of operation and sudden, drastic reductions in cost
- Major efforts by joint customer and supplier teams to improve overall capabilities
- Long trips out to the airport to meet customers passing through town and attending to customers' every need on trips and visits
- Monthly trips overseas by top management to visit major customers and regularly scheduled quarterly meetings at all levels—operations, support, technical, and manufacturing
- Walking customers out to their cars to see them off, and the giving of elaborate gifts throughout the year

PROFILE OF A SALARYMAN

At the backbone of Japan's corporate machinery is the salaryman, the selfless, group-oriented corporate employee. In business dealings with a Japanese company, one most commonly interacts with a salaryman. It will be important to understand the mindset of the salaryman if working relationships are to be successful. Some have compared the salaryman to the organizational man in the 1950's novel, *The Man in the Gray Flannel Suit.* However, as we have suggested, the societal and cultural influences on the salaryman are quite different from the American experience. The salaryman does share many of the traits of his American counterpart—a college education, a position achieved by working up through the ranks, an ingrained love of country and family, need for fulfillment, and so on. Yet, despite the parallels, the salaryman is different. Japanese society and the world of the salaryman reflect a strong Confucian influence stressing "a rational natural order of which man is a harmonious element, and a social order based on strict ethical rules . . . governed by men of education and superior ethical wisdom."[1]

At the risk of gross oversimplification, we have ventured to sketch a portrait of the basic cultural foundation and major influences on a salaryman in Figure 4.2. In this illustration, his life is a temple with a value foundation shared by virtually all Japanese. The structure is shaped by a variety of societal influences and external pressures.

In and of itself, the status of salaryman is not a formal social group,

Figure 4.2. Profile of a Salaryman

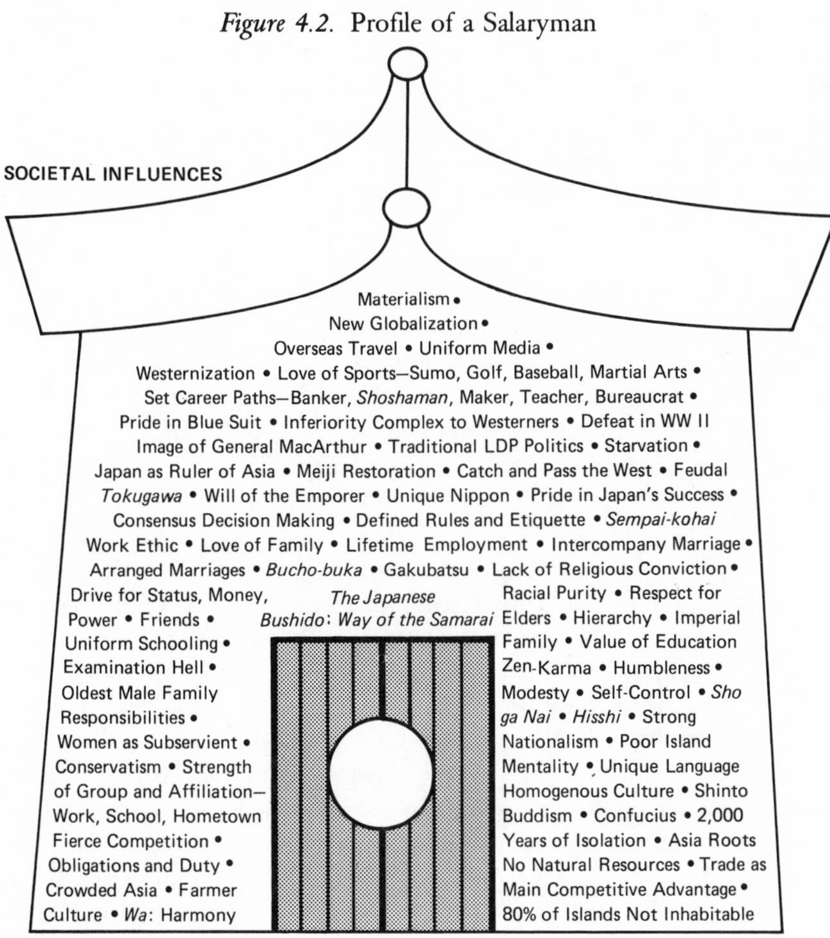

yet almost everyone you are likely to meet in Japan works for a company, and wears the prized uniform of the business suit. The salarymen reflect the unique values and environmental pressures of Japan—a lack of options and flexibility in life, stiff competition for limited resources, lack of space, and limited personal freedom. Every salaryman feels the intense competition for limited resources in Japan, especially good jobs with top companies, and land. Impossible housing prices are making the dream of owning a home beyond the reach of most Japanese. Large companies in Japan spend hundreds of millions of dollars on housing loans and dormitories for their employees, further increasing the interdependency between a company and its workers.

With the high degree of association the Japanese have with the companies they work for, a salaryman's life is likely to revolve around the job and the workplace. After-hours are typically spent with co-workers. This close camaraderie is an essential part of the team-building process that makes the *kaisha* a corporate family. Dependency on the company as the center of life is developed early, with the recruitment and "re-orientation" of fresh graduates into the company's culture, the provision of almost all the workers' needs—salary, housing, food, and affiliation, and continual pressure to meet a certain image of the "Mitsui man," or the Mitsubishi man. The differences in values and style between people of different companies in Japan is remarkable, and each company is unique in its traditions.

To enter an *ichiryu*, or first-tier, company is the goal of most Japanese from their early days in school, and explains why competition to enter the right university is so fierce. This step will largely determine a person's status and quality of life for the remainder of his life. The conservative traditions of most Japanese major companies puts many younger, more free-spirited Japanese in a difficult position of carrying on the traditions of the past, while expecting to find meaning in life other than work, and setting a new vision for Japan's role in the world. Because of the demands of the office, few in the better companies have time for many outside activities, and this is, in large part, the reason for the absence of such American traditions as community volunteerism in Japan.

A friend of ours, Takeshi Ikuta, is a typical salaryman and an examination of his life gives us a telling glimpse of the world of the salaryman. Ikuta works for the giant *sogo shosha,* Mitsui. At age 32, he has worked for Mitsui for eight years—since graduation from Kyoto University, one of Japan's premiere universities. Typical of most of the Japanese working in a large corporation, Ikuta is fiercely proud of his company, grateful even for the opportunity to be among its ranks. He is dedicated to his work, his division at Mitsui, to his *bucho,* or manager, and to his fellow workers. His days are often ten to twelve hours long. For its part, the company has trained him and provided him with numerous opportunities to prove, and improve, himself. For three years, Mitsui sent him overseas to train in French and then to work in the Paris and Geneva offices.

For most of his time at Mitsui, Ikuta lived in the company-owned dormitories in Nishifunabashi, about an hour away from the office in Tokyo. His was an all-men's dorm and he led a bachelor's life. Recently, however, he met and married a co-worker from Mitsui. Since so much of a salaryman's life is spent at work, such interoffice marriages are the norm. In fact, it was his general manager who introduced him to his wife. At his wedding, attended by his entire section at Mitsui, the general manager served as the "man of honor," giving both the bride and groom away. At the wedding, the co-workers occupied the front rows in the hall, the family members sat in back. After the wedding, Ikuta and his bride moved out of the dormitory and into a "mansion"—a two-bedroom condo in Nishi Kasai. To pay for such accommodations, Ikuta obtained a loan from his Mitsui, thereby tying his destiny even more closely to his company—along with his ability to pay a $3,200 per month mortgage.

Because the company is the strongest community in Japan, salarymen put a great deal of pride and energy into reinforcing and supporting the group they work with and its members. Ikuta spends at least three nights a week out with his group, boss, and customers at different celebrations and gatherings, many for new members or for old members taking assignments overseas. This investment in others—introductions, late nights helping co-workers, attending weddings of co-workers, and other mutual obligations—are extremely important in developing the Japanese group spirit and joint destiny. Since joining Mitsui, Ikuta has worked for the same *bucho.* He hopes to be promoted to the *bucho* level when his present boss is promoted. His ultimate dream is to someday fill the role of his general manager and gain the prestige and power associated with being a top manager of one of Japan's most respectable companies. Unfortunately, he senses the increasing difficulty in realizing this dream as the top of the corporate ladder in Japan becomes ever more crowded with the graying of the population and slowing economic growth.

Yet Ikuta was fortunate to enter a growing division at Mitsui, so the opportunities still linger out there on the horizon. He knows that key to his personal success will be the success of his upline management.

He will do what it takes to ensure that success. This ethic reinforces the strong group orientation and causes factionalism within Japanese society. Intercompany factions are more pronounced because of this power structure which is based on strong life-long father-son relations between managers and their employees.

Ikuta works hard. It is arguable whether he works harder than his American counterparts, but it is inarguable that he works longer hours. The salaryman at a top bank, *shosha,* or manufacturer has a strong ingrained work ethic from college. Within two years after starting his career, he has been molded for his role in the Japanese corporation. Orientation and formal training shape young workers to corporate standards of loyalty, respect for elders and customers, and hard work. The work ethic is so ingrained that many Japanese are dying from overwork, called *karoshi.* Ikuta suspects this was one reason his father, whom he saw little of when he was a child, died when he was only sixty while on assignment in Taiwan with a major construction company. On the average, the Japanese salaryman puts in 500 more working hours per year than business people in countries like West Germany; and, in the leading companies, the late hours and pressure is even more severe. Some companies, like Sony, now require their employees to take one to two weeks of vacation a year—not a major accomplishment by Western standards, but quite remarkable in a land where many older managers boast of never having taken a day of vacation in their lives.

It is the salaryman's long hours that most Westerners hear about, and these are undeniable. To this day, it is considered shameful for a husband to be home before ten o'clock in the evening on a workday. Even weekends are spent in the office or on work-related outings—golf trips, company meetings, and travel with customers. When not at work, most Japanese salarymen get together with co-workers in favored nightclubs and bars. *Mizu shobai,* or the water trade, is one of the biggest industries in Japan, employing some five million people. Ikuta and his co-workers spend many worknights drinking together, venting steam from the pressures of the office, and bonding. The *nomiya,* or drinking house, is probably the second-most frequented place next to the office in a salaryman's life in Japan.

But the positive side of a salaryman's commitment is evident as well. Ikuta's division has won major projects for new plants and equipment throughout the world, and this is a great source of personal pride for him and his co-workers. He feels a sense of fulfillment from his work and his company and cannot imagine ever leaving Mitsui. Life-long employment, another hallmark of the Japanese system, is as much a reflection of employee loyalty as it is a policy. Yet things are changing. While leaving one's company is still considered by most to be akin to divorce, a recent Recruit survey found 25 percent of 10,000 of the salarymen polled had changed jobs within the last three years, and 38.5 percent are considering a move.[2]

As we stated, there are many differences between the Japanese salaryman and his American counterpart. However, there are also many similarities. Appreciating the common ground is as critical to your success in Japan as are the areas of differentiation. Like American workers, the salaryman:

Has a reverence for family, nation, and country

Desires a good income, and has the same basic wants and needs—food, fuel, housing, consumables, appliances, and transportation

Places an emphasis on education and learning

Has a need for comradery, affiliation, recognition, security, and career opportunity

Needs to identify with a successful organization

Lives in an advanced industrial society

Has a love of business and the profit-based capitalist system

Has an interest in the international marketplace

In the world of business, the real focus should be on sharing these similarities. Success can come from adept navigation of the Japanese Way, and from gaining advantage through these cultural and operating differences. Many foreign companies in Japan have used the ingrained uniqueness of the Japanese business structure to their own advantage. By not having existing binding commitments, foreign companies can sell across every industrial group. Others have exploited their foreign or American image as an advantage, applied American marketing or European style, and used their own unique product introduction and promotion techniques. By emphasizing the similarities your company has with Japan, promoting areas of joint interest and mutual potential benefit, while capitalizing on the differences, foreign companies can thrive in the Japanese market.

We have tried briefly to give an overview of the many cultural and historical forces which shape Japanese society and by extension, the Japanese company. As we study the market itself in subsequent chapters, these forces should be taken into consideration. The distinction between insider and outsider, between Japanese and *gaijin*, is central to understanding the Japanese business machine. The group mentality, the values placed on loyalty and dedication to the system, the rigidity of hierarchy, and the almost mortal need for all elements of the organization to prosper are all components of the Japanese way of doing business.

Inside the Japanese Company: Summary for Understanding

- The Japanese *kaisha* is organized like a clan, or extended family. Personal identity, prestige, and self-worth are largely derived from membership in a company or organization. This results in intense loyalty to the company.
- As they do throughout society, relationships provide the underpinnings of the Japanese organization. The focus on group interests results from an inescapable, life-long feeling of interdependence and interconnectedness.
- In dealings with a Japanese organization, expect highly formalized and rigid rules of order and protocol. These rules and ways will not likely change, so do not fight them; make them work for you.
- Do not expect quick decisions from a Japanese organization. The *kessai* consensus-based decision-making process is necessarily slower than the American model of responsibility and authority-based empowerment.
- Expect to receive—and give—higher levels of service, commitment, and quality dealing with a Japanese organization. These values run deeper than company policy, and without understanding and reciprocating in like terms, your success will be limited in Japan.
- The Japanese salaryman across the negotiating table has both similarities and differences. Learn to identify, understand, and appreciate these: emphasize the similarities, exploit the differences.

Given an understanding of the Japanese Way, foreigners can be successful in Japan. Yet, what receives the most attention are the flops—the failed attempts to penetrate the Japanese market. These failings can be useful; they can instruct us on what not to do in Japan. However, most often these failings are used to reinforce feelings that the Japanese do not play fair and have made their market impenetrable. Both of these myths are wrong as we will see in the next section. Japanese do not "play fair" by American standards. What we have not yet come to grips with is that the Japanese are now setting the standards in global trade. Winning in Japan is definitely possible—with many great and intriguing success stories both foreign and Japanese to prove it. What is critical is to understand the Japanese as competitors inside and outside of Japan, and how foreign companies are winning—and losing—in the Japanese market.

PART

II

Doing Business with Nihonsha

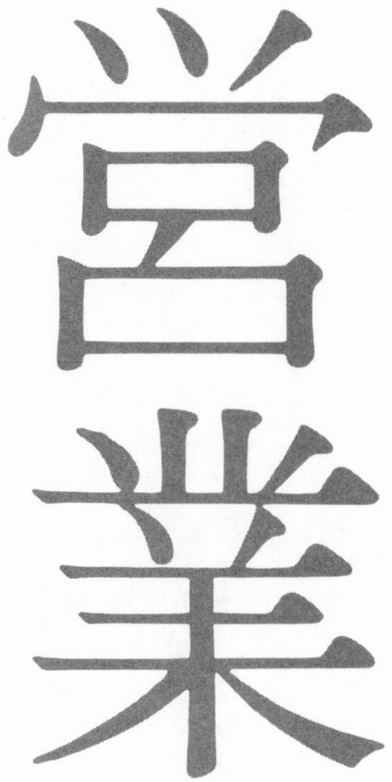

5

Bushido: Way of the Samurai

The Japanese as Competitors

Hardware needs software.
AKIO MORITA

The Japanese are consumed by an ancient board game called *Go,* played by placing small stone pieces on a grid-marked board. The object of the game is to capture territory across the entire board stone by stone until gradual dominance and defeat of the opponent is achieved. The game's strategy involves placing the stones initially in supportive groupings, and keeping one's opponent's stones isolated so they are ineffective. *Go* is wildly popular in Japan and the rest of Asia; it is as much a staple of childhood as checkers or Monopoly is in the United States. Not surprisingly, many parallels exist between the game *Go* and the Japanese approach to business. Japanese businesses are market-share driven and territorial, are willing to sacrifice profit here and there in the short term for long-term gain, and tend to operate in orchestrated groupings. And, they work their industries from a solid home base outward. It is well worth understanding Japanese strategy before attempting to take them on in their own market and internationally.

THE QUIET COMPETITORS

The first thing a businessman must understand is that he is already competing with the Japanese, whether he realizes it yet or not. If he has not faced Japanese competition, at home or abroad, it won't be long. The typical Japanese new-product marketing plan calls for achieving a foothold in the home market, learning from the experience of beating fierce domestic competitors, and selling enough units at inflated prices within Japan to generate operating efficiencies and profits. High markup selling at home, in effect, subsidizes a company's entry into the global marketplace, where margin may need to be sacrificed until a strong position is realized. Since Japan's domestic market is an arena where heavily armed Goliaths do battle, over the years Japanese companies have honed their battle skills by surviving its rigors. Japanese companies are typically the most successful worldwide in areas where they faced the most intense domestic competition. "Industries thrive," echoes Michael Porter, "when they are forced to overcome high labor costs or a lack of natural resources, when their customers won't accept inferior or outmoded products, when their competitors are many and murderous."[1] For this reason, the average American sees only the very top Japanese companies—the ones that have survived. Most are high-visibility, brand-name product corporations in consumer electronics, autos, cameras, motorcycles—companies that first competed fiercely for years selling their products in their own home market.

The Japanese companies that succeed in this "expand or die" atmosphere have given intense scrutiny to strategic competitive fundamentals. As James C. Abegglen and George Stalk point out in their landmark study, *Kaisha, the Japanese Corporation,* the Japanese are succeeding by pushing the fundamentals to the extreme:

- A bias toward growth
- A preoccupation with competitors
- The creation and ruthless exploitation of competitive advantage
- Supportive long-term financial policies

Abegglen and Stalk conclude that Japanese strategy follows a pattern of "rapid growth of the Japanese market; fierce competition in Japan for market share; steadily improving cost and quality position of the leading Japanese companies; then an export drive by the domestic winners from 'fortress' Japan's maturing industry, their base position protected from the lack of foreign competition in the Japanese market."

They go on to assert that "competition from the *kaisha* can best be met, and in many cases can only be met, by market competition *inside* Japan."[2] Thus, the only real way to compete with the Japanese is to limit a competitor's free ride at home.

It is also important to remember that Japanese companies rarely begin with a frontal attack on a market. History has taught them the folly of this gesture, and the Japanese work hard at not competing. In other words, winning without confrontation is the best, least costly, and the most satisfying way to win. If this kernel of wisdom makes sense to us now, its logic was doubly valuable to the people of postwar Japan. In the 1950s, the American automobile industry must have looked godzilla-like in size and power. Japan, on the other hand, was still a nation on the mend, with little in the way of advanced manufacturing capability and virtually no marketing savvy when it came to global opportunities. Confrontation avoidance was the only Japanese option. At the time, small, inexpensive cars were not the stuff of Detroit. German automaker Volkswagen was the only competitor in this segment of the market. In the late 1950s, Toyota Motors attempted to penetrate the American automobile market by launching a small, box-like car inauspiciously named the Toyopet. It sold only 258 cars in its first year. This grand failure did not dissuade Toyota from its mission and subsequently the Japanese automobile maker went back to the drawing board and the boardroom. Next, the little company from Nagoya introduced the Crown in 1960 and the Tiara in 1964, both of which were also less than well received. But Toyota enjoyed the ongoing support of the Japanese government and the major banks and a protected domestic market; automobiles were a strategic industry.

USING MARKET AND TREND ANALYSIS TO NIBBLE AT THE EDGES

What Toyota did next has been repeated thousands of times by the Japanese in all fields in which they compete: they reverse-solved the problem confronting them. Unlike American companies that once believed that anything they build at home would also sell in Japan, Toyota knew that their cars were not satisfying American customers. They took to asking themselves what it was that the consumer wanted, then went about supplying it. In the wider scheme of things, they could not afford to be wrong. Toyota set about surveying American consumers and dealers about technical requirements, design tastes, and unsatisfied needs, either directly or through American research firms. They also studied American style through the ages, American road conditions across various regions, and the accoutrements that comprised the American definition of "creature comforts." Toyota also studied the Volkswagen to determine what Americans liked about it—and more importantly, what they did not like.

Toyota found that Americans wanted roominess and a comfortable interior. Power was a must, but that they also liked fuel economy and a vehicle that dealt more adequately with the growing congestion created by urbanization. They also learned that consumers' greatest concern with buying foreign-made cars was the problem, real or imagined, of having repairs made and getting spare parts. The 1965 Corona reflected all that Toyota had learned. Unlike the Beetle, the Corona was Americanized in styling and in operating features and its engine offered twice the horsepower of the Volkswagen, yet dramatically greater fuel efficiency than American models. It was the only small car import to offer a fully automatic transmission; and it was also affordably priced, with larger built-in margins for dealers. To allay consumer concerns, Toyota spent years to build its service network to make sure that parts and after-sale service were widely available. Toyota built on its success in the low-end of the automobile market, growing to where it competes today in almost every segment of the market.

Japanese companies understand better than others the power of information. From the worldwide networks of the *sogo shosha* to the local R&D centers of Japanese manufacturers in the United States, thousands of overseas Japanese are constantly feeding the newest technologies and business opportunities back to Japan. It is hardly surprising to learn, then, that two of the most popular words in the Japanese language are *joho* (information) and *chishiki* (knowledge).

FROM COMPONENTS TO SYSTEMS

Growing a business from components to subsystems and then to advanced systems is a staple of Japanese strategy. To tackle the upper end of a market straightaway would have exposed the Japanese to an experienced field of competitors and the prospect of certain failure. By selecting ignored or underserved segments, the Japanese develop a market position, technical expertise, name recognition, brand loyalty, and the financial strength to carve out the next circle in the ring. The Japanese marketing and manufacturing matrix is nothing if not pragmatic. Products are mass produced in highly focused but flexible factories where production efficiencies can be maximized. With an established low-end product, they move up the value curve, adding features and getting the most out of the factory before a model change and subsequent retooling must take place. When demand for old main-line products weakens, they will often expand their product offerings with many variations on the existing theme, develop new distribution channels, and cut prices to stimulate sales. The risk of falling behind a competitor is seen as far more dangerous than the financial risk associated with rapid growth. For virtually every industry in which it now excels, Japan has worked to understand the base technologies and then moved up the value chain into higher margin areas.

In electronics, with leadership built in semiconductors, disk drives, display technologies, printers, and other peripherals, and with established sales channels throughout North America and Europe, the Japanese will soon move to dominate the electronics systems market from workstations to supercomputers. Across numerous other industries, the story of Japanese strategy is being similarly played out: a critical mass is developed at home by way of government backing and higher pricing; niche markets are selected; appropriate products are manufactured for each geographically targeted market; short-term profits are sacrificed to gain market share; and once a market conquest is completed, pricing moves up to build profits for the next stage of incremental growth. From VCRs to consumer audio equipment, the cycle is being repeated in almost every market segment, virtually unchecked by American manufacturers. Many American companies today seem to believe business is merely assembly and distribution of Japanese and Taiwanese components.

Commitment is also key. Even in firmly established markets, Japanese companies will aggressively take aim at a market and publicly announce five- and even ten-year market-share forecasts (often with targets of 25 percent or more) with confidence. An article in the *Nihon Keizai Shinbun* discussed in frank terms the goals of Okamoto Industries, Japan's leading condom maker. With a 63 percent market share in the Japanese domestic market, Okamoto sees great opportunities in the United States with increased safety consciousness following the AIDS crisis. In 1988 Okamoto opened its own U.S. subsidiary and boldly predicted that with its quality products and innovative packaging it would capture 10 percent of the American market within two years—despite starting from an indiscernible position—and expand to 25 percent within seven years. "The Japanese philosophy is that once we have committed ourselves, we will do it," says Hisayuki Naito, general manager of Okamoto U.S.A.[3] Contrast this upfront commitment to the American entrepreneurial approach. Venture capitalists and many executives are emotionally (and financially) committed to a rapid rate of growth early on via technological differentiation. Rapid exploitation of the early market and immediate emphasis on profit maximization are stressed in order to justify a high-market valuation at the time of a public stock offering. The result is a "hollow" organization without the foundation of competence needed to overcome long-term adversities and to build a lasting presence.

BURROWING, EMERSION, AND KNITTING

By obtaining proven technologies and eyeing already-proven markets with quantifiable consumer demand, the Japanese can enter a market on the cheap. A propensity to reverse engineer—or obtain license or patent access—has led to an image of the Japanese as copiers. We believe that this image is outdated in most respects. However, historically the Japanese achieved leadership in many fields through imitation thereby bypassing the expensive stages of initial research and development and marketing. The concept of copying and improving upon existing ideas is nothing to be ashamed of and should be a key strategy of Western companies, with the key differentiator becoming design, quality, and ability to manufacture.

A logical extension of this approach has been the campaign to purchase outright established American companies, many with blue-blooded lineage. As a result of their "burrowing" beneath the surface, the Japanese now own some of the biggest names in American business (see Table 5.1). The benefits of burrowing are twofold. By purchasing an existing company, they buy an ongoing, presumably successful enterprise, with all the consumer loyaties, market identity, and goodwill that comes with it. Secondly, they buy an American face.

In the same way, the Japanese have come to pursue a strategy of blending their wholly owned operations into the American landscape. No corner of the nation, from Hollywood to downtown Manhattan, has escaped the attention of Japanese industrialists who see numerous advantages to melting into the pot. For most industries, it brings the Japanese even closer to the turf they are working, giving them even

Table 5.1
Japanese Acquisitions of, and Investments in, American Companies (1987–89)

Japanese Company	*U.S. Company*	*Purchase Price (in $millions)*	*Date*
Sony	Columbia Pictures	$3,450	1989
Dai ichi Kangyo Bank	CIT Corporation	1,280	1989
Mitsubishi Real Estate	Rockefeller Group	870(51%)	1989
Fujisawa Chemical	Lyphomed Inc.	798	1989
Kyocera Corp.	AVX	561	1989
	National Advanced Systems	398	1989
	Shaklee Corp.	395	1989
	Guber-Peters Entertainment	270	1989
Toshiba	Diasonics	168	1989
Bridgestone Corp.	Firestone Tire & Rubber	2,600	1988
Seibu/Saison Group	Intercontinental Hotels	2,150	1988
Nippon Mining	Gould, Inc.	1,100	1988
Paloma Co.	Rheem Manufacturing Co.	850	
California First Bank	Union Bank of Calif.	750	1988
Shiseido Co.	Zotos Int'l Inc.	315	1988
Onoda Cement	CalMat Co.	242	1988
Sony	CBS Records	2,000	1987
Aoki	Westin Hotels	1,350	1987
Nippon Life	Shearson	508(13%)	1987
Sumitomo Bank	Goldman Sachs	500(12.5%)	1987
Dai Nippon Ink	Reichhold Chemicals	525	1987

SOURCES: "Japanese Firms Hunt Big Foreign Game" *Wall Street Journal* (November 10, 1989), reprinted by permission of the *Wall Street Journal,* © 1989 Dow Jones & Company, Inc. All rights reserved worldwide; *Asian Wall Street Journal* (January 22, 1990), p. 6.

greater insight into the sensibilities, tastes, and needs of their consumers. This is a model which American companies should study and follow. Through the formation of intricate joint venture arrangements, Japanese are effectively wedding their long-term interests with those of American companies—most particularly competitors, thus creating allied interest groups and becoming part of American life. U.S. firms are readily welcoming the onslaught of joint ventures with the attendant large bankrolls. By such means, the lines of nationalism are blurred by economic interests.

This "knitting" of interests is clearly the strongest force sweeping in change. Hybrid organizations woven across industrial and national boundaries serve Japanese companies in numerous ways; principally they provide a long-term growth opportunity distinct from, yet auxiliary to, their central operating entities. Changing eco-political conditions in the United States and Europe pose a threat to the Japanese, who are promoting extensive joint venture programs to minimize the threat of a political backlash against Japan's success. And perhaps most importantly, local manufacturing operations, even jointly maintained, offer a less costly way to produce products for local consumption. As a result, it has become difficult to distinguish who really is running the operation or the amount of local content. In the past five years alone, Japanese automakers have spent on U.S. plant facilities an amount in excess of the GNP of Hong Kong. As we can see from Table 5.2,

Table 5.2
Japanese Auto Plants in the United States and Canada

Manufacturer *Parent Company/Location*	*Yearly Capacity* *(number of units)*	*Employment*
1. NUMMI Toyota (50%)—GM (50%), Fremont, Calif.	300,000	3,400
2. Toyota Motor Cambridge, Ontario	50,000	1,000
3. CAMI Automotive Suzuki (50%)—GM (50%), Ingersoll, Ontario	200,000	2,000
4. Honda Motor Alliston, Ontario	80,000	850
5. Mazda Motor Flat Rock, Mich.	240,000	3,400
6. Diamond-Star Motors Mitsubishi (50%)—Chrysler (50%), Normal, Ill.	240,000	2,900
7. Fuji Heavy Industries (Suburu) Isuzu (49%), Lafayette, Ind.	120,000	1,700
8. Honda Motor Marysville and E. Liberty, Ohio	510,000	8,000
9. Nissan Motor Smyrna, Tenn.	440,000	5,100
10. Toyota Motor Georgetown, Ky.	200,000	3,500
Totals	2,180,000	31,850

SOURCE: "Shaking Up Detroit." Reprinted from August 14, 1989 issue of *Business Week*, p. 76, by special permission, copyright © 1989 by McGraw-Hill, Inc.

Japanese auto plants in North America will employ over 32,000 people and produce over 2.3 million autos, in addition to the 2.7 million vehicles exported to the United States every year.

Japanese also are spending millions of dollars to befriend other nations and to polish their image around the world. It is reported that Japan spent $25 million on a three-month "Europalia '89" cultural festival in Europe to show Japan has more to offer than just economic self-interest, and as a collective group of corporations, spend millions of dollars on joint advertisements organized by JETRO and other agencies in leading magazines expounding the virtues of their global strategies.

DEEP-POCKET COMMERCE

The Japanese are obsessed with market share at any cost. Even as the yen appreciated by 60 percent in the late 1980s, Japanese companies raised their United States prices only nominally, basing prices on America-bound goods on dollar-dominated "costs." Able to continue charging high prices to consumers in Japan, and with rocketing local demand, a sky-high stock market, and the near-absence of foreign competition, Japanese companies have beat the high yen and are today even stronger and more profitable than ever.

As soon as the strength of the exchange-rate ranges became apparent, Japanese companies set about to develop operations capable of profitability at an exchange rate of 100 yen to the dollar. The primary vehicle was cost cutting of a ferociousness and scope few, if any, Western companies have undergone. Among the techniques employed was the movement of labor-intensive subassembly operations offshore to lower cost areas where currencies were more closely tied to the U.S. dollar, such as Korea and Taiwan. Significant increased efficiencies were also achieved in Japanese-based operations through techniques such as "just-in-time" and automated manufacturing. At the same time, advertising and distribution expenses in the United States in terms of the yen declined proportionately, and imported raw materials became much cheaper. As a result, Japanese manufacturers were able to achieve record levels of profitability when the worst fears of yen strengthening were not realized and the dollar regained ground throughout 1989 and into 1990.

Japanese companies in the past have tended to be highly leveraged, financing fast growth with debt from friendly, supportive banks, and equity holdings by group or friendly long-term stockholders. Japanese companies are expected to earn smaller profits as a percentage of revenues, and pay less in dividends than do companies in North America and Europe. Success in the past decade, coupled with favorable financial markets, has built up the equity base of most Japanese corporations. The long-term bias of Japanese banks and stockholders and the low cost of capital have been key to the strong growth. These structures promote the pools of "patient" capital.

The diversified operations of the giant Japanese companies and their close banking relations give them access to many forms of stable capital. Accordingly, the sources that a corporation may have available for investment need not depend on the quarterly earnings of its operations or the price of its stock, factors that bedevil American competitors. Also, the extensive use of long-term credit from friendly banks encourages long-range planning and investment. The low prime lending rate in Japan is possibly its biggest competitive advantage and allows for aggressive investment in new plants and equipment. Collateral, equity, positions of lenders, required compensatory account balances, and the relatively stable capital supply in Japan allow continuous financing even in recessionary times for capacity expansion, R&D, price competition, and expansion of market share in domestic and foreign markets.

Japan still thinks productivity can be increased by investing in R&D (see Figure 5.1). Achieving a technology monopoly means Japan will have to worry less about protectionism. One economist estimates that over the past five years Japan's value-added per unit of exports has jumped by almost 70%.[4] One example of aggressive investment is Toshiba, which at the end of 1989 raised $3 billion for internal investment, and $600 million for semiconductor plants and equipment. This represented one of the largest fund-raising efforts ever by a single business on the Tokyo and Eurobond markets.[5]

JAPANESE STRATEGY IN ACTION

While in many ways unique from other Japanese companies—those spawned by the large *keiretsu* or nurtured by MITI—Sony Corporation provides a prototypical example of Japanese strategy in action. Established in 1946, Sony is a new company by Japanese standards. Since its founding, Sony has cultivated an image as a technology leader with a solid export strategy. Because it was an outsider in the Japanese business community, it focused its efforts on global operations, and pioneered

Figure 5.1 Key Indicators of Comparative Competitiveness: Capital Investment, Savings, Cost of Capital

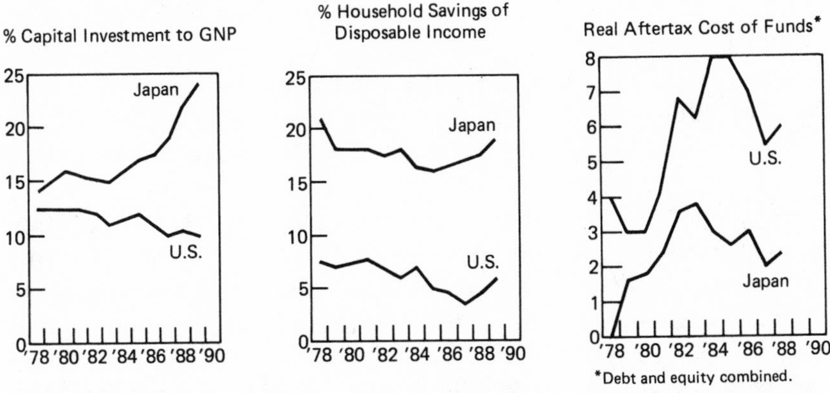

SOURCE: Andrew Tanzer, "How Do You Shut the Darn Thing Off?" *Forbes* (November 13, 1989), p. 39; Kenneth Courtis, Deutsche Bank Group; Organization of Economic Cooperation & Development; Federal Reserve Bank of New York, as published in *Forbes.*

new products for new markets. Not being one of the traditional members of Japan's industrial elite, or blessed by MITI, Sony must continue to pioneer to survive and has accepted for years that it will always have major competition globally.

Akio Morita, Sony's chairman and founder, is a true entrepreneur who targeted markets neglected by the big electronics manufacturers—personal electronics and entertainment. "Research Makes the Difference" is Sony's motto. With the solid-state radio, Sony was one of the first companies to embrace applications for the everyday use of new solid-state transistor technology. Now diversifying into professional and industrial equipment, electronics, and software, Sony is continually evolving, moving away from its former image as a maker of the Walkmans and other audio equipment. After a long 15-year relationship, Sony's $2 billion acquisition of CBS Records shows the importance it places on software; and, as well, Sony now owns the rights to many major artists—Madonna, Bruce Springsteen, Michael Jackson—which it believes will give it a major advantage in sales of CD compact disks, a technology Sony pioneered.

Sony's entry into the engineering workstation market is the most recent example of its pioneering spirit. In the last two years, Sony has gained tremendous market share in Japan (over 20 percent) being the only Japanese player to challenge American companies. Its ability to move early and swiftly may be due to Sony's early exposure to what was happening in the U.S. market by being insiders and closely watching the developments at Apollo Computer and Sun Microsystems.

Until recently, Sony had almost no channels for its new computer products in Japan; it had to pioneer brand new relationships. This is the same difficult task foreign companies face in Japan, and Sony has had to put a great amount of effort into developing programs and incentives for previously unrelated distributors and resellers to become interested in Sony workstations. Sony's pricing strategy is aggressive, no smaller company could afford it. These new products required a large amount of development, training of new people, even hiring experienced computer executives from the outside—an act almost previously unheard of at Sony. Sony's investment may not pay off for some time, and is very risky, especially if expected sales volumes cannot be achieved in the United States, but it is now well on its way to becoming a significant player in the advanced information systems market.

This diversification strategy is paying off. Through concerted efforts, nonconsumer goods sales increased from $640 million in 1985 to over $4.64 billion in 1989. Even after difficult years adjusting to *endaka,* the high yen, Sony had sales in 1988 of $7.6 billion and over 60,500 employees worldwide. Now decentralizing production, planning, and marketing into three regional headquarters, Sony may become Japan's first truly global electronics company, with full design, manufacturing, and marketing functions in every major geography. Sony is one of the few companies to have locally hired presidents and top management (rather than Japanese), and it has a large component of its manufacturing done locally in each country in which it operates. As a result, sales are distributed around the world in relation to the potential business of each region of the Triad—a powerful statement few other companies can match: 33.5 percent in Japan, 29.8 percent in the United States, and 22.1 percent in Europe.[6]

The world's leading supplier dedicated to the once-niche market for robotics and numerical control devices, Fanuc provides another example of a newcomer's strategy in action. Over the past five years, Fanuc has exploited its rivals' weaknesses to consolidate its position as the world's number one supplier of programmable numerical controllers and robots, the workhorses of the automated factory. First, General Electric surrendered, forming a fifty-fifty joint venture in the United States with Dr. Inaba's company. Despite the fact that "GE had more software experts than all of Japan," and that it vowed not many years earlier to crush the Japanese in factory automation, GE's major assaults failed and it lost $200 million in its abortive attempt. Then General Motors capitulated. In the area of robots, Fanuc once had almost no market share but by forming a joint enterprise with General Motors, GM Fanuc Robotics Corporation suddenly became the world's largest supplier.

Fanuc used technology from others to gain entry into the market, and readily admits that much of its technology came from other companies, in both Japan and the United States. But it crushed the competition by picking a small niche and being the lowest-cost producer of top-quality components. Now, by taking a far more aggressive global position than any of its rivals in Japan, it has two of the world's largest companies as equal partners and continues to grow, year by year, in the world of factory automation. Just like its products, employee uniforms, and buildings, Fanuc is painting the world yellow with its ever-expanding presence.

Even in markets created by American companies, the Japanese have come to gain tremendous leadership positions. In three markets which it pioneered—laptop computers, hand-held calculators, and electronic test equipment—Hewlett-Packard has watched as its first-place position was eroded with the entry and subsequent dominance of Japanese majors. Using HP's pioneering technologies, Japanese competitors have become the world leaders in each area—NEC, Sanyo, and Toshiba in laptops; Sharp and Casio in calculators; and Advantest and Ando in test equipment.

In an ironic twist of fate, HP has found it easier to purchase competitive knock-offs of its systems and merely put its name on the finished system. The back panels of much of HP's computer product line have the "Made in Japan" imprint. These systems are not made by HP's Japanese joint venture, Yokogawa Hewlett-Packard, but built by major Japanese competitors such as Canon (laser printers), Hitachi (disk drives), Sanyo (laptops), and Sony (monitors). And each HP computer system is fueled by Japanese DRAM semiconductors. In this sense, HP has become, in many ways, merely a distribution company. One of the most serious results is HP's dependence on Japanese semiconductors. Despite being a $10 billion company, HP has only a limited semiconductor capability, with no manufacturing capabilities for advanced memories, and is building for internal use only, which makes it impossible to reach the economies of scale needed to become profitable and drive such a critical technology to the leading edge.

THE FUTURE: KOKUSAIKA AND INOBESHION

"We've never seen figures like this for an economy this size," remarks Kenneth Courtis, senior economist at Deutsche Bank Capital Markets (Asia). "Japan is positioning itself to become the new product laboratory for the world in the 1990s, like America was in the 1950s and 1960s. When you are investing two and a half times as much of your GNP on capital equipment as the U.S., that is an enormous long-term competitive advantage." It is not consumption that will drive Japan's growth, says Courtis, "Capital investment is now the main economic engine in Japan, generating over half of real GNP growth. Last fiscal year (which ended March, 1989) spending on plant and equipment rose 18 percent, the highest rate in 19 years and quadruple the growth of private consumption."[7] Investment by Japan's manufacturers is exploding 28 percent in 1989, and again 20 percent in 1990. While the growth in domestic demand is helping imports, the majority is being filled by Japan's own production machine.

Kokusaika, or globalization, is Japan's new rallying cry and Japanese companies are moving faster than any other country to diversify overseas. The Japanese are using IBM, NEC, Sony, Fujitsu, and the *sogo shosha* as models for building world-wide information networks, local production and management systems, common corporate images and R&D structures, and company-wide value systems. The Japanese send thousands of managers to the United States (and Europe) on study tours of major American companies, to see how they operate and to accustom their employees to dealing with overseas environments and organizations.

Investment is booming and going international. In translations of oveseas information, and in English and foreign-language training alone, Japanese companies spend billions of dollars. Company sessions are given on how to deal with foreigners, manage Western staff, and promote Japanese manufacturing systems in overseas plants. The growth in global partnerships reflects this, as does the hiring of local management and the building of worldwide communications networks. The Japanese are also developing local government ties, participating in community programs abroad, and engaging in multiregional product development.

For Toshiba, forging linkages with foreign firms is a key part of its globalization plans which it has given code names—"I" and "W." The I plan, which started in the mid-1980s, was aimed at strengthening Toshiba's information and telecommunications resources, while the W plan is a global strategy to promote Toshiba's semiconductor business in new world markets. In a discussion several years ago, Tsuyoshi Kawanishi, executive vice-president of Toshiba's worldwide electronic component and materials semiconductor operations, said he believes that partnerships with the world's leading firms, while expensive, are in the company's long-term interest in order to foster technology exchange and complementary distribution channels. "It is impossible for one firm to supply all the products needed to meet the needs of a rapidly diversifying world market," says Kinshi Kadono, Toshiba's senior vice-president. Now Toshiba has built partnerships with twenty-two major overseas firms in the last five years—with Siemens of Germany in semiconductors, with Sun Microsystems for computer sales in Japan, with another German company in industrial robots, and with Motorola for the production of memory chips and microprocessors in Japan. Through these connections, Toshiba is gaining a better international vision, and most Toshiba employees working abroad will agree that "they cannot conduct business overseas from an isolated Japanese point of view any longer."[8]

Innovation is more than a new buzzword in Japan; it is a sweeping change in ethics with society-wide dimensions. Innovation (or *inobeshion,* as it is written in *katakana,* the Japanese phono-language used for foreign words) is seen as the means for leaping from the old ordering system onto a new plane of being. It implies that the Japanese no longer are satisfied with improving upon the past; they desire to be molders of the future. Like previous campaigns we can be assured that the Japanese will pour their souls into the effort. One reason for this drive to quantum improvement, as we have suggested above, is that innovation as a marketing weapon is practically indefensible. A wholly new product around which a wholly new market springs up has no competition. It is a goal not without risk due to its inverted structure: innovative products often precede customer demand. But where a company has the production and global distribution the rewards of cultivating demand with a small window for competitive response can be great.

Innovation is everywhere in Japan. When we asked a friend at Konica, the third-largest photographic supply company in Japan, what the goals of his company are as it fights head-on with Fuji Photo and Kodak (not to mention the likes of Toshiba, Fujitsu, Canon, Ricoh, and many others in the area of diversified office equipment), he said, "Innovation—new products, new design, and new manufacturing." And what the Japanese cannot develop themselves, they are tapping from American universities and by investing in start-up companies.

Nikon is a classic example of how Japanese companies have been successful by diversifying through R&D and determination into growing new markets, however unrelated to past business. While some companies have used their vast hordes of money to buy their way into new business fields, such as Nippon Steel into electronics, Nikon used existing technical strength in optics technology to become the world leader in wafer steppers used in manufacturing integrated circuits. Nikon, long known as a producer of 35mm cameras, actually saw its stepper division sales outpace its traditional business in 1989. Carefully positioning Nikon beyond its past role as a cameramaker, Chairman Shigetada Fukuoka refers to Nikon today as "a precision machine maker." Nikon's sales grew from 20 units in 1981 to 530 units in 1988. Despite losses in both 1986 and 1987 due to the high yen, a saturated camera market, high fixed costs, and a semiconductor recession, Nikon weathered the storm by continuing to invest during the downturns and building direct marketing organizations. Due to this persistence and to internal development efforts of new advanced technology, Nikon today is the world leader in this critical market—a market in which American companies—such as GCA and Perkin-Elmer which were once the leaders—have nearly collapsed in the face of fierce competition.

Competitive Profile: Summary for Understanding

- Regardless of what product or services you offer, you are competing with Japan—today.
- Japanese companies are market-share driven and committed to the long term. Those that survive the fierce battlefield at home are tough, seasoned fighters. Short-term profits will often be sacrificed for market share. Competing with a Japanese company can be a war of attrition.
- The typical Japanese strategy is to first attack neglected or underserved markets and simple, repeatable technologies and/or components. From there, they move to more sophisticated, higher value-added, and more competitive markets.
- With a lower cost of capital and less pressure for short-term performance, the Japanese company can sustain longer battles for market share with such powerful tools as predatory underpricing and dumping.
- The Japanese companies are integrating themselves into the heart of the American market by linking their interests with competing

and complementary companies, and by buying big name American firms. They are also buying into promising American start-ups pressed for cash.

- To survive against your Japanese competition, you have to have success in Japan.

These and other considerations paint a profile of a very tough set of competitors arising from the East. As a result, most American and European companies have worried themselves—and rightly so—about fending off the Japanese competition at home. Far fewer have seen the absolute necessity of competing in Japan. Still, many foreign firms have established operations in Japan in search of a share of its huge market opportunity. It is enlightening to study in the next chapters those firms that have bravely ventured forward behind the shoji screen.

6

The Japan Success Quotient

American Companies in Japan

He who is shut inside is a pheasant. He who enters to arrest is a hawk.

MIYAMOTO MUSASHI

The foregoing chapters have described the very real challenges for foreign companies competing with Japan. But this should not lead one to believe that success is not possible. The good news is that many foreign firms are succeeding in Japan, have achieved handsome rewards in the Japanese market, and are gaining a foothold in other parts of the booming Pacific Rim. In Japan today, you can find such well-known names as IBM, Hewlett-Packard, Xerox, Weyerhaeuser, McDonald's, Texas Instruments, Digtal Equipment Corporation, Applied Materials, Proctor and Gamble, Goldman Sachs, Sun Microsystems and even Domino's Pizza. Some are even market-share leaders:

- American Express is the most popular credit card in Japan. The company has 3,500 employees and had $800 million in 1988 revenues.
- Coca-Cola produces 60 percent of all carbonated beverages sold in Japan and had 1988 sales of over $3.4 billion. Japan is their most profitable operation.

- IBM's wholly owned subsidiary today employs more than 26,000 people and had sales of $9.2 billion in 1988. Some 20 percent of its Japanese sales were exports to 70 other countries.
- McDonald's has over 600 franchised outlets in Japan, with 2,750 full-time employees and 50,000 part-timers.
- Fuji-Xerox's 1988 sales topped $3.5 billion, and today it claims 50 percent of the copy volume in the Japanese market.
- American Insurance Union (AIU) revenues in Japan are larger than those of its U.S. parent.
- The market has grown so big for Upjohn Pharmaceuticals that it opened a $113 million R&D facility in Tsukuba.
- Salomon Brothers made pretax profits of $57 million in the first half of 1989 in Japan, while its U.S. operations lost $27 million in the same period.
- Nearly half of the $115 billion Japanese software market last year was controlled by distributors and subsidiaries of American companies.

More than 50,000 U.S. products are being sold in Japan. The American Chamber of Commerce in Japan (ACCJ) now has more than 500 member companies. The policy bureau for Japan's Ministry of International Trade and Industry (MITI) estimates that more than 1,000 American firms are doing business in Japan, either through subsidiaries or joint ventures with Japanese companies, and they realized combined sales of nearly $60 billion in 1989.[1]

Unfortunately, by most other indicators, foreign companies are far from reaching their potential in the Japanese market. An analysis of Yano Research Institute's *Market Shares in Japan: 1989* points out that of 1,400 categories of products and equipment, there are less than thirty companies with market shares of over 10 percent in any category or market. The few that do have strong positions, we have listed in Table 6.1. American direct investment over the last forty years is still less than one-eighth of Japanese investment in the United States during the past five years. In 1988 alone, U.S. companies invested only $1.8 billion in Japan, while Japan invested $21.7 billion in the United States.[2] The United States Chamber of Commerce estimates that some 50,000 American businesses could export their products to Japan, but do not. Only 120 of the Fortune 500 companies have affiliates in Japan. A 1987 study by *Electronic Business* magazine found that only forty-six American electronic companies reported taxable income to the Japa-

Table 6.1
Foreign Companies with Leading Market Shares in Japan

Foreign Company	*Product*	*Market Share in Japan*	*Ranking in Industry*
Ajinomoto-General Foods	Instant coffee	24.8%	2
Applied Materials Japan	IC etching equipment	32.0	1
Caterpillar-Mitsubishi	Crawler tractors	37.4	2
	Bulldozers	38.9	2
Coca-Cola Japan	Soft drinks	60.0*	1
Eastman Kodak (Japan)	Color photo film	11.2	3
Fuji Xerox	Copiers	19.2	3
IBM Japan	Large-scale computers	30.0*	2
	Personal computers	5.6	4
International Rectifier	Discrete Si Thyrister devices	12.1	5
Johnson & Johnson	Adhesive Band-Aids	39.5	1
Levi Strauss	Jeans	10.2	2
Lipton	Black tea	28.7	1
McDonald's	Fast food	30.0*	1
NCR	Cash registers	28.2	2
Nestlé	Instant coffee	65.1	1
Nippon Lever Industries	Shampoos	12.0	3
Nihon Otis Elevator	Elevators	12.4	4
Nihon Sun Microsystems	Engineering workstations	30.0*	1
Pyrex	Cookware	30.0*	2
Procter & Gamble	Disposable diapers	15.0	1
	Sanitary napkins	10.1	3
Schick	Safety razors	70.0*	1
Sumitomo 3M	Magnetic tapes	20.0*	3
Texas Instruments	Bipolar digital ICs	12.9	3
Tupperware	Kitchenware	20.0*	3

*Estimates.

SOURCE: "Market Shares in Japan: 1989," Yano Research Institute, Ltd. (July 1989), 12th Edition.

nese government of more than $1 million, and of that number only eighteen companies earned $10 million or more before taxes.

Among those companies that do participate in Japan, most pass their products "over the fence" and rely on Japanese distributors to take things from there, content to send their management to Tokyo once or twice a year. Sadly, many firms merely license their technology to Japanese companies to manufacture and distribute in the local market, without even establishing an office in Japan to manage the relationship. A few hearty souls enter into joint ventures with Japanese companies by providing a new product or technology. But the Japanese partner typically controls the show in Japan, staffing the office, working closely with the customers, and determining strategy with minimal active participation from overseas. From such an arrangement the American company enjoys little in the way of reciprocal technology transfer. The unfortunate fact is that the vast majority of American companies still fail to consider Japan a market worth their time and effort. Much is yet to be done.

CHARACTERISTICS OF WINNERS IN JAPAN

Over the past three years we have followed and researched a number of American companies in the Japanese market, mostly large corporations, but also a number of smaller and medium-sized operations. While a large number of these companies are technology-related, we feel that the lessons they provide are applicable to any business being established in Japan. In determining a success quotient for the companies we reviewed, the following criteria were used:

- Percentage of worldwide revenues generated in Japan
- Percentage of worldwide employees located in Japan
- Market share in Japan
- Industry ranking in Japan
- Sales revenue and profits
- Growth rate
- Percentage of revenue for new product development in Japan
- Image in the market
- Leadership in technology and innovation—real and perceived
- Engineering resources in Japan
- Sales offices and sales force
- Direct customer, supplier, and banking relationships
- Extent of product adaptation and market targeting

- Number of Japanese on corporate board of directors and in top management
- Number of new college graduates hired
- Partnerships with first-tier Japanese firms

While actual performance in Japan was a significant factor in our study, we were principally interested in relative performance in Japan compared to overall corporate performance and, more importantly, the impact of participating in Japan on the wider corporate culture. In fact, building their Japanese business has given these companies an understanding of how to compete on a global basis in the world's most demanding business environment. In light of these demands, these companies have adopted truly global marketing strategies and organizational structures and have pushed their people to be the best in product development, manufacturing, quality, and delivery. They are gaining access to the world's most technologically advanced suppliers, and close, long-term relationships with valuable global partners, major customers, and banks.

As this list indicates, the number of foreign-owned companies meeting their potential in Japan is small. For most of these companies, revenues from Japan represent a small percentage of worldwide revenues, in most cases less than 5 percent. Not surprisingly, beyond the top ten in our analysis, there were almost no companies with greater than 5 percent of their employees in Japan.

Clearly the numbers in Table 6.2 cannot fully reflect the actual situation for every company, and many companies have rapidly increased their commitment to Japan over the past three years in hiring and sales, but the overall impression of limited commitment is unmistakable. For companies with strong Japanese performances, we find that they are also successful in most other parts of the world. The distinct advantages to participating in the Japanese market include access to new products originating in Japan, the opportunity for global partnerships with Japanese companies, and the ability to closely monitor competition and to apply pressure on Japanese rivals in their own markets. A number of Western companies are doing well in Japan, and not all of them are big companies. Many smaller firms and cooperative ventures are reaping profits and growing market shares. These companies demonstrate common traits which have enabled them to be successful: a genuine commitment to the market, a carefully honed image, and a product strategy tailored to Japan. Significantly, they are learning from the experience and are translating this knowledge into greater competitive strength worldwide. We believe these stories of success and failure

Table 6.2
Leading Foreign Subsidiary Performances in Japan,
1987–88 Estimates

Company	*Employees in Japan*	*Employees Worldwide*	*%*	*Revenues in Japan ($in thousands)*	*Revenues Worldwide ($in millions)*	*%*
1. Applied Materials Japan	310	1,765	17.56	135,165	362	37.26
2. Molex Japan	1,030	5,900	17.46	174,635	502	34.78
3. Fuji Xerox	12,646	99,032	12.70	2,977,078	10,866	27.40
4. Shin Caterpillar Mitsubishi	6,370	53,770	11.84	1,513,814	10,423	14.52
5. Banyu Pharmaceuticals (Merck)	2,700	31,100	8.68	554,664	5,061	10.95
6. Nihon Unisys	7,686	98,300	7.81	1,196,521	9,713	12.31
7. NCR Japan, Ltd.	4,332	62,000	6.98	782,264	5,614	13.86
8. Amway (Japan), Ltd.	450	7,000	6.43	553,571	1,800	29.61
9. Texas Instruments Japan	4,700	78,000	6.02	720,943	5,595	12.88
10. Nihon Data General Corp.	876	15,565	5.62	122,143	1,364	8.95
11. IBM Japan, Ltd.	20,630	387,112	5.33	8,484,621	59,681	14.21
12. Avon Products Co., Ltd.	1,715	34,500	4.97	154,757	2,763	5.56
13. Samsung Japan Co., Ltd.	210	4,300	4.88	575,000	27,386	2.09
14. AMP (Japan), Ltd.	1,050	21,800	4.81	362,143	2,318	5.62
15. Johnson Co., Ltd.	590	12,300	4.80	211,071	1,500	14.07
16. Yamatake-Honeywell Co.	3,697	78,097	4.73	683,071	6,679	10.22
17. Sony Tektronix Corp.	950	20,252	4.63	182,142	1,412	12.89
18. Teisan, K.K. (L'Air Liquide SA)	967	25,000	3.86	322,421	20,639	1.56
19. Japan Upjohn (45 Sumitomo)	770	20,500	3.76	205,143	2,521	8.14
20. Revlon	900	24,700	3.64	220,000	2,456	11.16
21. Yokogawa-Hewlett-Packard	3,000	87,000	3.44	834,443	9,831	8.48
22. Nippon Roche, K.K.	1,600	47,498	3.37	283,571	5,502	5.43
23. Teradyne K.K.	160	4,750	3.37	30,950	377	8.20
24. Bristol-Myers	1,140	34,900	3.26	380,000	5,401	7.00
25. Nihon Digital Equipment	2,700	94,700	2.85	521,428	9,389	5.55
26. Measurex Japan, Ltd.	67	2,540	2.64	15,000	227	6.60
27. Mitsubishi Monsanto	1,357	51,702	2.62	458,378	7,639	6.00
28. Squibb Japan, Inc.	440	16,915	2.60	85,714	2,588	3.31
29. Sumitomo 3M	2,135	82,818	2.57	729,157	10,581	6.89
30. Coca-Cola Japan	684	28,030	2.44	2,000,000	7,658	26.11
31. Dow Corning	170	7,000	2.43	35,078	1,303	0.01
32. Ciba-Geigy (Japan), Ltd.	2,088	86,109	2.42	786,300	12,059	6.52
33. Cray Research Japan, Ltd.	85	4,000	2.12	20,000	687	2.80
34. Merck Japan, Ltd.	175	8,606	2.03	61,678	1,000	6.10

SOURCES: "Foreign Affiliated Companies in Japan," *Toyo Keizai Shinposha* (1989); "You Can Make Money in Japan," *Fortune* (February 12, 1990), p. 85.

offer valuable lessons to all companies seeking to crack the Japanese market.

REVERING THE CUSTOMER AS GOD

Many of the companies in our study used service as a strategic weapon. The concept of serving the customer, and transforming this capability into a point of differentiation, takes on a whole new dimension in Japan. Japanese customers demand the very best in quality and service. Since it is an intensely competitive world, the giant Japanese companies have learned to make service a unique definer. As William Davidow and Bro Uttal explain in *Total Customer Service,* "In all industries, when competitors are roughly matched, those that stress customer service will win." Any company, whether American or domestic, which cannot meet the Japanese standards of service soon finds a bevy of capable competitors waiting in the wings. The best way for Americans to be successful is through the continual involvement of world-wide personnel with Japanese accounts and an on-going commitment to service.

We often use the analogy of the "flying wedge" to describe the role of service in the overall corporate strategy. Service must precede all products, regardless of how advanced and unique they are, in the relationship between supplier and customer. The service vanguard teaches the entire organization about what the customer really wants—not just what the supplier thinks he wants. We tell our employees that "Americans have always believed that if you build a better mousetrap, the customers will beat a path to your door. We believe if you beat a path to your customer's door, you will build a better mousetrap."

Molex is a prime example of a medium-sized American company which has demonstrated extreme commitment to service in the Japanese market, and as a result has become a major player among a field of giant competitors. Molex entered Japan in 1968 through a trading company, just as the consumer electronics industry was taking off, and well before other companies in its field even dreamed of going to Japan. At that time, foreign companies were not allowed to set up wholly owned subsidiaries. Establishing a joint venture originally, then incorporating Molex Japan, Molex was able to begin full operations in 1972 with a factory in Yamato, which has since been expanded to three other plants in Shioya, Shizuoka, and Okayama.

Molex's humble beginnings in Japan began with its first plant in a former bowling alley. Today, Molex Japan has over 1,200 employees under a charismatic president, Mr. Goro Tokuyama, and ranks in the top five electronic connector companies in Japan. Family-owned, and based in the Midwest, Molex was not your typical small company and seized the market opportunity in the days when Japan was still known for toys and cheap radios, rather than as a leader in high technology. Today, the products of Japan's major electronics companies such as Fujitsu, Sony, Matsushita, and Pioneer depend on Molex's high quality connector products, just-in-time delivery, close cooperation, and design expertise. Sales, service, and customer product design are handled through Molex's ten offices throughout the islands.

Molex made an important decision to hire people exclusively from the outside when they initially formed their joint venture. This was a critical decision as most of the people stayed with the company when they bought out their Japanese partner and have stayed loyal to Molex over the years. Also, from their first relationships with Sony and Matsushita, Molex learned early how to be successful in partnerships as a loyal Japanese vendor. Molex's CEO and vice chairman, Mr. Fred Krehbiel, points to the major re-education throughout the company which took place as Molex strove to meet the strict customer demands of its Japanese customers. "In quality, product design, delivery, and miniaturization, Japan was setting the pace throughout the 1970s and 80s. We were required to reduce new product cycles to six months for our Japanese customers, while in the United States, twelve months was the norm, and eighteen months was acceptable in Europe. Today, though, we find that almost all of our customers which are global companies have the same demands, and operate more or less in the same way. Our years in Japan gave us a jump on our competitors in this regard."

Molex has a large engineering group of hundreds of design, materials, and sales engineers in Japan dedicated to develop optimal parts in close partnership with its customers. With over $300 million in revenues in Japan in 1990, Molex has proved the payoff of having strong local sales, service, and manufacturing operations dedicated to serving its customers. A primary strategy is to strategically locate design centers for the fast turnaround of new prototypes and to answer immediate customers needs. As well, Molex has fostered a company ethic for fast response to customers. "We bend over backwards for our customers," said David Johnson, a Japanese-speaking design engineer from the United States, who has worked for Molex Japan for five years.

The second component of Molex's strategy is to operate locally as a fully Japanese company, while being integrated with the world-wide

Molex organization. Almost all parts sold in Japan are manufactured locally and Molex, Inc. has encouraged local decision making and decentralized corporate management. "We encouraged actions which would be expected of a Japanese company in Japan," says Krehbiel. "As well, Molex Japan personnel participate in worldwide functional training programs. Many Japanese employees have lived and worked in other Molex operations overseas and vice versa." Molex Japan continues to reinvest a large percentage of earnings back into new product development, design systems, and new production in Japan. As well, Molex Japan will be able to take advantage of Molex's global capabilities for serving any of their customers who move production facilities offshore. Says President Tokuyama, "This is extremely important as we have the ability to support Japanese companies wherever in the world they may want to locate."

Doing business in Japan for Molex has for many years involved concepts which are recently becoming popular worldwide: delivery of quality products on time using very quick product development cycles, working closely with the customers to fill their need in initial product development, and partnering with the customer as part of a joint team over the long haul. "These ways of doing business were at one time quite particular to Japan," says Krehbiel.

In the early days, recounts Krehbiel, "We didn't even know we couldn't be successful." Today, Molex is expanding their product lines even further beyond their traditional *minsei,* or home electronics, market into office electronics, industrial, and automotive connector markets based on their customer's own changing requirements. Mr. Krehbiel and Molex management have learned a great deal from their Japanese experiences, and this is reflected in Molex's approach to his global growth strategy. "It is our duty to supply our customers with the highest quality and the most innovative products we can, and to deliver them exactly when the customer wants them. We must be able to move quickly to meet the exact needs of our customers no matter how fast these needs may change. Our goal is to work to make sure our customers prosper, and in turn it will mean that Molex will prosper."

CONTROLLING YOUR OWN DESTINY

In order to truly succeed in Japan, a company must have a direct presence. The successful companies in our study invariably had a direct operating subsidiary with its own Japanese management and a local sales, marketing, manufacturing, and development capability. While direct sales may not make sense for every company or industry, the goal should be to move as close to the end customer of your products as possible. By doing so, the opportunity to influence the public perception and dealer and supplier channels will also increase. Since relationship-building is central to business-building in Japan, developing direct links to customers is essential. The strength of relationships, what we call the "vital link," directly correlates with a company's access to markets and industrial groups, and ultimately to positioning for long-term survival and growth. If a trading partner is used as a go-between, the distributor controls the customer; when he goes away, so does the customer, and in Japan customers are less likely to change relationships once they have built them. Your history as a supplier begins when you know your customer and his needs intimately, not in an insulated way from behind a Japanese company selling your product. This contrasts starkly with the American relationship which begins with the sale. In Japan, sales only come after a relationship is built.

There are also defensive considerations. By not having a strong direct presence in Japan, by not responding to the local market demands, and by failing to apply pressure in Japan's domestic market, American companies such as those in the automobile industry have allowed Japanese competitors to expand unchecked in Japan and then use that uncontested base to move into other world markets. Even though the Japanese have the highest per capita income in the world and a hunger for symbols of status, American automakers still largely ignore it. Until this year, no American car makers have had Japanese management or a Japanese sales force aggressively beating the pavement in Japan.

Albert Seig, Eastman Kodak Japan's president, admitted in an interview, "For too long we granted our Japanese competitors a safe haven. Because we didn't give them any real solid competition in their home market, we allowed them to amass enormous resources that they can use strategically against us in the rest of the world." In recent years, Kodak has aggressively built its operations in Japan, establishing a large R&D center in Yokohama, consolidating a number of various operations under Kodak Japan, and increasing investment and advertising. Today, after years of hard work, Kodak Japan is flourishing. Now, the Kodak blimp even rivals the Fuji Photo blimp for airspace over Japanese sporting events. A symbol of its growing sensitivity to local culture, Kodak fashioned its airship in the shape of a giant *koi,* or Japanese carp, a revered Japanese symbol. "Our strategy in Japan isn't just profit motivated. It is also to learn how to do business against our competition in their home territory. We believe this will be a major asset as we compete with (our rivals) in the rest of the world," concludes Seig.[3] This is the same strategy being used by Procter and Gamble, which is planning to build a new Asia headquarters in Osaka and invest millions in new product lines aimed at serving the local market. P&G hopes to keep its competitors in a reactionary mode, with resources and energies tied up in the domestic market and out of North America and Europe.

IBM is possibly the best example of how a direct presence pays off, both as a means of producing profit and as a way to maintain the technology edge in the face of aggressive competition. Obviously, IBM's size makes it one of the only companies that can afford to go head to head with the giant Japanese corporations, a fact which continues to earn "Big Blue" enormous respect in Japan. Maybe more important than its size, IBM has served as a model for Japanese corporations as they build global organizations and manufacturing strategies. For all these reasons, IBM is a compelling model for any company interested in doing business with Japan. It has truly earned insider's status in Japan, and has built close relationships with the government and a number of Japan's major corporations, including its own largest competitors. IBM learned better than anyone else that a good offense is the best defense.

IBM started in Japan in 1925, and secured its first major order for adding machines with Mitsubishi Shipbuilding. In 1937, it was established as Nihon Watson Computing Machines and built its first Japanese factory, for computer cards, in Yokohama just before World War II. Even then, IBM understood the importance of going direct overseas, of adapting its products to regional markets, and providing a truly local company environment for IBM's Japanese employees. Thomas Watson's own corporate values blended well with Japanese company culture—an emphasis on group accomplishment and employee development, and its policies of trying to provide lifetime employment. All of these characteristics have merged well with the Japanese management style. In 1985, IBM was ranked by graduating university students as one of the top five companies to work for in Japan. Today, most Japanese feel that IBM Japan is a Japanese company, and, in fact, IBM Japan produces a large percentage of the products sold in Japan and throughout the world.

By being a consistent innovator and by licensing its technology (even though much of the licensing was forced by the Japanese government), IBM has positioned itself as the market leader in the Japanese computer market. By virtue of its trend-setting stature, IBM effectively controls the technological direction of its largest Japanese competitors, including Hitachi and Fujitsu, whose machines are compatible with IBM mainframe computers. By hanging tough in Japan, IBM has become a better company overall, and against the fiercely competitive backdrop, its commitment is unflagging. IBM presently has over 26,000 employees in Japan, several major factories, a world-class semiconductor fabrication center, a large headquarters in downtown Tokyo, sales offices throughout Japan, and a number of technology development centers and central research laboratories nationwide. The company continues to be one of the largest technical recruiters of Japanese new college graduates, competing quite favorably against Japanese companies.

The pharmaceutical industry provides other examples of success through a direct presence. Foreign pharmaceutical companies in Japan have performed better than companies in almost any other industry. They have been among the most aggressive in taking control of their own operations, building direct sales forces, and investing for the future. As a result, they are cashing in with a 15 to 20 percent share of Japan's $37 billion drug market, a market second in size only to the U.S. and remaining among the few industries in which the United States maintains a trade surplus with Japan.[4] Bayer Yakuhin, a subsidiary of the large West German chemical company, is an excellent example of the recent trend. Bayer ended its longstanding sales agreements with Japan's largest pharmaceutical company, Takeda Chemical Industries, and will cancel another with Otsuka Pharmaceuticals to begin selling most of its product directly.[5] In Japan, doctors sell the drugs they prescribe, thereby making most of their income not on services but on prescription sales. This may explain why Japan has the world's highest per capita drug consumption. Foreign companies have realized that a large direct sales force is critical to providing the personal attention demanded by Japanese physicians. Building relationships is vital; selling product requires a great deal of legwork and frequent customer visits.

RESEARCHING AND MANUFACTURING THE RIGHT PRODUCT FOR JAPAN

Japanese consumers have different tastes than those of Americans and Europeans. They also have more stringent definitions of quality. And they expect more in the way of service. A benefit of having a direct operation in Japan is a powerful understanding of these important differences, which will positively impact expectations and levels of quality and service throughout the entire company. This can, and should, result in the development and marketing of products appropriate to the demands of the Japanse buying public. An American product transplanted directly to Japan will not likely be successful without skillful adaptation and repositioning. Sometimes entire product lines may need to be reconceived for this market, and at other times may require only simple modification. For instance, adding miso soup flavoring to potato chips has created a growing demand for this classic American snack food. When Swatch entered the Japanese market, the Swiss watchmaker of colorful, low-end time pieces made the nearly catastrophic mistake of using the same advertising campaign and concept it successfully employed in the United States. With sales floundering, the company quickly stepped back and reintroduced the watches, customizing the product and the appeal to Japanese tastes. The key difference? Swatch found out through market studies that it needed to educate Japan's young people about how to wear watches as a fashion coordinate. Today, custom Japanese-designed Swatches sell in over 500 stores in Japan with growing success.

Procter and Gamble has realized significant gains after years of hard work in Japan. "When we entered Japan we were well armed with statistics, but we did not have an in-depth understanding of Japanese consumer need," said Far East President Ronald Pearce, in a speech to the ACCJ in March 1989. "Now we not only know what Japanese consumers are doing," he continued, "but increasingly why they are doing so." Five variations of the Pampers product line of disposable diapers, fifteen years, and $360 million in deficits later, P&G is making large profits in Japan, having achieved strong brand-name recognition, and forged an integrated operation tuned to the unique needs of this market, all the way from product design through distribution.

Japan is now a leading center of innovation for a broad range of technologies, some of which are available nowhere else in the world. Japan has already become the leading supplier of most of the components for the Information Age—semiconductor chips, displays, and printers—as well as becoming a driver in other areas like biotechnology, advanced materials, manufacturing, and electronics. Virtually any company in any industry can benefit from exposure to this dynamic environment, and this can only be accomplished through research, development, and engineering in Japan, with Japanese scientists, technicians, and market experts. Only by developing local technical leaders, and building networks with leading laboratories, research institutions, universities, and associations, can American companies expect to get in on the ground floor of emerging technologies emanating in Japan.

In the pharmaceutical field, Upjohn has benefited from its Japanese research and development capability and is working to bolster its presence. Realizing the tremendous market potential, Upjohn established a wholly owned direct subsidiary in 1985, Upjohn Pharmaceuticals, and in 1988 it opened a $113 million R&D center in Tsukuba Science City, north of Tokyo, designed for advanced research in vascular and central nervous system disorders. The center serves as an integrated component in Upjohn's network of R&D centers in Europe and America. Upjohn Pharmaceuticals is using its Japanese presence to monitor new developments in Japan, to work closely with Japanese hospitals and pharmacies to get feedback on product requirements, to gain acceptance for new products through the regulatory process, and to research new chemicals and processes. Its local presence also helps Upjohn win the confidence and trust of Japanese doctors and researchers. The new facility and the commitment it represents have not gone unnoticed, and Upjohn officials believe it will play a key role in the company's long-term success in Japan.

Bayer Japan Ltd., formed in 1911, today has twelve affiliates in Japan. In recent years, Bayer became determined to be a leader and to bring its name out front in Japan's highly competitive pharmaceutical market. Theodore Heinrichson, president of Bayer Japan Ltd., believes that although restrictions and barriers could impede his business, coexistence is the key to success. A German, Heinrichson adds his own perspective to the current debate on Japan's "closed" markets: "I would not accept Japanese companies coming to Germany trying to change the German system." The company's aggressive investment plans, says Heinrichson, "reflect the growing importance of Bayer's Japanese operation as the center of the Asian market and as one of the three polars—together with Europe and the United States—in its global network. "Our philosophy is not only to sell, import, manufacture, but also to distribute and make real R&D in Japan. This is one of the cornerstones of our corporate strategy," he says. "Be patient, spend a lot of money, expect good returns, not quick ones, build your personnel and have continuity. Short term, quick, cheap, and fast are not adjectives which are going to be successful in Japan. Bonsai does not become beautiful in a few years."

Heinrichson expects to begin distribution soon of Bayer brand pharmaceuticals through its own distribution route, ending an 80-year-old sales contract with Takeda Chemical Industries Ltd. This will represent $430 million in lost business for Takeda: "We have grown up as a man to do our own business." Bayer now owns 76 percent of Bayer Yakuhin, steadily buying Takeda's shares. The twelve-company Bayer

Figure 6.1. Registration of Foreign Automobiles in Japan, 1975–90

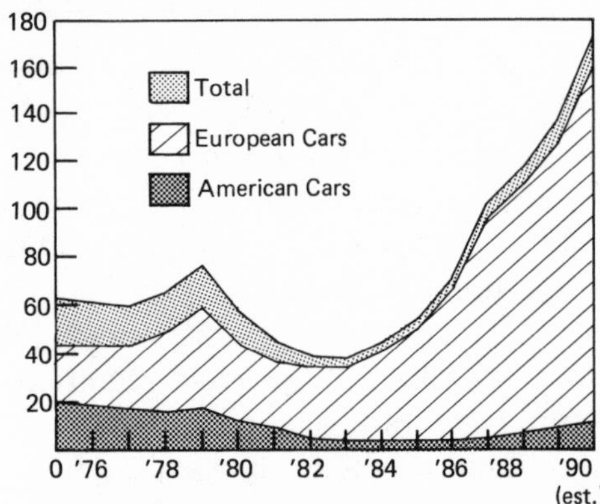

SOURCE: Japan Automobile Importers Association, adapted from Access Nippon, 1990.

group plans to spend $250 million over the next few years to expand its Japanese engineering plastics plant and development facilities.[6]

Kentucky Fried Chicken (Japan), a joint venture with Mitsubishi under the leadership of president Loy Westin, customized its American product and strategy to suit the tastes of the Japanese consumer. It positioned the stores as trendy and high class, not as fast-food stores. After conducting basic market research, french fries were substituted for mashed potatoes, the sugar content in the coleslaw was reduced, and KFC Japan introduced a menu of fried fish and smoked chicken, much to the chagrin of the headquarters office. Japan even had a few ideas of its own and tried to introduce the Japanese concept of small-store layout and flexible kitchen design to the home office, which could be suitable for U.S. shopping malls. KFC Japan was even experimenting with chicken nuggets as far back as 1981—until it was told to stop.

Shin Ohkawara, general manager of KFC Japan, became quite cynical in regards to the home office misunderstanding of his local strategies. "What worries me, though, is that despite this constant pressure from the United States for improved margins, Mitsubishi has never asked us for more profit. People at headquarters want to know why we have not raised our prices for four years now, and only twice in the last twelve years. By pricing our products just 20 percent above supermarket fresh chicken prices, we have expanded demand tremendously. If we use the U.S. pricing formula, we will just invite competition."[7]

While imports of European cars skyrocketed in Japan, American sales have remained dismal, and the corresponding lack of presence by

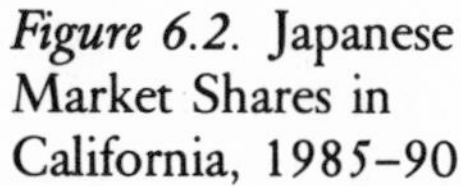

Figure 6.2. Japanese Market Shares in California, 1985–90

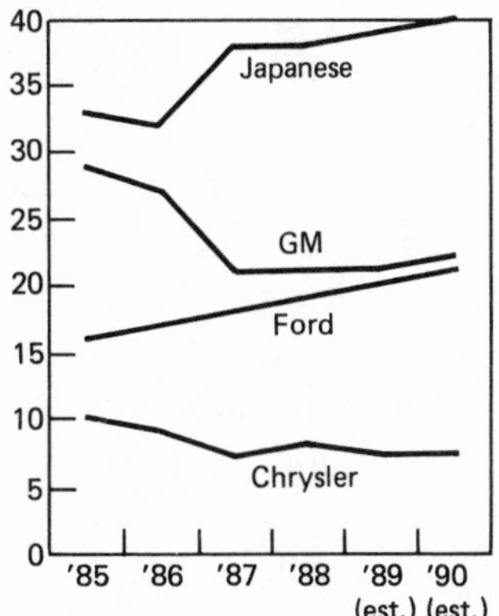

SOURCE: *Fortune,* "Can American Cars Come Back?" (February 26, 1990), from J.D. Power & Associates. © 1990 The Time Inc. Magazine Company. All rights reserved.

the American "Big Three" in Japan (see Figure 6.1) has allowed ten Japanese auto manufacturers to expand in the United States and other markets throughout the world virtually unchecked. American car makers are quick to point to "structural impediments" which hinder their efforts. Yet, in 1989, European models sold over 120,000 units and increased over the preceding year at a double-digit growth rate. BMW alone is predicting to be a billion-dollar business in Japan within three years. Across the Pacific, Japanese passenger car makers have more than a 26 percent share of the United States market (in California, over 40 percent—see Figure 6.2) and operate ten large factories in North America turning out 2.4 million automobiles per year in addition to the 2.7 million already being imported from Japan. Many estimate that Japan will have a 33 percent market share in the United States within five years.[8]

BUILDING A WORLD-CLASS ORGANIZATION AND MANAGEMENT

Successful companies in Japan realize that they are not competing just in Japan, but globally. Therefore, they have organized for this reality.

The operation in Japan requires—and gets—attention by the entire corporation. Division managers have responsibility for product success, not only in the United States, but in overseas markets as well. Each group throughout the company knows its job depends on success in Japan and other overseas markets, and each manager is evaluated by how well he performs in every region. The integration of Japanese managers into the worldwide organization represents one of the biggest advantages to a presence in Japan. Many American companies have found the Japanese to be their top performers in managing worldwide R&D centers, overseas manufacturing operations, and entire business units. Also, Japanese customers are global customers requiring Japanese employees in each region to support these accounts throughout the world.

Texas Instruments provides a good example of how integrating Japanese executives can be effectively achieved. In addition to running a major operation in Japan, Nihon TI President Akira Ishikawa is a senior vice-president of the parent Texas Instruments, with global responsibility for all of TI's semiconductor memory products worldwide. Under his leadership, Nihon TI sales revenues in 1988 were $591 million, a 46.7 percent increase over 1987.

EMBRACING COOPERATION AND COMPETITION

Many of the new movers and shakers in the Japanese market have reached their status by joining in strategic alliances with both complementary and even competing companies. For some, partnering has added value as a short-term bridge to direct operations—as part of the learning curve. In this respect, the Japanese can be among the best partners in the world when the alliance is properly structured and communication, technology, and information is shared and reciprocal by design. Enhanced market access, increased sales and marketing opportunities, and new sources of financing can all result from a well-conceived partnership with a top-tier Japanese company. The problem is that in partnerships with Japanese companies the lion's share of advantage has gone to the Japanese side. This usually manifests itself in lopsided access to critical technology, exclusive sales rights in Japan, and too much control. Good partnerships allow both parties to retain a fair degree of autonomy and independence, with minimal restrictions on complementary business opportunities. Problem partnerships are nearly always the result of poor communication or of wedding two organizations of unequal strength and differing management philosophies. Failing to clarify objectives, strategies, and methods of operations at the start of an alliance can be ruinous down the road when the honeymoon is over.

Sun Microsystems, a Silicon Valley maker of computer workstations, is today one of brightest stars in Japan as a result of strategic partnering. Just seven years since its founding, Sun reached sales in Japan of over $250 million in 1989, comprising over 12 percent of the company's total revenues. Leveraging partnerships to access the Japanese market and gain critical technology and components has been key to Sun's success. The giant trading company C. Itoh was Sun's first partner in Japan. This relationship began in 1983, when Sun's international operation was only a five-man group. But Sun was not satisfied with this initial success, seeing that major markets were unaccessible through a trading company. Company management decided instead to build a number of alliances with major industrial companies. First with Toshiba in 1985, Sun followed with alliances between itself and diversifying Nippon Steel Corporation (NSC), Fujitsu, Seiko, and Fuji Xerox. Because Sun believed no one partner could adequately reach the entire market, it found that multiple partnerships was the right strategy. Each of these relationships was targeted to a major untapped market, either a different industrial group or a vertical technology segment, like VLSI design or mechanical engineering. The Fujitsu relationship helped Sun move into mainframe networking, Seiko got it into graphics, and Fuji Xerox provided an entre into the office market. Each partner understood the role it had in the Sun strategy, so as additional channels were added, Sun did not lose face.

Seeing its business grow, Sun set up its own subsidiary in 1986 to support its major sales partners in Japan and to sell directly to universities and research labs—markets not being served through existing channels. It also began to develop a base of value-added resellers (VARs), usually smaller software or trading companies in specific vertical markets, such as electrical and mechanical design, software engineering, publishing, finance, office automation, and construction engineering. By using a large trading company to get started, then building channels with a number of leading industrial conglomerates, expanding from there to forge new alliances in each industrial group and application area, and then building its own operation in Japan, Sun has rapidly paved its way to insider status in the Japanese market.

A key to Sun's success in Japan was its ability to remain independent of any one industrial group and to maintain only nonexclusive relationships with its partners. The ability so far to prevent major multibillion dollar partner companies, each of which are Sun's fiercest competitors worldwide in their own right, from locking up its business in Japan has been key to getting to its current position. Sun has a powerful image in the engineering community as the market leader and market creator. Technological superiority gave Sun an entry to Japan, but only with its aggressive partnership strategy, diversification of channels, and commitment to a direct operation, has it been able to multiply its initial success.

Sun's commitment to a direct manufacturing, service, and engineering presence will be essential to its long-term survival against the giants of Japan's computer industry. Not only is Japan Sun's second largest market, but it is also the primary source for the majority of the components it uses in its products. Sun has already built a large service and receiving inspection center in Atsugi, and in 1989 announced plans to manufacture in Japan though this has not yet materialized. A commitment to these projects and an increased emphasis on technical engineering capabilities in Japan are seen by top management as the only way to maintain leadership. Like the situation for many global industries, increasingly Japan's requirements will dictate the worldwide standards in design, quality, and delivery.[9]

NINGEN KANKEI—HUMAN RELATIONS

"I can see why some American businessmen get frustrated in Japan," observes Charlie Perrell, former director of international sales at Sun Microsystems and now with MIPS Computer. "You arrive in Tokyo and expect to get down to business discussing accounts with the distributor the first day. Instead you find the time is loosely organized, that there are dozens of meetings, lunches with mid-level people and dinners with senior people. But if you stop listening to your inner voice that keeps asking 'when are we going to get down to business?,' you will realize that this *is* business, and you will be far more successful."[10]

As we have asserted, human relations are at the foundation of business in Japan—business built on a long history of networks and association, and past working relations. The Japanese like to deal with people and companies with whom there has been built a bond of trust. Loyalty, friendship, and mutual obligation between suppliers and customers "make the deal" in Japan, far more so than price or performance considerations alone. The reason that this is particularly true in Japan is that many companies have financial and historical cross-relationships involving distribution, equity investment, personnel and management which cement long-term joint destinies. In the "Japanese Way," customers and suppliers are long-run partners who will work together to attain maximum mutual value. These relations go far beyond contractual bonds; shared management philosophies and styles and gut-level feelings are very important.

C. Peter McColough, who was CEO of Rank Xerox from 1968 to 1982, talks about the early days when he and his colleagues were picking partners in Japan for what was to become Fuji Xerox, one of America's most successful joint ventures, and the importance of human considerations in the decision process. "When we went to Japan, we had a list of twelve companies that would be possible partners. Toshiba was high on the list. Fuji Photo was well down on the list. We didn't know anyone over there, but we thought other companies that were more into electromechanical devices would be a better partner. Fuji Photo was a chemical company, like Kodak. The reason we made a deal with Fuji Photo was that we had a deep trust in Mr. Kobayashi's ability, his honesty, and his integrity, and we really picked our partner on the basis of personal qualities rather than company qualities, not that Fuji Photo is a bad company. It is a good company. But it was not the ideal company for us in some ways."[11]

GETTING BACK TO BASICS

From the examples provided by our study companies, it is clear that success in Japan is only possible if the company's fundamental business practices, the "block-and-tackle" aspects of quality, continuous improvement and cycle-time reduction are in sound working order. These three performance indicators are shown to largely determine the levels of customer satisfaction and performance needed to survive and thrive in Japan and, by extension, the global marketplace.

Motorola has been one company to focus on the basics, both at home and in Japan. Tight controls by the Ministry of Post and Telecommunications and a stranglehold on the market by NTT makes the telecommunications market perhaps the most difficult Japanese market to crack. But by keeping its focus on quality and continuous, incremental improvement, Motorola has remained a powerful force in electronics in the face of large Japanese competitors, which are making inroads into every one of Motorola's markets. Chairman Robert W. Galvin frequently travels to Washington, D.C., to stress the need for the U.S. government to put pressure on Japan to open its markets further. George Fisher, Motorola's CEO, remains adamant that Motorola will succeed. "We intend to be the best manufacturer of electronics hardware in the world." As a result, the company is a strong competitor in Japan's growing markets for products such as pagers and mobile telephones. By pushing the basics—sticking to its main lines of business, investing in R&D and manufacturing, and uniting the company around quality—Motorola hopes to continue to strengthen its position.

In order to increase sales in Japan and gain access to technology, Motorola has entered into a joint venture with Toshiba. Through this venture, the company is investing heavily in new product design, miniaturization, faster introductions, and in higher standards of quality for the Japanese consumer. By mobilizing the entire company to reduce turnaround and improve quality, Motorola has already won big in Japan. Motorola has used MicroTac, its new shirt-pocket telephone, as a rallying point for quality and design improvements. The MicroTac has only 400 parts, and is assembled in only two hours using both robotics and manual labor at Motorola's advanced facility in Arlington Heights, Ill. In 1985, it took forty hours to assemble the over 3,000 parts of previous models. For its two-way radios and new cellular phones, Motorola reduced delivery time from thirty days to three. Production times went from two years after design to six months, and defects were reduced from 3,000 per million to less than 200. Since its inception, Motorola estimates its "Find It and Fix It" campaign against impediments to quality has saved the company $250 million annually. Due to its company-wide emphasis on quality, Motorola received the first Malcolm Baldridge Quality Award from President Reagan in 1988.[12]

U.S. Precision Lens (USPL), a division of Corning, Inc. since 1986, learned that meeting Japanese standards for servive and quality was not only essential for success in Japan, but in maintaining leadership worldwide. Today, one-third of its $37 million business in lenses for projection televisions comes from Japan. But things were not so rosy back in the early 1980s. From his first encounters with Japanese customers, USPL President David Hitchman realized that it was a different world behind the shoji screen. The customers he approached with offers to provide multisized plastic lenses—Sony, Toshiba, Hitachi, NEC, and Sharp—were among the giants of the Japanese electronics industry. "We had just sent one of our first shipments to a customer in Japan. Soon afterwards, we travelled there for a meeting. In the conference room, three of us faced twenty-five of them. In no uncertain terms, they told us that among their nearly 2,000 vendors, they had found only two with unacceptable quality. We, of course, were one of the two." With Hitchman's personal commitment to improve, the Japanese customer soon began to teach USPL how to be better, how to provide better quality and better service.

"The Japanese customer had found obvious defects in workmanship and quality control, but took USPL step by step through analysis of the problem. It was a great lesson for us," Hitchman recalls, "We guaranteed it would not happen again." When they returned to Cincinnati, USPL virtually shut down the plant, assembled all the employees together, and explained that everyone had to work together to meet new standards of excellence, standards demanded by Japan. USPL management accepted full responsibility for past failures and promised to communicate expectations throughout all levels of the company, and to give workers the tools to meet new standards. As a result, USPL instituted a company-wide quality program and focused on Japan through internal training and daily contact maintained through direct sales to the customer. Today, USPL is respected in Japan as a high-quality, loyal supplier to a large number of major Japanese firms. The company attributes its success to dealing directly with Japan through the top management of the company, by being very careful not to disclose trade or manufacturing technology or secrets, and working closely in Japan with the customer.[13]

THE ATTACK/COUNTERATTACK RESPONSE

Japanese companies move rapidly toward a new opportunity. In fact, most companies with a successful product or service in Japan find that they are never alone in the market for more than six months. Sony can be sure when it introduces a new portable CD player or television, five to ten other companies will soon have similar products on store shelves. This capability—to respond quickly to competitor challenges and to introduce new products to undermine or complement the competition's offerings—is seen as a key attribute for the successful companies we examined.

Even an industry leader like IBM has come to understand the speed by which competitors like Fujitsu and Hitachi can ramp up a production in the market for mainframe computers. Faced with growing threats to its business base, IBM is aggressively counterattacking in

Japan with new products and partnership strategies aimed at retaining its leadership position. A clear recognition of the competitors' growing influence came in 1989, when IBM announced that it would market new products to convert Fujitsu and Hitachi system software to run on IBM machines. By doing this, IBM began to offer a migration path to the IBM world for the thousands of Hitachi and Fujitsu customers.

After McDonald's entered Japan, it saw some ten new hamburger chains spring up within a five-year period, all vying for a piece of the booming fast-food market. To keep ahead of these challengers and to retain market share, McDonald's Japan has continually had to introduce aggressive advertising and discounting campaigns. Discounting and price wars in recent years have become so prevalent that many in the industry wondered whether any company could make any money. But only by being in the market, and counteracting the competition move for move, has the Golden Arches been able to continue to grow and retain any semblance of leadership.

From its introduction in 1977 until the early 1980s, the Pampers brand of disposable diapers made by Procter and Gamble had a stranglehold on its market. But by 1985, competitive products from Japanese companies brought P&G's market share down to 5 percent. Durk Jager, vice-president of P&G's Far East Group, says the rapid introduction of new, improved products by Japanese competitors nearly crippled P&G. "The Japanese companies simply offered products that were better than ours. We had to change our product and fight back." P&G learned that, unlike American housewives, Japanese housewives readily shift from brand to brand in search of improvements. This opened the door for domestic companies to get a toehold and forced P&G to introduce changes at a far more rapid pace than it did in the United States. Today, Pampers has regained a 25 percent market share.[14]

As Xerox looks back on the 1980s, its management will readily admit that Fuji Xerox's leading position in Japan was probably the only thing that saved Xerox from losing the entire low-end and mid-range of its business. Xerox was able to limit the overseas growth of Canon, Ricoh, Minolta and others only by having a strong offense in Japan which kept the Japanese at bay in their own market. Fuji Xerox has its own development and marketing teams and a direct sales force of over 3,000—all with their fingers on the pulse of the market. By being an insider in the market, with fast response to competitive moves, Xerox was able to fight back against an onslaught against which many predicted it could not win.

At one time, Fuji Xerox was only a fledgling company, and for many years, strictly a marketing organization. During that time, it became painfully obvious that these Fuji Xerox machines from America weren't designed with the Japanese consumer in mind. For example, when the Xerox 7000 arrived in Japan, secretaries had to stand on a box to reach the print button. It had been designed with the taller American secretary in mind. But in recent years, all that has changed, and Fuji Xerox remains a leader in the Japanese market with over 50 percent of the copy volume in Japan, where Ricoh and Canon together have less than 30 percent.

Fuji Xerox today has a number of major sales channels in Japan: direct sales through over fifty branch offices throughout the country, together with 206 locations and close to 3,000 salesmen; 500 dealers, which it plans to expand to over 1,000 by 1988; its own downtown showrooms; and around thirty marketing subsidiaries set up as joint ventures, which are 51 percent owned by Fuji Xerox. Some of these—with Suntory, a major distillery in Japan, for instance—have more than 1,500 salesmen. Fuji Xerox's sales territory is limited by the original contract with Rank Xerox to Japan and some parts of Asia with the exception of Singapore and Hong Kong. This may be a source of contention in the future. In fact, Fuji Xerox is so aggressive, it often feels it is being held back by the parent corporation, due to its inability to participate in the worldwide market. For instance, Canon is exporting almost 80 percent of its production while Fuji Xerox is able to export only 20 percent, the lowest rate among Japanese copier makers. Until it is allowed to become a more active company worldwide, Fuji Xerox feels it will have a hard time reaching the scale required to beat major Japanese competitors in Japan.

As Xerox's market position in the United States rapidly deteriorated in the late 1970s, a painful realization developed in Xerox's Rochester headquarters; executives knew radical action had to be taken. One of the most important counter-strategies was to increase the company's investment in Japan and the independent power of Fuji Xerox within the Japanese market. Another step in Xerox's counterattack was to get to know the competition better. An entire team was formed at Fuji Xerox just for competitive analysis, and annual conferences were initiated worldwide to discuss developments at major competitors, which, with the exception of Kodak, are now all Japanese. Xerox gleaned critical information from Fuji Xerox research studies, Japanese newspapers, and government statistics. Top executives went to Japanese trade shows and conducted special investigations of end-users. They analyzed patents and summarized information from Fuji Xerox salesmen and vendors. The ensuing analysis of competitive products enabled Fuji Xerox to counter the many strategic moves being made weekly by its major competitors in all different product areas. The strategy has paid off royally: for example, Xerox was on the ground running when Canon announced a new deal with Kodak to develop and market high-speed, low-end copiers, as it was when Ricoh and Canon announced a joint marketing partnership in Japan in 1988.

When Xerox began its intensive competitive analysis and benchmarking of the products coming from Japan, it became a rallying point to increase the level of cooperation and joint product development between Rochester and Fuji Xerox. This cooperation eliminated duplication of development efforts and allowed the parent to more easily incorporate the knowledge base of its Japanese subsidiary. Among other things, Xerox learned the Japanese philosophy that simpler is better—in design, maintenance, and pricing. Xerox also made major improvements in the manufacturing process itself as a result of the lessons learned at Fuji Xerox. By designing the products for mass production, using continuous flow lines, modular subassemblies, supplier reduction, total quality control, reducing inventories, and improving flexibility and cost cutting, Xerox was able to introduce a successful new line of mid-range products.

By 1985, Xerox had made a complete reversal and was even taking major market share back from Canon and Ricoh in Japan and in the American market. Fuji Xerox also stopped IBM in its tracks in the Japanese copier market by identifying early on where IBM was testing its new machines. To those customers, Xerox salesmen were given the power to commit to aggressive sales terms, including giveaways, a strategy which prevented IBM from becoming more than a negligible factor in the market (in 1989, there were fewer than 100 IBM copiers in Japan). Atseo Kasuda, a Minolta vice-president, was quoted recently as saying, "It appeared that we could kill Xerox too. Now I don't think so. Japanese people don't talk about it, but Xerox is taking more and more market share back."[15] Fuji Xerox is probably the best success story of any American partnership in Japan. It is now over twenty-five years old, and has had the fastest growth of any subsidiary or related company in the Xerox Group. With sales approaching $4 billion, out of total sales of Xerox of over $17.6 billion worldwide, Fuji Xerox shows that Japan is a market critical to the company's very survival.

EMPHASIZING SIMILARITIES/TAKING ADVANTAGE OF DIFFERENCES

For so many years, the media and American business people have been emphasizing the major structural and cultural differences which are closing off opportunities for American firms in the Japanese market. But what we have found is that many companies are using these differences to their own advantage. By being an independent company outside of the traditional Japanese structure a foreign enterprise can move more quickly to build a broader range of relationships across many industrial groups and large partners than can older established Japanese companies and members of a Japanese *keiretsu* organization.

Coffee consumption is an example of an area in which basic differences in tastes and traditions between the United States and Japan was at once both a challenge, and an opportunity. While Americans enjoy a hot cup of coffee whenever they can, at home, the office, or out at a restaurant, the Japanese traditionally drink *ocha,* or green tea. This difference in tastes could have been seen as an impediment to purveyors of coffee. But Coca-Cola found a way to turn the dearth of coffee shops into a big opportunity. Noting that many Japanese enjoy coffee but just can't get it as readily, Coca-Cola popularized the idea of canning it and making it available through vending machines. In Japan, vending machines are a common form of retailing, and in public places rows of vending machines sell everything from shampoo to batteries, from beer to whiskey. Today, Coca-Cola's Georgia brand canned coffees (and seemingly hundreds of other brands now) can be bought from many of the thousands of vending machines and stores throughout Japan, right beside Coke Classic and Fanta.

Even small start-up companies can achieve large sales in Japan by capitalizing on the differences in the market. One company, an American developer of high-end graphic supercomputers, found Japan's interest in advanced graphics and design, and its moves into basic research and advanced software development, provided the makings of a booming niche market. Its experienced executives set up offices in Japan, England, and Germany simultaneously and closed three multimillion dollar, "exclusive" deals in Japan within a year. Especially in Japan, this type of arrangement is possible where there is a tradition of upfront commitments for distribution rights. The Americans were very skilled in negotiations, giving each partner in Japan so-called "exclusive" rights, but only exclusive in each of that company's areas of expertise and channels of access—a major trading company for access to its industrial group and investment in the American parent, a large chemical company for its internal application expertise, and a small value-added reseller for its entry into the graphics market. Within three months of signing these deals, the company was then able to establish its own Tokyo office to manage the business generated from these upfront commitments and hire an experienced manager from Nihon Digital Equipment to run the office. The key here is that top management had vision and experience in Japan from which they knew that Japan would soon be one-third of their market. They knew the market well enough to find partners and local management quickly and used structural differences, such as up-front commitments, to their advantage, enabling them to guarantee a strong revenue stream to cover the high costs of the Japanese operation in their very first year of operation.

The cosmetic industry is another place where a few shining stars, such as Clinique Labs, are breaking all the rules in Japan's entrenched, monopolized channel market. Clinique's main competitor—Shiseido—is Japan's largest cosmetic company, with a tight grip on its *keiretsu*-like group of thousands of stores and wholesalers throughout Japan, in addition to a 25,000 store-strong chain which sells only Shiseido products. Clinique Labs, a division of American Estée Lauder, has been effective in Japan despite a distribution system dominated by Shiseido and other Japanese majors. How did the company overcome these obstacles? Clinique saw that the cosmetic specialty shops would be too tough to crack and instead chose to focus its energies on developing a merchandising policy to work primarily with ninety or so large department stores, mostly newer firms, concentrating on a few which would give it large counters and demonstration areas. The plan worked, and Sogo, one of the largest of the department stores, set aside 100 square meters of its Tokyo store, about 20 percent of the total cosmetic floor, for Clinique. By targeting investment in a few major retailers, supporting them with a top team of Japanese managers and beauty advisors, and spending a high percentage of its sales on advertising—upwards of 12 percent versus the industry average of 10 percent—Clinique has built great name recognition and a profitable operation for itself and its partners.[16]

Amway, Avon, and Tupperware have found that success in Japan can follow much the same model as at home, and by transplanting their direct distribution systems to Japan, each has achieved great success in their market. Today, Amway is ranked the seventh fastest growing of among more than 3,000 foreign companies in Japan by *Diamond*

Weekly, a leading business magazine. One-third of Amway's 1987 worldwide sales of $1.8 billion came from Japan. In1989, Amway celebrated its tenth anniversary in Japan with profits of $186.6 million.[17] Amway's strengths in Japan come from its generous sales incentive programs to its over 70,000 independent distributors, an efficient nationwide distribution system (including a six-story Tokyo Distribution Center), and highly computerized packaging and processing. Amway sells close to 150 products, 80 percent of which are made in the United States. Today, Amway in Japan has a staff of 450.[18] Avon's revenues in Japan in 1989 were $277 million. The company has thousands of sales managers and distributors for its products throughout the nation. Tupperware, which has an even longer history in Japan, has 590 full-time employees, over 5,000 managers, and 60,000 individual dealers selling its U.S. and domestic-made products in the traditional Tupperware way.

Children the world over love toys, and Japanese children are no different. Seizing upon this basic commonality, the American company Toys R' Us has entered into an 80/20 joint venture with McDonald's Japan to open six stores by 1992 and 100 within ten years. Toys R' Us will be the first major U.S. retail company to establish direct operations in Japan. In January 1990, Toys R' Us announced plans to open a 5,000-square-meter store in Niigata City on the Sea of Japan. Toys R' Us, which has 580 stores around the world and annual sales of $5 billion, has created a major reaction in Japan, and nationwide toy retailers associations are organizing a major anti-Toys R' Us campaign, saying it would devastate the Japanese toy market. "In Britain, the number of toy stores decreased from 6,000 to 1,500 in ten years due mainly to Toys R' Us expansion," complains Takashige Seki, president of the All Japan Associated Toy (AJAT), an association of independent toy retailers. Joseph R. Baczko, president of Toys R' Us-Japan Ltd., said his company had "been looking for a chance to enter the Japanese market for many years." When MITI published a report, "Vision of the Japanese Distribution Industry in the 1990s," which indicated a willingness to relax the Large Retail Store Law, it felt the time was right. Baczko believes that consumers are ready for his type of store, and has high hopes for the future of Toys R' Us in Japan.[19]

The Japanese buy more life insurance per capita per year than any other people in the world, more than twice the U.S. average. A study commissioned by The Equitable predicts the Japanese market will double by 1995. Ten U.S. life insurance companies are already operating in Japan; seven have been there for more than a decade. Together, their share of the market is 3 percent, and most have continually lost money. The Prudential Insurance Company of America, the largest American insurer, set up its subsidiary in 1988, but does not expect to make a profit until 1995. Metropolitan Life Insurance Company, the second largest in the United States, spent two years and a million dollars on a feasibility study before giving up in July 1989 and instead targeting South Korea.

By coming in early and offering an innovative product, American Family Life Assurance is today one of two companies (the other is Alico Japan) making any kind of a profit in Japan. Established in 1974, American Family received an exclusive license to sell cancer insurance in Japan, because the Ministry of Finance deemed that such insurance is not "appropriate" for Japanese companies to sell. This window enabled American Family to earn $6.8 million in net profits on $1.8 billion in premiums in 1988—75 percent of the company's worldwide revenues—and win it a 90 percent market share in Japan.[20]

BELIEVING THAT SUCCESS IN JAPAN LEADS TO GLOBAL EXCELLENCE

Since Japan is increasingly setting the standards in quality, manufacturing, service, response, product innovation, and globalization of operations, a valuable side benefit to participating in the Japanese market is the exportation of experience. Texas Instruments' experience in Japan has enabled it to remain one of the only surviving American makers of dynamic random access memories (DRAMs), the largest single segment of the semiconductor market. TI executives readily admit that they have learned a lot about manufacturing from their Japanese subsidiary, and constantly promote the lessons company-wide through assignment rotations and cross-training of personnel between Japan and TI's other locations in the United States, Italy, and Taiwan.

TI had not always been able to satisfy the Japanese, and as late as 1980 the company was being haunted by a reputation for poor quality and delivery among Japanese customers. Faulty chips were still slipping through quality control, and at least one major customer complained that TI's defects were worse than those of any of TI's four major Japanese competitors. Growing threats to stop purchasing TI parts by its top four customers echoed loudly throughout Nihon TI and back to Dallas. This presented a grave challenge, especially to the Nihon

TI's Hiji plant, because 95 percent of Hiji's chips were sold in Japan. In response, the company resolved to push a major program for total quality control. It brought in Japanese consultants to teach its workers and implemented a number of Japanese programs, such as employee suggestions. The company also defined a *kaizen*-like incremental improvement plan, built statistical data bases to track yields and identify ways to improve them, and empowered workers to take control of production and improve processes.

The results were breathtaking. By 1985, Nihon TI's defect rates had fallen to fewer than 20 parts per million, from more than 5,000 parts per million in 1980. TI's reputation for quality now matches that of the best Japanese companies, prompting a Toshiba official, recently quoted in the *Wall Street Journal*, to deliver the supreme accolade: "We don't think of TI Japan as an American company. We think of their chips as 'Made in Japan.'" Infusing "Made in Japan" quality and a corresponding understanding of customer needs for perfection back into TI factories worldwide has been a major challenge. Due to this kind of commitment and an aggressive pursuit of quality and excellence, major customers such as Canon and Sony have found TI to be an excellent supplier. As a result, Nihon TI was awarded the Deming Quality Award, a highly cherished prize in Japanese industry, making it the first non-Japanese company so honored.

By learning from its exposure to Japan, TI has also developed many strong relationships with Japanese suppliers, the government, local prefectures, universities, and major banks. Even with its largest competitors, TI is forging new alliances, like a deal with Hitachi for joint development of 16-megabyte DRAMs. This alliance combined their prowess in design and manufacturing and advanced process capabilities. TI is continuing to expand globally with its own memory plants in Italy and Taiwan. TI has been able to remain one of the few American survivors in the DRAM marketplace by having access to the inner circles of Japan's research and technology, by promoting Japanese management to run its memory operations, all of which was made possible by maintaining large plants in Japan itself.

The Japanese have an old proverb that goes, "If you understand everything, you must be misinformed." That is precisely true of doing business in Japan. It is a moving target: in order to succeed, you must be ever diligent in learning, adapting, and evolving, and never for a moment assume you have mastered the marketplace. The companies we examined each endured a great deal in order to stay alive and to achieve some modicum of success in Japan. Their trials and tribulations cannot—must not—be minimized. The experiences of each company profiled tells a common story:

- You have no choice but to compete in Japan.
- It will be harder, more grueling than you ever imagined.
- It will be an ongoing battle—you have to want every advantage, no matter how small.
- It will cost more than you think, in terms of money and other resources.
- What you gain from the battle, however, will revolutionize your business worldwide.

Each of the lessons learned from the companies in our study, in one way or another, is capsulized in our own experiences in the Japanese market. Critical issues such as presence and persistence will be re-occurring themes. Courage and conviction will also be reinforced. And, as our story unfolds, the common characteristics of success—and of failure—will make themselves even more pronounced.

7

Applied Materials Japan

A Brief History of a Long Journey

It is better to err on the side of daring than on the side of caution.

ALVIN TOFFLER

In late 1989, the *Wall Street Journal* ran a feature story on the top exporters in the American electronics industry. Ranked by percentage of overseas sales to overall sales, the list included such familiar giants as IBM, Intel, and Hewlett-Packard. At the top of the list was a Silicon Valley semiconductor equipment maker, Applied Materials, Inc. In annual revenue Applied Materials may have been dwarfed by other companies on the list, but it had over 64 percent of its sales coming from overseas, more than 40 percent in Japan alone. Drawn by this extraordinary performance, George Bush, on his pre-election campaign trail, visited Applied Materials' campus in Santa Clara, California, a week before he was elected President of the United States in November 1988. Speaking to employees and a large group of Silicon Valley business leaders, Bush hailed the company's success in Japan as a model for all of America. That success, the steps Applied Materials took to achieve its unique position, and the all-too-common mistakes it made and avoided along the way, provide valuable lessons for Western companies looking to break into Japan.

Applied Materials manufactures processing equipment essential to the making of integrated circuits—silicon chips. It was founded in Mountain View, California, in 1967 by a flamboyant young engineer named Michael McNeilly. The company quickly found itself in the right place at the right time in the semiconductor industry's young history. The late 1960s were heady times for the technology-rich valley forty miles south of San Francisco. Inspired by the successes of those who had started out before them, hundreds of young entrepreneurs busily took to transforming a plethora of scientific ideas into marketable products: instruments, computers, and most importantly semiconductor chips. Since chip making was a new technology, a support industry did not yet exist. In typical Silicon Valley fashion, McNeilly saw a need and filled it. By supplying chip makers with "front-end" manufacturing tools, McNeilly figured correctly that chip makers could concentrate on doing what they did best, making chips. A young Applied Materials began its early life with healthy sales and a good prospect for growth—until it got off track.

Mike McNeilly had a talent for turning a vision into a business. But like many successful entrepreneurs, he was better at starting the company than managing it. When he uncovered the semiconductor supplies niche for Applied Materials, he saw a good opportunity ready for the taking. The problem was, it may have been *too* good. The business of supplying support products and services to the semiconductor industry seemed boundless to McNeilly—and he wanted it all. Almost from the very beginning, he diversified the company into varied segments of the business—materials, chemistries, and equipment. As a result, the young company did not acquire a critical mass of talent and technology in any one area. When I (Jim Morgan) first encountered McNeilly and Applied Materials, it was as a partner with WestVen, a venture capital firm associated with the Bank of America. McNeilly was looking for financing to expand the company's operations. I had examined the company's portfolio and had determined that it had some good businesses, but was suffering from willy-nilly diversification. Involved in a half dozen different businesses, its resources were spread thinner than a silicon wafer. And the strain showed. Its board of directors was also concerned, and was pushing for a change. WestVen opted not to participate in a financing deal, but the rapport I had developed with McNeilly resulted in him asking me to join the company as president. This was a tough decision for him to make: Applied Materials was his baby and it was not easy to give up that much control.

I have seen that happen many times in Silicon Valley—young, energetic entrepreneurs wrestling with the decision to let go of the reins of a company they had created because it was in the best interests of the business. That is a bitter pill for many company founders to swallow. It takes a big person to vanquish the demons of ego and paternalism in favor of permitting the enterprise he (or she) founded to move forward without him. Seeing that his company was in trouble, McNeilly let it go. In 1976, when I became assured that I would have the authority to make the necessary moves to turn the company around, I moved into the president's office.

Our first task was to bring Applied Materials back from the brink upon which it teetered. We did that by imposing a sense of focus. Of the company's six ventures, only one, the semiconductor equipment business, possessed products with a reasonable market share—and it accounted for 50 percent of the company's revenues. The other business were either marginal or outright liabilities, and the company was hemorrhaging cash. It became clear that Applied Materials needed to concentrate what resources and energies it had on the equipment businesses. I spent the first two years making the required decisions to save the company. This meant spinning off or closing down the unprofitable businesses, while at the same time throttling up the efforts in support of the semiconductor equipment unit.

In the early days, I spent a good deal of time analyzing the business, educating myself about the technology, the customers, and the geographic markets. The company marketed its products through a direct sales force throughout the United States and Europe. However, in Japan it had had a distributor relationship since 1970 with the Kanematsu Electric, a subsidiary of Kanematsu Gosho. I found out that the company had chosen this route to Japan, as opposed to the direct approach it employed everywhere else, because the Japanese historically had been reluctant to purchase equipment from outside of their companies and related suppliers. By contracting with a Japanese trading partner, Applied Materials as a very small company was afforded access to what might have otherwise been a closed market. The trading partner provided the Japanese chip makers with an acceptable interface, while at the same time assisting Applied in navigating the unfamiliar nuances peculiar to the Japanese way of doing business. In six years of distributing through Kanematsu, Applied Materials enjoyed healthy, yet unspectacular, growth in Japan. The company's most successful year there brought sales to a modest $3.8 million.

Kanematsu was a general trading company, and at the time sold a large catalogue of foreign products in Japan ranging from simple testers to the most advanced equipment. Because of the complex technologies involved with Applied Materials' systems, I assumed that Kanematsu must have a very technical team of sales people who were specialists in the semiconductor processing field. The technology seemed to me to be too complex to sell without some degree of expertise. However, as I came to learn, this is not necessarily the case with a Japanese trading company. A salesman in the electrical group might represent anything from a soldering gun to sophisticated processing systems like Applied's epitaxial reactors. Although the Japanese semiconductor industry was still in relative infancy in the early 1970s, I was convinced that there was a very real opportunity to grow our business in the market. At that point I judged my best move would be to meet personally with Kanematsu officials to see how we should proceed. That required a trip abroad.

INNOCENTS ABROAD

I was born and raised in the Midwest. As a child, America's heartland seemed to roll on forever. It was difficult to imagine other worlds beyond the horizon. After all, my hometown seemed so complete and self-contained. There well may be other places in the world, but who needed them? But I was always adventurous, and became an exception in my town when I ventured off to attend college in New York. Later, I traveled extensively throughout the United States as part of management assignments with high-technology divisions of Textron. But in 1977, at age thirty-eight, I had never traveled outside of North America—never even imagined it. When I did think of places overseas, I saw them in my mind as ethnic neighborhoods in an American world. On the eve of my first trip to Japan, this was very much the way I expected to find Tokyo—an expanded version of San Francisco's Japantown. I am afraid my experience is not unique. The conceits of Americanhood have colored the thinking of many otherwise-able businessmen and women who sail into international waters. As they return less than triumphant, they can do nothing but wonder about where they went wrong. For those who follow, let me suggest a bit of advice: preconceived notions, leave home without them.

My first trip to Japan was in 1977 to attend the industry's first trade show there and to make a first face-to-face meeting with our representatives from Kanematsu. The trade show was not impressive. There were a few undistinguished booths in a very large domed exhibition hall at the Harumi Center on Tokyo Bay. The visit to Kanematsu was even more discouraging. I figured with a short meeting, possibly over lunch, I could explain to them some of my strategies for improving our sales in Japan. The way we saw it, Applied Materials should have been able to achieve a better market share. During the flight itself, before I had even landed on Japanese soil, I was impressed by the Japanese people and their service ethic. The JAL attendants provided a level of attention which far surpassed that of any experience I had had on an American airline. I would later recall that this same attention to detail was evident everywhere I went in Japan, be it in taxi cabs, hotels, restaurants, train stations, wherever. The Japanese concern for the wants of the customer, I am afraid to say, was in striking contrast to standard practice in America.

Yet even in light of this service ethic, within moments of my arrival at Tokyo International Airport in Narita I felt out of place. As I disembarked the plane, I was directed to a customs area marked "aliens" (that choice of wording has since been changed to "foreigners"). The customs agents were very polite, but not exactly friendly. They were stoic and businesslike. This is typical of the Japanese approach. Japan has a way of making you feel at home and unwelcome at the same time. On a person-to-person level, the Japanese cannot be rivaled for courtesy and cordiality. But in manners, expression, and in their detached brand of courtesy, there is an underlying resentment of foreigners that cannot be seen as much as it is felt. After a long cab ride to the hotel, I decided to get out and do some walking around. A friend had mentioned a few places to check out when I got there, and I thought I might walk there in order to get a better sense of the city. But getting to a destination in Tokyo can convince you that the Japanese are deliberately trying to discourage you. Buildings are numbered in the sequence built or by lot number, which means you can be in front of the address you are seeking and never know it. I was lost several times. However, I found that if you look confused, someone will invariably come up to you and offer help. One gentleman, a snappily dressed young salaryman, went far out of his way to bring me to one of the addresses I was looking for. Just walking those densely peopled streets taught me about the two Japans—the one that lets you in and the one that doesn't. It was a lesson I never forgot.

On arriving at the trading company's offices the next morning, I was taken through the usual ritual of being introduced to each of the key people on our account and being briefed on the status of their activities. That day I spent most of my time with Ikuro Yusui, who was then head of the equipment sales department, and Tetsuo Iwasaki, an aggressive young salesman. Both sat with me and explained some of the problems and opportunities facing our company. Overall, I would describe the meeting as cordial and informative—up to a point. Once the introductions and pleasantries were dispensed with, the trading company representatives reverted to speaking Japanese among themselves, which naturally I didn't understand. When I had substantive concerns about operations and customers, I was reminded that the Japanese way of doing business was, well, different. I would need to adapt to these differences if I was going to make progress, which of course would be made slowly. That first meeting ended five hours later with almost no better understanding or agreement on the future of our business in Japan. As we were ushered into the elevator, one of the other Applied Materials executives who accompanied me said, "We're going to have to get everything in writing." I wondered if that really even mattered.

APPLIED MATERIALS JAPAN

Yes, my first visit to Japan was very discouraging. I didn't understand the market, the customers, or the distribution system, and I wasn't convinced that the trading company had a good understanding of how to develop a broad-scale technical systems business like ours. Yet, we were at a total loss without them. After my return to California, I discussed with several members of the executive staff what our options might be in improving our interational businesses, particularly in Japan. During the next couple of months, we sought the counsel of as many executives as we could find who had had any experience in Japan. We also talked with the few Japanese customers who visited us in Santa Clara, and got to know them on a more personal basis. We spent many evenings with them trying to learn their true requirements and what we had to do to become a supplier halfway across the world. They were reassuring: they confirmed just how ignorant we were.

Increasingly, I was coming to the conclusion that we needed to sever ties with Kanematsu and form closer relationships with our customers. But, as I looked around to see how we might go about structuring our own operation, I had nothing to use as a model. What few foreign success stories we could look to were not relevant to our particular circumstances. Each American company participating in Japan had over a billion dollars in annual sales and were in totally different businesses. We were considerably smaller. What we did next was guided by some basic assumptions:

- *Success in Japan would be critical to our overall success.* We saw the global marketplace for our products segmented into three spheres: the United States, Japan and the newly industrialized countries (NICs) of Southeast Asia, and Europe. We would not be a truly international player without proving ourselves in Japan.
- *Success in Japan would give us the wherewithal to succeed anywhere.* Since Japan was increasingly setting the pace for global business activities, what we learned in Japan would be exportable to all our other operations.
- *Sales of our products in Japan would be based on two factors: technology and relationships.* These are the two principal determinants of success in the world of Japanese business.
- *Without a direct operation to sell and support our products—developed and manufactured outside Japan—they would be successful only as long as they maintained technological superiority.* The Japanese will typically buy from outside sources as a last resort, and only until they can gain equal capability domestically. Technological superiority tends to be short-lived and alone is not enough to sustain a long-term business in Japan.
- *Direct operations would be essential to building lasting relationships with our customers.* Being once- or twice-removed from the selling/service process, the manufacturer cannot truly understand customer requirements nor allow those requirements to drive the business. Such relationships not only lead to success in established areas, but will lead to success in later-developed products and businesses. Indeed, the trading representative gets all the benefits of this critical competitive advantage.
- *In order to succeed, our subsidiary should conform as closely as possible to Japanese management style, values, and behaviors.* A foreign-based company using non-Japanese in key management positions will not be able to develop the advantage of Japanese business relationships because very few, if any, foreigners will belong to the social institutions from which strong relationships are derived in Japan (family, community, school, job). Applied Materials' Japanese operation needed to be indistiguishable from any other Japanese company.
- *We must be committed for the long haul.* In Japan, as elsewhere, relationships develop over time and blossom from long-term exposure and involvement in the community. One of the things that causes Japanese customers to develop their own resources is the tendency

by many foreign firms to cut and run when the market starts to get tough, either in Japan itself or in other parts of the operation outside Japan.

Operating through the trading company, our customers did business with us out of need, because we were the technological leader in the market segments we served. The business we wanted to build—in fact, needed to build—was one that could only be sustained on the basis of lasting relationships. In order to begin establishing the kind of trust which would result in increased market penetration, we knew we had to convince our customers that we were making a long-term commitment to them, and that this commitment would be evidenced by superior equipment and support, no matter what the condition of our business in other geographic markets. As I mulled over what to do, I had much to consider. By 1978, Applied Materials was back in the black—its first profitable year since 1974. Yet, with revenues of only $28 million, we weren't quite positioned for a global expansion. Dedicating the kinds of resources it would require in order to create a substantive presence in Japan was a risky proposition. But, as so often happens, fortuitous events helped galvanize our decision.

Since that first visit to Japan, I had been fortunate in having good rapport with Tetsuo Iwasaki, the dynamic young executive from Kanematsu. About two years after my first visit, Iwasaki informed us that he and six others wanted to leave Kanematsu and form their own company, Nippon IC. When Iwasaki told us of his desire, I saw the opportunity we were waiting for. Impressed by Iwasaki's spirit and knowledge of our business, we agreed to establish a partnership with Nippon IC. And although I had no idea whether breaking away from Kanematsu might not lead to recriminations and the risk of total failure, for me there was no turning back. Besides, the partnership structure was a far less risky approach to the problem, benefiting us with an organization of people practiced in the needs of the customer base. One of the partners had a fairly strong financial and management background and he became Applied Materials Japan's (AMJ) first president. Iwasaki was in charge of sales and service. On October 1, 1979, AMJ was born running.

I couldn't have been more pleased about the way we solved the problem. The initial employees were all talented men willing to put their careers on the line to make the business prosper. And best of all, Applied Materials was not on the line by itself. Within a year, however, the honeymoon was over. Iwasaki and another executive came into conflict over growth strategies. Our management supported Iwasaki, and we decided to make the operation a wholly owned subsidiary. In 1981, AMJ became Japan's first wholly foreign-owned semiconductor equipment company. If I had known then what I know now—about how important a market Japan would eventually become—I would have been less fearful of this commitment, but at the time Applied Materials was relatively small (with only $42.6 million in sales) and venturing across the Pacific into a strange new land and forming a standalone business was not without its dangers.

GROWTH AND COMPETITION

Iwasaki turned out to be every bit as able a leader as I read him to be. After the first full year of operations, AMJ's revenues rose to over $6 million, a 100 percent increase over the previous year operating through Kanematsu. Moreover, we were building long-term relationships with customers directly, something we were unable to do through the trading company. Doors opened to us initially based upon the strength of our technology, and as the depth of our relationships blossomed, trust and mutual respect kept those doors open. As we began to work directly with our customers in Japan, we gained a better understanding of ourselves, of our capabilities (and limitations), and of the competitive situation. What we saw was not always pleasant. It quickly became clear that we had to make some major step-function improvements if we were going to be truly successful in Japan and the rest of the global market.

For the first few years, AMJ struggled with the demands of the Japanese integrated circuit (IC) industry, which proved far more extreme than those of the United States, especially in the areas of process technology, process repeatability, and equipment reliability in high-volume production. Japanese companies demanded constant modification, and we were expected to comply with their every request. Initially, our U.S. executives found the demands hard to accept and resisted. Americans have a strong NIH or Not Invented Here syndrome to their personalities. But, after extensive visits to Japanese customers by our engineering staff, we realized that our Japanese customers were willing to work in partnership with us to develop new equipment and adapt our products to their needs. By showing that we could support their special requirements, and by proving that our entire organization was dedicated to their success, we overcame the most difficult barrier to business in Japan: the customer's fear of noncommitment by foreign companies.

It is also important to understand the situation of the industry we were in at the time. In the early 1980s, no one could have guessed that Japan was about to leapfrog the United States in the production of semiconductors, come to dominate the entire integrated circuit memory market, and be rapidly moving up the entire silicon food chain to produce increasingly sophisticated electronic products and systems. The same went for the equipment business, where for an entire decade before, Applied Materials and its American competitors were the leaders, supplying almost all of the equipment used in Japan. At the time Japan was quietly ramping up a government-sponsored effort to build an indigenous and self-sufficient "next generation" semiconductor industry, eyeing everything from materials to equipment and, ultimately, to IC devices.

Actually, Japan's strategic targeting of semiconductors was a boon to Applied. While much of our equipment was being used to re-engineer and build Japanese machines, Applied Materials stayed on the leading edge in new system development with many of our etchers and epitaxial reactors going into the major production lines that were sprouting up all over the islands. At first we did not realize how significant our direct presence was. While we grew closer and closer to our customers, our American competitors were insulated from them and the demands of Japanese industry by their trading companies. A turning point came when the industry hit a recession in 1982. Investment by American chip makers virtually stopped. The Japanese market however, spurred on by government assurances, and guaranteed demand from parent and sister companies, grew by 66 percent in that period. In the equipment business, scores of foreign companies abandoned the Japanese market altogether. While others turned and ran, Applied Materials stuck it out and earned a reputation as a loyal, committed supplier. It was during this time that Japan began to take the offensive in building its semiconductor capacity and in wresting the top market positions from American companies. At this point Applied was still rather fragile financially, and this expansion greatly benefited us because the markets in the United States and Europe declined significantly. Figures 7.1 and 7.2 show the dramatic changes which took place in the industry and our customer base.

Each of the top IC manufacturers in Japan is part of a larger, vertically integrated organization. Many of our biggest competitors were

Figure 7.1 Top Worldwide Semiconductor Manufacturers

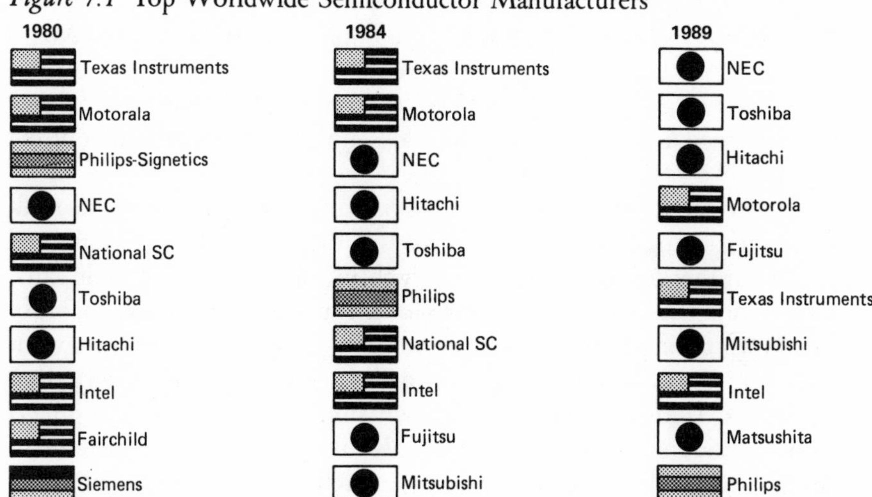

SOURCE: Dataquest, Inc.

financed and spun off from our customer companies. Anelva, a maker of etch equipment, was an outgrowth of NEC. Two of Japan's largest IC tester companies, a field in which we do not compete, were similar spin-offs: Advantest, a progeny of Fujitsu; and Ando, another product of NEC's vertical integration. Other companies in the equipment field, such as Tokyo Electron, began as trading companies and bootstrapped themselves through joint ventures with foreign firms. Nikon Camera used its expertise in optical and mechanical areas to become a leading

Figure 7.2 Worldwide Integrated Circuit (IC) Market Shares

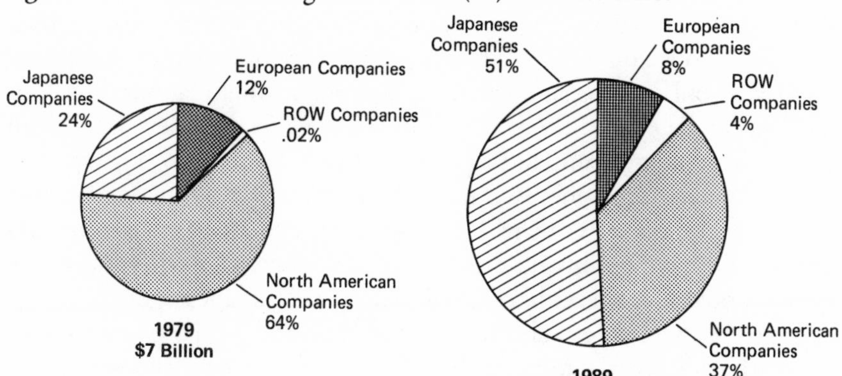

SOURCE: Dataquest, Inc.

supplier in the photolithography field with a successful direct step on wafer (DSW) systems which is a line complementary to Applied Materials' systems. Each of these companies are part of a bigger, more powerful parent or sister organizations that give them huge war chests, a guaranteed customer base, and close links with the broader R&D divisions.

Applied Materials has succeeded against these well-heeled, well-connected competitors because many of them have had only limited success in markets outside Japan, which in turn has limited their capabilities in Japan by minimizing the global experience they have incorporated into their product development. The Japanese chip makers want (and can afford to buy) only world-class equipment. Ironically, that demand excluded many of their own domestic equipment suppliers from consideration. Applied Materials enjoyed the added benefit of being "independent." By not being a member of a *keiretsu* or other large industrial group, we are not limited regarding which companies we can sell to and, in fact, are able to have working relationships with all the major chip makers. Many of our Japanese competitors cannot do this for obvious reasons.

A BREAKTHROUGH

By 1983, AMJ accounted for 33 percent of Applied Materials' total sales, and we had begun to receive multiple orders from our Japanese customers as our systems were qualified and welcomed into full production facilities. With this success, it became increasingly obvious that we needed to go to the next stage; AMJ needed a local applications laboratory, customer demonstrations centers, and a facility for product service and development to serve as a long-term base. Up to that point, AMJ was only selling and servicing equipment manufactured back in California. To extend the partnership relations we had developed with our customers in Japan, and to make it easier to build to our Japanese customers' requirements, we needed to actually modify systems and begin development work in Japan. We decided to gamble again. As fate would have it, this time assistance would come from what at the time seemed like the unlikeliest of places—the Japanese government.

By 1983, we had established ourselves not only with our customers, but with some very influential Japanese organizations such as our bank in Japan, the Bank of Tokyo. In fact, in the early 1980s when we were beset with the ill effects of the semiconductor slump, Applied Materials received more patient support from the Bank of Tokyo than we did from our founding bank, the Bank of America. In order to show Applied's true commitment to our customers and to the Japanese semiconductor industry as a whole, in early 1983 we began to examine the options available to finance the building of what for us was a massive technology center in Japan. As we looked at possible financing arrangements, a number of Japanese business associates encouraged us to apply for a loan from the Japan Development Bank (JDB), the quasi-governmental finance organization that funds strategic Japanese enterprises. No wholly non-Japanese firm had ever received such funding, but our advisors sensed that a policy change was in the works. I figured we had nothing to lose by applying.

Our representative at the Bank of Tokyo arranged for the bank to formally introduce the company to the JDB. As we prepared for this process, we took measures to assure that we looked "local." AMJ's finance director was Japanese and Applied's corporate treasurer spoke the language fluently. They were the lead representatives in the loan application effort and conducted all direct dealings with the JDB. The importance of having Japanese employees spearheading our dealings with the Japan Development Bank cannot be overstated. Although we clearly were not a Japanese company, the bank felt more comfortable interacting with people they understood and trusted. This scenario was borne out many other times in our early days in Japan. While unlikely to embrace a foreigner completely, Japanese appreciate it when an outsider tries to assimilate his efforts or "put on a Japanese face." The process took several months, which gave us the opportunity to line up supporters. One of the best things we did was target the city of Narita in the Chiba Prefecture as the site of the technology center. Since our locating there would be a source of revenues and jobs for the prefecture, and because the local government was very interested in attracting high-technology companies, we got the immediate support and assistance of the governor of the prefecture. He sent letters to the JDB on our behalf and even lobbied in person.

For some reason, I felt confident we would get the loan, even though our case would be precedent-setting and even though we were in competition with 80 other companies, from all over the world. Five months after it all began, I received a phone call while touring our Implant Division in England telling me that we had been selected. As a testament of our acceptance in Japan, few honors could have been more timely or more critical to our future success. Our selection by the JDB made the front pages of many of the world's leading newspapers, and literally every publication in Japan. Coincidentally, the following day I had been scheduled to speak at a meeting of Japanese stock and industry analysts. The roomful of people was impressive—we had attracted a larger audience than turned out to hear from the chief executives of General Electric and Schlumberger earlier that year. This presentation would prove fortuitous in many ways. It resulted in an expanding base of long-term investors in Applied Materials, including leading Japanese insurance companies, banks, and trust companies. And in 1987, when the company held a public offering, we were fortunate in placing about 25 percent of the shares sold with Japanese institutional investors, although we were then a much smaller company than they normally invested in. Most of those shares are still held (and, in fact, the Japanese have increased their position) because these investors look for long-term growth in their portfolios.

THE NARITA TECHNOLOGY CENTER

With the loan from the Japan Development Bank, we began construction in 1983 of the Narita Technology Center, a 65,000-square-foot, state-of-the-art complex. When we conceived the center, several areas were considered but the Narita area near the Tokyo airport was an attractive place for a company with our long-term objectives. We thought housing would be reasonable, and even though the local facilities had not been developed, over the long term the area would develop satisfactorily to support business and industry in the area. The one drawback was its distance from Tokyo—forty miles—which made it a little harder to attract top engineers who considered Narita to be *inaka*, or the countryside. But with the crowds and expensive housing of Tokyo, Narita has become more attractive and has also proven convenient for people traveling into Japan from other parts of the world. Proximity to the airport has made the location a good base of support for business throughout Asia.

Construction on the center was completed in 1984, a year in which Applied Materials Japan's revenues jumped from $34 million for the previous period to $52 million. The technology center was built at a total cost of $9.2 million, with a $3.2 million loan provided by the JDB. It was clearly a major investment for Applied Materials, but the center provided a major center of activity for customers to jointly develop and test new processes, and to demonstrate equipment—activities which in the past could only be done in California. The center also inaugurated the equipment industry's first "Class 10" clean-room development laboratory. A clean room's degree of "cleanliness" is measured in terms of particulates per cubic foot of air. Among the cleanest environments in the world, a Class 10 clean room permits only ten particulates per cubic foot. Our clean room was designed and installed by a subsidiary of one of our largest customers, Hitachi, a contractor renowned in Japan for this specialized type of construction. This experience gave us the wherewithal to establish similar advanced clean rooms at all our facilities and resulted in our leading the industry in manufacturing within a clean room.

Today, the Narita Technology Center serves as a fully functioning R&D laboratory and plays an important role in the worldwide success of Applied Materials. As Japan continues to focus on its R&D strengths in the semiconductor industry, exposure to the latest breakthroughs benefit our products and their worldwide performance. To ensure that we are on the cutting edge, AMJ has already started several research projects with universities and leading semiconductor manufacturers. We are also taking steps to make the center even more functional. In 1991, the expansion of the technology center will be completed, tripling its present size. We are also considering a second technology center elsewhere in Japan.

THE 'TOUGH OLD SAMURAI'

When I look back at my experience in the Japanese market, among the most gratifying aspects were the relationships I developed with the customers. Always willing to teach as well as to learn, our Japanese customers have had an outstanding impact on the quality, reliability, and overall capability of our systems and the performance of our company. One of the most memorable characters I had the pleasure of befriending was a man named Kirachi Tomura, the legendary president of Shin-etsu, Ltd. Tomura was a demanding old codger, lovingly referred to by friend and foe alike as, "that tough old samurai S.O.B." Until his untimely death of a heart attack on a business trip to Korea in 1988, he was every bit the epithet. But he was also a compassionate, principled man who would easily extend his hand in help whenever and wherever he could. I had the pleasure of first meeting Tomura in 1979 when I approached him about buying Galamar, one of the Applied Materials' divisions I moved to divest the company of when I came on board. Although the deal didn't stick, our friendship did. Already in his early 60s when we met, Tomura was a classic Japanese success story. Like most senior managers in Japan, he had worked his way up the ranks, always learning, always teaching. By the time we became friends, he had guided the small, little known silicon wafer division into a major, world-class player in its field in a little over a decade. His oft-repeated explanation for his success was 1) always setting challenging goals for his people; 2) always investing in the future; and 3) always working closely with his suppliers to let them do what they were best at. I can truly say it was a pleasure to become a supplier to Shinetsu. Not always easy, but a pleasure nonetheless.

As a customer, Tomura demanded excellence. But he was always reasonable in that expectation. In fact, he felt that it was the customer's responsibility to help the supplier achieve excellence. For Applied Materials, Tomura challenged us to outperform ourselves at every step. He worked us as hard as he worked his own people. In return, he did everything he could to ensure our success by imparting a set of values which launched us into a leadership position which we still maintain today. Tomura always let us in on the ground floor of his new development plans, always shared technology with us, and assigned his top engineers and operations managers to assist us. He also purchased our prototype systems and worked out the bugs with us. Then he would follow up with volume purchases once we had together perfected the processes. To old Tomura-san, I will forever be grateful. We have since used the model of this relationship to build relationships with other customers throughout the world.

HARD TIMES IN TOKYO

When discussing the essential role of the manager in an organization, I often use the analogy of the circus juggler who spins plates on top of dowels. In order to be effective, a manager has to give continuous periodic attention to each area of responsibility. Without such attention, the plates will surely fall, one by one. Inertia usually succumbs to gravity. Nowhere is this truer than in Japan's marketplace, a world that is generally moving on a fast track. Change occurs rapidly, and often in unexpected areas. This means paying close attention to the information gathered from the field and responding to it quickly. Applied Materials wasn't always good at that, but we learned.

In the early 1980s, our Japanese marketing group started warning us that their customers were making noises that they would bypass the five-inch wafer for the six-inch, and were encouraging the company to rapidly automate our 8100 etcher to process the six-inch wafers. The technical staff in Santa Clara didn't believe the Japanese would make that jump, and were not ready to pursue that opportunity so quickly. Clearly, they knew the industry would move to the six-inch wafer, but the technical staff believed that move was some time off. As it happened, the Japanese customer did transition to six-inch wafers, and we were not ready. While we scurried to catch up, our Japanese competitors, who did listen to the feedback from the street, beat us to the punch. We watched for nearly a year as our competitors won the sales. As a result, we lost early position and market share, and only through a massive technical and marketing push did we turn it around and regain our leading position. From that time on, we have been uniquely sensitive, company-wide, to the input from the Japanese marketing staff and our Japanese customers.

The Narita Technology Center made an enormous impression on our customers. By the mid-1980s, Applied Materials Japan was one of the larger and more visible semiconductor equipment makers in Japan, foreign or domestic. We had established ten customer support centers around the country. We had some of the best systems and one of the best support apparatus in the business. As a result, sales and market share steadily rose each year (see Figure 7.3). But, we could not rely on this momentum to keep us moving in the right direction. As you move along, a bridge one day becomes a wall the next. For Applied

Figure 7.3 Applied Materials Japan Employee and Sales Revenue Growth, 1980–89

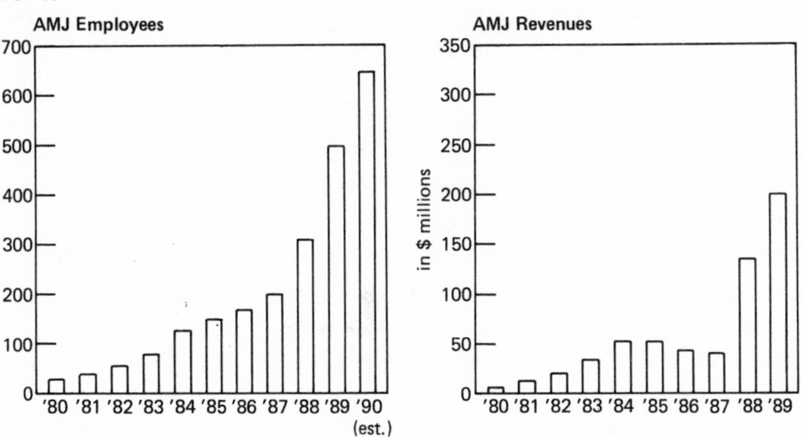

Materials, remaining sensitive to the marketplace and to our customers' rapidly evolving needs was key. And, in 1985, as the worldwide semiconductor industry lurched into the most severe and lengthy recession in its history, good, accurate, smooth communications was a must.

The semiconductor slump lasted nearly two years. In that time many of our American competitors abandoned the Japanese market outright, even though it had become the largest center of semiconductor activity in the world. As demand cooled, development costs in the market became too heavy to bear. Struggling in their own home markets, and with the recession so taxing, most companies could not afford to invest in the future. But, in a time when our worldwide sales were slowed to a crawl, we remained committed. Applied Materials never lost its resolve to support the Japanese operation and stayed its course through three consecutive quarters virtually without orders from Japan.

For our Japanese executives, and even for our Japanese customers, it was a very depressing period emotionally. Prior to the slump, the Japanese market had only known one direction, up. This was something disorienting for them. I remained positive, however, firm in the belief that difficult times have a way of illuminating existing weaknesses in an organization. I looked at the downturn as an opportunity to strengthen the company. As the old saying goes, "That which doesn't break you, builds you."

The 1985–86 recession was a real test for our industry in Japan. It resulted in management shake-ups, the redeployment of employees to other divisions, and significant losses for many Japanese and foreign companies. It was also a time when the aura of Japanese management prowess was put to the test. It was just prior to this time when, at a company luncheon, a very capable young sales manager asked me about the superiority of Japanese management. I replied that I thought that there were indeed outstanding Japanese managers, but that there were also outstanding American and European managers. I added that there were also poor Japanese managers and poor American and European managers. One day, I chided, we'll see which is which. I didn't say so at the time, but I knew we had good managers by and large, and they would earn their stripes during this recession. Overall, it was interesting to see how the Japanese managers dealt with the blow. Many customer and competitor firms suffered from an outbreak of what became known as "booking sickness" among their management ranks. Nothing humorous about it; the downward spiral of orders and the intensive competitiveness of the market resulted in many managers suffering from stomach ailments which, for some, ended up as ulcers.

At first, the downturn caused quite a shock at AMJ. But it was not long before the managers and employees rebounded to meet the challenge. Iwasaki and his team struggled bravely to hold market share with existing products and to position the company for the next generation of systems. He also implemented a number of cost controls which vastly improved the bottom line. The rest of the company also showed it support by rallying behind Japan. It was a period of genuine bonding across geographic and cultural boundaries, and resulted in a more focused, more cooperative global organization. I consider this period to be a turning point in the company's history. Whereas in the early days, AMJ felt like a stepchild, the show of faith from around the world let the Japanese know the true extent of our commitment to them and to the market. As we accelerated our development in new systems, rather than simply hire locally, we assigned AMJ employees to those areas around the globe to better utilize them. This was a huge morale and confidence booster. The confidence would prove essential in regaining ground as the downturn ended. In general, I believe the difficulties of this period brought the company closer together, forging a global operation which could withstand just about any difficulties. Through these actions, we gained momentum and market share (see Figure 7.4). AMJ built its infrastructure and learned on an emotional and visceral level what it was like to be a part of a growing, global enterprise. For my

Figure 7.4 Top Worldwide Semiconductor Equipment Manufacturers

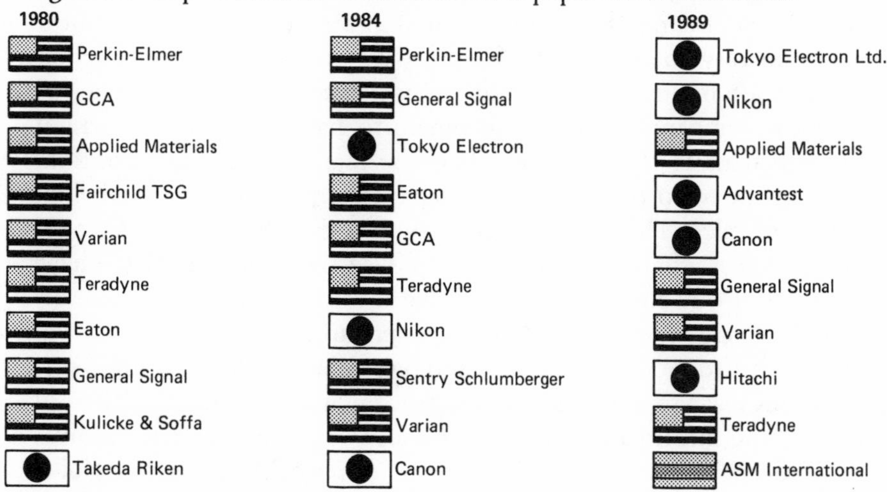

SOURCE: VLSI Research Inc.

Table 7.1
Applied Materials Progress in Japan

- Began sales in Japan, 1970
- Established Applied Materials Japan, 1979
- Japan Development Bank loan for Technology Center, 1984
- Elected Dr. Hiroo Toyoda of NTT to board of directors, 1985
- FY 1989 Sales in Japan 26.8 billion yen ($200 million)
- 11 sales and service offices, Narita Technology Center
- 630 Employees in 1990
- Japan market share leader in Etch, CVD, and Epitaxial Equipment
- 8.1 billion yen ($58 million) facilities expansion underway

part, I knew we had built a team I could count on in both times of opportunity and adversity.

We won a lot of supporters in Japan because of the courage we displayed during the recession. And when it finally ended, the Japanese market rebounded wildly. As Japanese manufacturers rapidly increased capacity to meet new demand for semiconductors domestically, and to provide foundry services for American companies caught short without capacity, Applied Materials was positioned to benefit handsomely. Applied Materials' sales in Japan in the subsequent two years soared by nearly 500 percent, from $40.8 million in 1987 to $200 million in 1989.

After ten tough years, Applied Materials has become the market-share leader in Japan in three of the five technologies in which we compete, and is rapidly gaining ground in the fourth and fifth. But it is not an easy road to travel. Even today, we are facing the toughest competition in our history, coming almost exclusively from well-heeled Japanese companies. We are fortunate to have established a critical business mass in the important Japanese market. With this position, we have the opportunity to build a Japanese organization with a billion dollars of sales. The great advantage we have is the years of learning how to work effectively together to utilize the global talent we have throughout our corporation (see Table 7.1).

By working closely with our customers around the world, we will continue introducing the new technologies that enable the leading corporations that use our equipment to reach new dimensions in advanced devices and information products. Clearly, Applied Materials Japan is a significant factor in the emergence of Applied Materials as a global growth company in the 1990s. I firmly believe our future success depends on globalizing what we've learned from competing in Japan.

In the first two sections of this book, we laid out the landscape of the Japanese market. We explored the historic, cultural, and societal influences that make the market unique, and have examined some of the key players you should know. We also looked at Japanese competitive strategy and foreign company performance in Japan. We studied strategies that have worked, and strategies that have not. For your organization's needs, no single strategy will provide all the answers. One thing is clear, your development in the Japanese market will likely be gradual. Like the stages of progression for a student of karate—from white belt to black—an organization seeking success in Japan will typically follow an evolutionary pattern. Each stage provides a platform and foundation for the next sequence of growth. These stages have been gleaned from the experiences of successful foreign operators in Japan. In the next section of the book, we examine each stage in detail: 1) kick-starting the global organization, 2) defining the Japan strategy, 3) growing the Japanese business, and 4) becoming a world-class competitor.

PART

III

Succeeding in Japan

8

Kick-Starting the Global Organization

Karate has become popularized worldwide as a sport and martial art form. It's the stuff of Hollywood movies, and is even an Olympic event. To the Japanese, karate is different; it is more a philosophical expression than a mode of combat. Considered as "moving zen," karate calls upon the practitioner to unify mind and body and to tune in to the surrounding environment. Doing battle is merely an outgrowth of the philosophical foundation: in a contest, this strength of mind permits the practitioner to exploit both an opponent's strengths and weaknesses for advantage. Becoming an effective competitor in Japan is much the same process. To succeed, a foreign company must be committed and coordinated in mind and organization; it must be sensitive to variations in the environment and must respond to these variations accordingly. Simply focusing on the mechanics will not do. Erecting an organization or signing a distribution agreement, without a sense of spirit and commitment behind it, will be seen by the Japanese as just going through the motions. If you are to have a prayer of success in Japan, you must painstakingly prepare your company for the market. And, as we have suggested, by doing this your organization will also be properly girded for global performance.

SEEING BEYOND AMERICA

A friend of ours who works in Tokyo for a major Japanese consumer electronics company relates a story that illustrates the shortcomings of the typical American attempting to sell in Japan. As a member of the company's International Procurement Department, he was requested by MITI to encourage the importation and "design in" of U.S.-made semiconductors in the company's products. As a means of generating interest, he invited senior executives from U.S. chip makers to make product presentations. As in many of such meetings, the president of a major military and aerospace electronics company spoke to a group of engineers responsible for consumer products, stereos, and VCRs. The American executive addressed the group in English. With great relish, not to mention attractive charts and graphs, he told the engineers why his company was the best in the world. He said the company's chips were used on the Space Shuttle and in nuclear missiles; they could go to Mars and back. The chips were highly advanced and therefore could only be manufactured in limited runs, maybe a few thousand wafers per year. Yes, they were expensive but they were worth the price.

In closing, the executive showed slides of his company's large U.S. plants and R&D centers, and capped off the presentation with a long list of achievements, including a world map showing the company's international operations dotted with a sales and field engineering force of over 800 people. When it came to the question and answer period, the executive got but a single query; he was asked how many of the company's 800 engineers were located in Japan. He answered proudly that the company had thirty people in its Tokyo office. With that, the meeting politely came to an end. In most situations, it would have been a fine presentation, but this was Tokyo, not Boston's Route 128 corridor. After the meeting the American executive was mystified; he could not understand why the Japanese did not show greater interest or even discuss placing an order. For their part, the Japanese were frustrated. They felt they had wasted their afternoon listening to puffery from a foreigner who had no idea of their lines of business. Moreover, the Japanese executives probably only attended at the insistence of the International Procurement Department, which organized the meetings in an effort to appease MITI. And MITI only needed appeasing because it was under pressure from the United States to open up opportunities for business exchanges—interactions the Americans claim will result in more sales.

What went wrong? Clearly, the American executive had not bothered to do his homework prior to the meeting. If he had, he would have known first to bring an interpreter, as most of his presentation was lost on the attendees. He should have researched the audience's needs. While he was trying to interest them in the latest semiconductor devices, capable of operating advanced systems, those in attendance

CRITICAL ISSUES—STAGE ONE

Kick-starting the global organization:

- Push your people to see beyond America
- Understand the Japanese market and customers
- Develop information sources
- Quantify market opportunities
- Develop market analysis and strategy
- Promote a champion of change
- Form initial team of leaders
- Implement orientation programs
- Follow six "Ps"
- Define your vision

were designers of consumer audio and video equipment. They did not need advanced devices. What they did need were reliable, high-quality chips. A few thousand expensive chips a year would not do: they needed thousands every week at twenty-five cents a piece. And to top it off, these engineers were accustomed to having twenty to thirty supplier engineers assigned to them exclusively, pampering them with hospitality and practically designing the chips for them. With only thirty engineers in all of Japan, this group was unimpressed with what the American company had to offer. Simply put, they preferred the Japanese way of business. This story of misadventure tells a great deal about how Americans have lost opportunities in Japan.

We believe the above lesson is simple: the Japanese are not interested in buying products they cannot use, and they do not want to rely upon products they cannot get in a timely, cost-effective fashion. Make things they can use, and the Japanese have proven themselves rich and willing (and becoming more willing) consumers. The first step in effectively addressing Japan's rich markets is to shatter old myths and broaden the field of vision within your organization. The goal is to develop an internal corporate orientation and mindset focused toward the world outside and gain an insight into what the Japanese want. It's not always easy to accomplish this.

Americans have a well-earned reputation of being ignorant of the world around them. In a study of California State College students cited in *The Economist,* only half of the respondents could even locate Japan on a map. This reputation of being "geo-blivious" has wide and dire ramifications. Certainly a travesty in the cultural sense, it is also the damning factor in America's failure to compete effectively in the global arena. General ignorance of other people and cultures extends to matters of market nuance and sensitivity. We have seen that too few businessmen carry with them either the desire to understand a foreign market or the wherewithal to respond to its differences effectively. A large part of the reason Japanese markets appear "closed" is our own failure to understand the markets and the needs of its consumers. When you look at the track record, Americans are most often tripped up by their own foibles when they go abroad. Only by focusing your entire organization on Japan and overseas business, by growing an intelligence and information data base, and by gaining direct experience with Japanese customers can your company adequately face the realities of Japan's marketplace. American businesses must take off their blinders and see how the world has been transformed.

STUDY THE JAPANESE MARKET

A good way to generate interest within your company about the Japanese market is to quantify your opportunities. We have found this to be one of the most potent inducements to action. The objective is to get to know Japan by geographic area, study its differences and similarities, and to develop a rough list of customers, partners, and markets where an initial entry could prove fruitful. Japan is a gold mine of information on worldwide markets and technologies, a great deal of it in English and much more in Japanese. It generates more market data than any other country in the world today. The Japanese Export Trade Representative Offices (JETRO) thoughout the United States provide a wellspring of relevant information about numerous industries. Other sources include industry organizations and analyst groups for your line of business. You will find some basic sources and a list of market research firms in the back of this book in Appendix D.

Even before going to Japan, we recommend subscribing to Japanese-oriented news magazines and newspapers in order to get in touch with the people and the places. Publications such as the *Far East Economic Review*, *Business Tokyo*, the *Asian Wall Street Journal*, the *Japan Times*, and best of all, the *Japan Economic Journal*, published by *Nikkei Weekly*, are English-language publications that focus on international business issues in Japan and around the Pacific Rim. They are excellent sources for news and commentary, tales of foreign companies in Japan, exclusive articles on your major competitors, and human interest stories—features wherein you often learn the most about the intricacies of the market and its potential. This kind of preliminary homework allows you to learn the industry structure for your products, potential partners, and customers, and the major influences affecting the Japanese market. The more you know about the lay of the land before venturing to Japan, the better off you will be.

A company considering participating in Japan might find it helpful to answer such basic questions as:

- Who are the customers?
- Who are the competitors?
- Who are the potential partners?
- What vertical markets and industrial groups should be targeted first?
- What product adaptation and local engineering must be done?
- Who is best qualified to lead the new venture in Japan?
- What kind of human resources and capital budgeting will be required over the long term?

MAKE A COMPANY-WIDE COMMITMENT TO JAPAN

After you have convinced yourself, and a few other key people in your company, that there exists a satisfactory market potential for your products or services in Japan, the next step is to spread the word widely throughout the organization. As with most matters of change, broadening the perspective will be met at first with cynicism and fear. The "but that's not the way we've done it in the past" syndrome is a powerful siren call to inaction and lethargy in any group. However, resisting change because it is change is an irrational and debilitating disease of the will. Dynamic and thriving organizations embrace and harness the power of change and turn it into a competitive advantage. Nowhere is this more the case than in the challenge of transforming the corporate mindset toward the Japanese market. New ideas usually have a modest genesis and are nurtured along by constant attention and reinforcement by an articulate agent of change working alone or with a small group of champions. If you are reading this book, we suspect you are the champion of change in your organization. Even within the largest organizations, one voice can be quite effective.

When I as president of Applied Materials made the commitment to address the Japanese market, for a long time there were few others willing to join. But because of my personal commitment and stature in the company, others began to sense my dedication to the issue. I still had to work to raise the general awareness level of company executives on my staff, peppering every conversation and discussion with a similar refrain about going global, and constantly circulating copies of articles, videos, books, and speeches to individuals under my signature. As I shared these feelings with others, my ideas caught fire.

At Applied Materials, we began by developing an educational program for the top executives—what I called the "Japan Program." To get this program off to an enthusiastic start, program planners established an orientation regimen which included considerable reading, a Japanese cultural orientation, and talks by Japanese executives who were in the United States on assignment. We also arranged for weekly visits by groups of four or five managers and engineers from Japan semiconductor companies. Through this process each executive was immersed in Japanese culture, customer demands, manufacturing technology, quality principles, geography, and everyday language skills. These preliminary sessions reinforced my belief that business must be built on our similarities with the Japanese and that, often, even our differences can be advantageous when properly emphasized. The next step was to take the entire group of executives to Japan.

Once in Japan, the tutorial began with a short seminar on the Japanese market organized by the Semiconductor Equipment and Materials Institute (SEMI), our industry trade group. The seminar included representatives from the Japanese business community, MITI, a lawyer experienced in Japanese law, and a representative from one of the major banks. This presentation provided a broad overview of what to expect when doing business in Japan. In subsequent days, Applied Materials executives visited the same Tokyo trade show which had a few years earlier made an impression upon me. There the Applied executives were able to see competitors from around the world and meet Japanese customers. Such face-to-face meetings with customers and other corporate executives in Japan provided a good look at the business environment, the possibilities and the pitfalls. The trip also included a number of side trips. One of the most memorable was a visit to the Tsukiji Fish Market in central Tokyo, the largest such market in the world. This excursion pulled the group out of bed at 4:00 a.m. into the heart of the Japanese food distribution system. The hustle of the marketplace, the innate sales ability of the fish mongers, and unique customs which we observed brought home an important point about the differences in our business styles. It added a good deal of color to the business side of what we studied.

But a visit to the Honda Motor Company was probably the highlight of the trip from a business viewpoint. The Honda production line was turning out a new car every twenty-seven seconds; each car a different color and bound for a different country. Some cars had four doors, some two doors. Some had steering wheels on the right, some on the left. All the cars were coming off the line built to order with each station being fed with exactly the right parts in exactly the right order. I had been attempting to significantly reduce inventories, improve quality, reduce overhead, speed up turn around and add to the variety of products at Applied Materials for several years, but my message seemed to fall upon deaf ears. The brief walk through the Honda plant did more to convince my executives about the possibilities and opportunities we had than the reams of memos and teams of consultants could back home. We all learned firsthand how a well-trained workforce, an effective employee suggestion program, just-in-time (JIT) manufacturing, intense planning and forecasting, quality programs, and building supplier relations with a few selected vendors could result in dramatic improvements in performance.

We also visited a number of customer plant sites and, after a week of education and being together with our Japanese colleagues, we all regrouped for a quarterly management meeting to chart our course in Japan based on our new perceptions. It was quite a changed group that entered that meeting room. Since that time, Japan became an issue at every top management meeting at Applied Materials, and today you will find that everyone at the company, from the shipping clerk to the director of marketing, knows that his job depends in large part on our success in Japan. The immersion into a new culture over an extended period of time and under such intense conditions brought the entire Applied Materials team together with a common base of understanding and with a Japanese point of view. Also, the bonds that were established during that initial and subsequent orientation programs have strengthened the company's culture and provided avenues of mutual trust which have proven significant in the corporation's long-term success.

Since it is impractical in a larger organization to send all employees to Japan, a Japan Program should be designed first for senior managers. But the real results will not come about without some form of companywide emersion. Japanese business and culture classes which outline the Japanese market and its importance and unique requirements should be routinely available as part of employee training. At Applied Materials, we established a much-heralded program some years ago. Eight hours in duration, the program includes readings on Japanese history, society and culture, and some training in rudimentary conversational Japanese. All levels of management are required to take the course and all other employees are encouraged to attend. The language portion of the program is not extensive, but does permit employees to demonstrate to their customers and fellow employees in Japan the *desire* to communicate. Showing this kind of respect is very important. By knowing how to appropriately greet and politely sustain a telephone conversation or electronic mail correspondence, our employees have universally reported positive results in their relationships with their Japanese associates.

Through televised classes offered at Stanford University, we have also made it possible for employees to attend beginning and intermediary Japanese language courses. And naturally, the company will pay for such courses or reimburse any employee who takes outside classes on Japanese language and related subjects. In general, at Applied Materials we are highly supportive of travel to Japan, encourage study projects there and other efforts by employees to develop firsthand experience and friendships with associates, customers, and suppliers. We believe airplane tickets, which make international business possible in the first place, should not be one of the initial expense items cut if belt tightening is required. Growing the international business is a long-term proposition and should not be shortchanged.

DEVELOP A JAPANESE MARKET PHILOSOPHY

Once you've taken a look at the Japanese market, and you are convinced there is a place for your product or service, you must develop a philosophical foundation upon which to base your strategy. Like a student of karate, this foundation will lie just beneath the surface of your battle plan. You should begin by developing a market orientation based on an analysis of the market structure in your industry—taking into account the competing and complementary industrial groups, distribution systems, and primary obstacles to entry and sustained success. We have found six simple components to keep in mind: presence, people, pioneering, piggybacking, partnering, and persistence.

PRESENCE AND PEOPLE

The successful foreign companies we have studied in Japan have been so because they made a direct investment in the market. A direct presence, through a subsidiary and by manufacturing and engineering in Japan, or even an on-site support operation when you are working through a distributor or joint venture, is the best way to gain and maintain market share, to adapt your product or service to rapidly changing consumer needs, and to build a lasting operation. Only by showing continually increasing commitment to the market through investment, local hiring, and developing a localized technical capability can foreign companies realistically expect to support local requirements and build essential relations with Japanese companies—both suppliers and customers.

PIONEERING

In simple terms, "get there first, get there fast." In Japan, an "original" product earns a definite distinction and normally has a longer life to it than a "me-too" product. Among the market innovators in Japan who have reaped benefits from their pioneering products are Sony, with miniaturized electronics, the now-legendary Walkman, and the more recent 8mm camcorders; Canon, in laser printers; Honda, in mid-size luxury cars; Sun Microsystems, in workstations; and Procter and Gamble, in disposable diapers. These companies were the first out of the gate with a hot new product, and each has been able to maintain a leadership position by keeping one step ahead of its competitors. But it has not been easy.

Maintaining a lead against giant Japanese companies, and other foreign companies now entering the market, requires diligence and constant attention. Things happen fast in Japan, faster than in almost any other market. This is a given. A technology pioneer like Sony knows that within months of launching a new product, a company like Matsushita will have a similar send-up of its own. The saving grace is that the marketplace will treat the pretender differently, with consumers preferring to own the "original," breakthrough brand name.

Be assured, your breakthrough product or service will never be alone long. In time, after one or more of the giant companies take a run at you, the second-tier companies will also identify the niche and follow suit. In Japan, this large second tier of companies tend to wait and follow the market leaders before entering the ring. Only after a clearly established demand has been created, and the market leader has spent heavily on initial product development and consumer education, do these smaller fish come to feed. This is a typical scenario, and if you successfully weather the first assault from a giant competitor, do not rest on your laurels. The next wave could come like a *tsunami.*

PIGGYBACKING

Japan's byzantine distribution system has been built on a long history of complex relationships. It is a web that has withstood the many tests of times. Therefore, it is extremely difficult for a newcomer to enter and attempt to build a proprietary distribution network or sales force. It is a long, arduous process, with no guarantee of success. One way to get into the market may be to use established channels. The practice of "piggybacking" is quite common, even among those with access to the distribution system. A good example of a successful piggyback is seen in the joint venture arrangement between Blue Diamond Almond Growers of California and Coca-Cola.

In 1970, Blue Diamond began selling almonds in bulk in Japan through trading companies, but things really didn't take off until the organization looked into a strategy for selling retail-packaged almonds directly to consumers and educating the market with recipe booklets and even classes on how to use almonds. However, it came up against the wall of the Japanese distribution system and nearly considered retreating from the idea of selling direct. Then Blue Diamond came across a partner in the Coca-Cola Bottling Company. It was a simple concept: snack foods and soft drinks were a natural combination. And, as the largest seller of soft drinks in Japan, Coca-Cola had nearly 600 sales offices and over 20,000 salesmen throughout the islands. By using Coca-Cola's well-established routes, Blue Diamond was able to reach all seventeen bottlers in Japan and approach its target goal of 40 percent market share in ten years.

In another example, General Foods had long been trying to make inroads into the Japanese market, with little success. They found a solution by teaming up with Ajinomoto, a Japanese food processing company, to form General Foods Ajinomoto (AGF). With its large group of wholesalers, Ajinomoto has adapted General Foods products for the Japanese market and today through these sales channels, AGF is a $300 million-plus company in Japan. Other examples include Federal Express' purchase of an equity interest in a medium-sized Japanese trucking company and Merck's majority interest in Banyu Pharmaceuticals. The key to piggybacking is to leverage Japan's people-rich companies and existing structures, many of which hungrily need new products and ideas.

PARTNERING

Striking partnerships with established Japanese companies can be another source of success in the market. Linking up with first-tier Japanese companies has given numerous foreign firms access to industrial groups, complementary product lines, financing, and new technologies. For Sun Microsystems, bridging three-way partnerships with Fujitsu, Toshiba, and Fuji-Xerox instantly gave it a powerful sales network across a number of industry groups and vertical markets. As a result, Sun was able to dramatically increase its market exposure and decrease its investment in local operations and direct marketing. Through its partners, Sun has also been able to obtain access to the best components and technologies Japan has to offer.

Finding partners in Japan with complementary technologies and marketing strengths can be a relatively quick avenue to success. It can help you build relationships across multiple industrial groups which may never be open to your company otherwise. Even giant companies like IBM and Texas Instruments, which have large direct sales forces, use partnerships for strategic advantage. IBM currently partners with over twenty major companies such as Ricoh and Nippon Steel which sell and service IBM equipment in Japan. TI's technology relationship with Hitachi enables it to remain on the leading edge in DRAM integrated circuit development.

Yet, partnering has its drawbacks. The case of Tokyo Electron, Ltd. (TEL) shows what can go wrong. TEL began as a general trading company with a division concentrating on advanced equipment. As a part of its business, TEL routinely arranged for joint ventures with leading American equipment makers which had little access to Japan and could see such a venture as a convenient way to manufacture locally. The American firms reasoned that some access was better than none. In actuality, the arrangement kept them isolated from any direct relationships with Japanese customers. In the meantime, TEL learned all it could from the process and went on to manufacture and develop its own competing products, which it is now selling against its former partners in both Japan and the United States, and many of its former partners are today bankrupt. The lesson to be derived from this story is not to be a silent partner with the Japanese counterpart; delineate responsibilities but watch the chickens in the coop.

PERSISTENCE

The Japanese value *gambate*—stick-to-it-iveness—like few other societies. Regardless of the approach you select to selling in Japan, you will earn the respect and trust of customers, suppliers, and competitors alike by hanging in there through good times and bad. And if you stand up for yourself assertively in the process, it's all the better. Allen-Edmonds, a small Wisconsin-based shoe manufacturer, provides a good example of sheer persistence paying off in the Japanese market. The company's high-quality footwear had consistently sold well in markets like Honolulu and San Francisco. It didn't take its market research department long to uncover that the demand was being created by Japanese tourists who flock to those cities on holiday. Considering this a sure sign of company potential in Japan itself, Allen-Edmonds President John Stollenwork began to look at why his distributor had moved next to nothing in Japan.

Having almost no prior contact with Japanese retailers and no formal strategy, Stollenwork began doing his homework. He soon found that pricing and lack of leading retail outlets for his footwear were killing his chances in Japan. Due to tariffs and high distribution costs, a pair of shoes that sold for $139 in New York were priced at over $400 in Tokyo. His retailers argued that, to maintain a high-status image in Japan, imported luxury products must be expensive. Stollenwork made it clear that he didn't consider a comfortable pair of shoes a luxury. He soon found out that there was more to it than that. The footwear industry in Japan is tightly controlled by the *Dowa*, Japan's largest minority group. The *Dowa* are descendants of the early butchers and tanners of Japan's feudal period. Because Buddhism forbade the killing of animals, the *Dowa* were social outcasts. Unable to find respect within traditional industry, the *Dowa* have accumulated political power in order to preserve their position in meat and leather products. Thus they have been able to keep import quotas low and tariffs high.

Even after negotiations between the United States and Japan lowered the tariffs, imported shoes remain on a low quota and carry a 27 percent tariff. Shoes entering above the quota carry a 50 percent tariff. Despite these barriers, Stollenwork sensed an opportunity and decided to take his company's products directly to Japan and, in particular, to the Tokyo Shoe Fair. When he tried to reserve a booth, he was told that only domestic manufacturers could exhibit at the fair. Instead of being discouraged he booked a flight to Tokyo, called a press conference in Milwaukee, and invited Japanese journalists to join him in his fight to gain access to the fair. With fifty pairs of shoes in hand and an entourage of reporters in tow, embarrassed show organizers not only relented, but gave him prime space in the foyer outside the main exhibit hall. But the challenges for Allen-Edmonds didn't end there.

Because he had stuck to his guns, Stollenwork's company earned the respect of the retail community and sales took off. Then the other shoe dropped. As sales began to rise, Allen-Edmonds soon found out that its trademark had been registered by a Japanese company—a company that made its business by registering thousands of foreign brand and company names in order to extract royalties. It cost Allen-Edmonds $30,000 to buy back the rights to use its own name. Today, Japan is a strong market for Allen-Edmonds. The company has found new channels for growth and has begun to build a real presence in the market, owing it all to the persistence of its president.[1]

OTHER CONSIDERATIONS IN MARKET STRATEGY

- Keep initial product introduction simple and easy to support
- Use market exposure to gain further market information
- Penetrate through components, move gradually to more sophisticated systems
- Understand rapid, boom-bust market dynamics
- Counterattack competition with model upgrades—avoid obsolescence
- Diversify early success

When developing a strategy for entering the Japanese market it is vitally important to keep the initial entry simple, maintain a high-status leadership image, maintain consistency, and keep abreast of the rapid "boom-bust" cycles of fickle consumer demand.

Many foreign companies make the error of believing that their products will sell well in Japan because they sell well elsewhere or because they are the most advanced technologically. Following this logic, they make their first entry into the market behind a state-of-the-art or new-concept product without first having developed a solid understanding of Japanese wants and needs. Not uncommonly, they have not even "seeded" the landscape with a basic support structure to sell and service their new products successfully. Other companies bury themselves by trying to sell too many different products right out of the chute. Companies like Applied Materials, and even IBM years ago, have proven that introducing a limited line of low-support products is the best way to develop strong relationships and a support apparatus which can serve these relationships before moving up to a broader line of more sophisticated products.

In status-conscious Japan, perceived value is a major determinant of product success. Qualitative images are far more important than value based on the typical cost model used in the United States. Automobiles are the ultimate status symbol in Japan, and BMW and Mercedes have dominated the foreign import market using these "images." Mercedes advertises in the very expensive *Nihon Keizai Shimbun,* something like our *Wall Street Journal,* which is read by almost every businessman in Japan. BMW spends close to $5 million a year on sixty-second, prime-time television spots that run weekly. Pricing is part of the image. Unlike in the United States, there are cases where products actually lost popularity and market share due to reductions in price. Johnny Walker Black and Red and Chivas whiskies have long cultivated high-status images in Japan. They are very expensive in bars or clubs, and are highly prized as gifts. Thinking that it could take advantage of the high yen, and hoping to gain market share away from Chivas, Johnny Walker dropped the price of the Black label brand. Instead of increasing sales, the move shot them through the cellar. Japanese consumers saw the price reduction as somehow related to quality problems with the beverage, and it suffered a drop in status. Yet while the Black fell out of favor, and still today is on the cheaper end of the drink menus, the Red label has maintained its status position.

When a product sells well in Japan, it really sells. The compact size of the country and the relatively homogeneous nature of the society makes Japan unquestionably the fastest moving market in the world. Unfortunately, a market boom can go bust just as rapidly. Given the quickness of demand creation, and the scale of the opportunity, a hot product will be duplicated in no time. This "lemming factor"—wherein competitors follow the leader en masse—has been the bane of many foreigners unfamiliar with the nuances of the Japanese market.

The successful competitor in Japan must possess the ability to ramp up quickly to satisfy rapid increases in demand, then ramp down production just as quickly as demand drops off. One strategy is to offer different versions and upgrades of a product as soon as the market begins to show signs of softening.

The story of the much ballyhooed Japanese home breadbaker provides an example of a boom gone to bust. Not much bigger than a toaster oven, the home breadmaker was first introduced by a small company in Osaka in 1986, and it took off like a rocket. It seemed like every Japanese consumer had to own one. Within the first three months, the demand grew so large that the company couldn't keep them in the stores. By that third month, however, a dozen competitors quickly introduced their own versions. By the end of the year, the market was saturated, and the demand weakened. Being unable to meet the demand it created, the company that introduced the product initially didn't get to enjoy the full life cycle of the product, and those companies which came in at the tail end of the boom lost a bundle. To expand to full market potential, a company in Japan must have product in volume and available throughout the entire island when the boom hits. Then, it must quickly introduce new, improved models in rapid succession, always staying a few steps ahead of the competition which will surely follow.

We have provided some of the key considerations to make when drafting a strategy for Japan. By understanding some of the dynamics which fuel the market, we hope you will select an entry approach which best suits your needs and capabilities.

9

Defining the Japan Strategy

On one of our first visits to Tokyo, a customer took us to a *sashimi* restaurant near the *Tsukiji* fish market. It was a small place in one of the alleys skirting the glittering avenues of the fabled Ginza district. We sat down at the counter surrounding the chef's alcove. In front of us, a glass case ran the length of the restaurant. It contained rows of raw fish and seafood, some we had never seen before. Back then sashimi, or prepared raw fish, was not that popular in the United States, and we were not yet familiar with the culinary art form it truly is. The customer ordered for all of us and we watched as the chef prepared a tray of items. Because there were so many sashimi restaurants in the area, I asked our customer if this was a favorite of his. He said it was, because it had a special license to prepare and serve *fugu*—which he had just ordered for us. The *fugu* is a small round fish, indigenous to the cold waters of the China Sea. A very delicate white fish, it is highly prized in Japan. It is also one of the most dangerous animals on earth. Sometimes called "blow fish" because of its shape and its ability to inflate itself to fend off enemies, the fugu's liver and ovaries contain tetrodoxotin—a potent poison. Less than a gram of this poison can kill a 160-pound man within a few hours. The rest of the flesh is safe to eat, but even a slight inaccuracy in its preparation can prove fatal. Owing to the great risk involved, chefs must be specially trained and licensed to prepare the fish. Most come from the same province on Kyushu island. Besides being tasty, eating *fugu* is thought by the Japanese to be an act of virility and manhood (and occasionally, we found out, used to test the courage of foreigners). When our order was served, we ate our first bites of the thinly sliced fish with considerable trepidation. Thankfully, it was properly prepared. In many ways, the fugu is a symbol of the Japanese market. When approached properly, it is a market which offers great opportunity for wealth. If, however, it is approached improperly—with the wrong strategy or the wrong product—a venture into Japan can prove ruinous.

THE MARKET MAP

Our analysis and experience indicate there are some very fundamental issues that precede the development of a Japan strategy appropriate for your organization. A basic starting point for a strategic and market survey of Japan should include:

- A summary of research on the economy and your industry
- Analysis of all potential customers and partners, end-user markets, and competitors in Japan
- Determination of how Japanese needs are different and how products are used differently/similarly in Japan
- A full report on Japanese requirements for product design and customization, service, quality, delivery, and support
- A forecast of investment and operating revenue and profit over five years; expected capital outlay for a long-term commitment
- A recruitment plan—sources of managerial, sales, and technical personnel
- The appropriate worldwide organization required to support the Japan operation
- Related industry associations and Japanese industry standards
- An executive commitment to the Japanese market; time allotted for personally meeting customers and partners, and for understanding market needs
- Analysis of sources for investment and key banking relations needed

MODES OF ENTRY INTO JAPAN

After reconciling the need to address the Japanese market, the biggest challenge for most executives is to figure out how to begin. This requires carefully selecting the best route to take in entering the market and determining the best mode to support initial business generated. The change from domestic to global thinking is a difficult step, but it provides dramatic opportunities that would previously not have been considered possible. A global orientation raises the entire company's expectations for revenue targets, market share, gross margin opportunities, technical partnerships, and acquisition of management talent. While there are exceptions, in our view the primary objective of any company should be to establish in its worldwide organization as many of the business functions in Japan as possible, from sales and global competitive analysis to product development and research. The emphasis should be on sales to build direct customer linkages, service to ensure repeat business, engineering to design the right products, research to take advantage of Japan's technologies, and manufacturing to ensure fast turnaround and delivery. *All other agreements and partnerships should be considered as stepping stones to a direct operations strategy.* Whichever method you choose to address the Japanese market, the criteria for results should be the same:

- *The operation should be designed to begin and support a close relationship between your company and your Japanese customers.* This means that it must provide an avenue for feedback so that continuous product and process improvements can be made. It should also provide a means for establishing future requirements for products and services, allow for mutually beneficial joint development efforts, and create an environment of intertwined destiny with the customers.
- *The Japanese operation should permit long-term control of company products, services, and technologies and a two-way exchange of benefits, either through partners or distributors, or through the local subsidiary.* Arrangements that offer nothing but short-term benefits and a certain obsolescence are undesirable.
- *The closer to the marketplace you can get, the clearer your understanding of the competitive environment, its needs, and its nuances will be.* The local operation is an intelligence base for both information gathering and processing.
- *The Japanese strategy has as its ultimate end the goal of participating effectively in a vast and growing market by building opportunity and limiting risk.* The closer you get to the opportunities and the customers, the more assured you can become that they will not get away from you.

CRITICAL ISSUES—STAGE TWO

Defining the Japan Strategy:

- Target markets, key customers, key partners (potential)
- Define product/service adaptation requirements
- Identify funding sources
- Determine entry mode
- Plan local support operation
- Hire core management

For different companies, products and market situations, the selected entry methodology will vary. Through our case studies and personal experience, we have found successful companies using each of the four principal avenues for selling to Japan: distribution agreements, licensing agreements, joint ventures, and direct operations. It is quite possible to attack the market through any one, or even all, of these entry options. For instance, a machine tool maker can sell products through a distributor, and thereby take advantage of a sizable, in-place sales organization, while at the same time embarking on a joint venture with one or several other complementary or even competitive firms. A retail outlet may franchise its concept, but also own and directly operate various locations. Flexibility is essential and in some respects an integrated approach may even be the most desirable end result.

THE DISTRIBUTION AGREEMENT

When Applied Materials first engaged the Japanese market, it did so with the idea that it was an extension of its primary market in the United States, a generator of incremental revenues beyond the company's strategic business with American customers. The company arranged with a distributor to represent Applied's systems along with its massive catalog of other products. That was perceived to be sufficient for the level of expectations at the time. If any systems were sold in Japan, they were considered "gravy." In retrospect, the reasoning may have been flawed, but the exercise of going through a distributorship provided a valuable learning experience for the company.

For American companies seeking a distributor in Japan, usually one of the first companies that will approach you with interest is a large sogo sosha, or general trading company, or one of the hundreds of *semmon shosha,* or specialty trading companies in your field. These huge conglomerates typically buy and sell thousands of products through various divisions in each industrial sector, and have their own unique networks of "group" companies and sub-distributors for a nearly unlimited variety of products. Before signing on with any trading company, it is important to fully understand the advantages and disadvantages to the distributorship approach.

ADVANTAGES

- Instant market access
- Minimal start-up costs and risks
- Accepted customer interface, trusted name
- Quick to pay, good cash flow

DISADVANTAGES

- May be insufficiently familiar with your product/technology
- Few real sales channels and industrial partnerships
- Limits opportunity for direct customer contact
- Products will be part of larger catalog—no special attention
- Impedes intelligence gathering
- Limited technical support

Applied Materials found that its distributor could never grasp the requirements to be successful in the advanced equipment business. Instead of helping the business grow, the distributor was, in actuality, a hindrance; it stood between the company and the essential feedback it needed to build long-term relationships with customers. Other companies have had more success with trading companies. C. Itoh & Co., Japan's largest sogo shosha, saw the potential for Sun Microsystems' engineering workstations and invested millions of dollars to build a 1,000-employee subsidiary to sell and support the product.

Foreign companies must take the time to carefully evaluate the true capabilities and upper management commitment to their business before jumping into a distributorship relationship, particularly where theirs will be among hundreds of products carried. Demanding revenue commitments, investment in your own Japan operations, and detailed business plans—backed by the word of top directors—is essential to making the distributorship work. *In all cases, exclusive relationships should be avoided.* In fact, multiple channels should be developed across each market and industrial group. And, of course, your company should have an office in Japan to manage these relationships. Getting locked into relationships with mediocre partners or major companies with little experience in your field has been the bane of too many foreign companies trying to gain access to Japan.

THE LICENSING AGREEMENT

Of the four main ways to address the Japanese market, product and technology licensing has proven the most dangerous and least effective avenue for American companies. For many years, restrictive Japanese laws made licensing and technology sharing necessary to even participate in Japan. For such giant American firms as IBM and Texas Instruments licensing was an unavoidable price of admittance to the market. Today, these demands have lessened, and for most companies the licensing option is the weakest possible strategy for entering the market—because it is really no entry at all. Once a Japanese competitor has rights to utilize or reproduce a technology, it will move quickly to absorb the technology and own it outright. RCA, for example, received $50 million a year for its color television technology, instead of pushing to gain access to the booming Japanese market through direct sales—and RCA was doomed from that moment, as Japanese companies dominated what was to become a $2.4 billion market. The U.S.-Japan Trade Study Group has estimated that as of 1982 U.S. firms had received license fees of about $800 million from Japan. If they had developed their own products and sold them in Japan, that technology might have accounted for sales of more than $60 billion. Today, the benefits to Japan may be double or triple this figure.[1] Clearly, this predisposition to license technology away without becoming an operating company in the local market to monitor and defend one's position has come back to haunt American firms. A dollar of licenses today will create ten dollars worth of another company's product tomorrow.

This is not to say there are no uses for a licensing strategy. Sun Microsystems has aggressively licensed its microprocessor technology to Toshiba and other leading computer manufacturers in Japan in a carefully aimed effort to promote its Sparc/Unix technology as a standard for the entire computer industry. For Sun, the advantage is obvious: by sharing certain "boiler plate" aspects of its technology with other, even competing companies, it grows the overall market for its products and therefore expands its own opportunities by not allowing standards to be made which bypass its approach. The risk, of course, is that the market will grow but in the face of fierce competition, Sun's market share will not, both in Japan and worldwide. The problem is, once the "genie" is out of the bottle and all the players have the same equipment and technology, the Japanese advantages of high-volume production, process control, quality, capital investment, and customer sensitivity come into play to trim the growth opportunities of the technology originator.

Licensing should be considered very carefully, and only as a strategic tool to complement primary direct sales strategies through your own operations and through partners. Technology might also be licensed under controlled conditions for contract manufacturers and as a base technology for a joint venture. Often, technology is used in exchange for equity participation in joint ventures. If possible, technology should not be licensed exclusively to maximize profits—and all projects must be managed closely from Japan.

Advantages

- Establishes market, operating standards for new technologies and products
- Provides short-term fees, with the promise of longer-term residuals

Disadvantages

- Gives competitors "free ride" to new technology with no R&D costs
- Creates no local presence for R&D, marketing, or manufacturing
- Offers no exposure to complementary opportunities
- Competitive obsolescence guaranteed

Southland Corporation's licensing of 7-Eleven chain stores to Ito-Yokado in Japan is one of the classic examples of how Americans are, for easy-money and short-term gains, losing out on major opportunities for global expansion. Southland receives royalty payments—to the tune of more than $200 million per year from Ito-Yokado. This is big money, no one can argue, but today 7-Eleven in Japan has thousands of stores and billions of dollars in revenues and is one of Japan's biggest retail success stories. Ito-Yokado, through its 7-Eleven venture, has built one of the largest networks of suppliers and local partners of any convenience store in Japan, and scientifically developed a product mix unique to Japanese eating and purchasing habits. Today, 7-Eleven serves *udon, oden, sushi* and a number of other traditional Japanese foods. Meanwhile, Southland has been kept virtually insulated from the business in Japan. As a result, the American company is missing out on the opportunity to build relationships with important suppliers, real estate companies, and distributors, and cannot adequately develop a reading of the unique tastes and buying trends of the super-rich Japanese consumer. With the demand for oriental foods in the United States, it is conceivable that specialized products from Japan would be successful at many 7-Eleven locations in America.

THE JOINT VENTURE AGREEMENT

One of the quickest ways to plug into Japanese markets is to form strategic partnerships with Japanese companies for joint ventures in sales and manufacturing, joint technology development, as technology suppliers, and as a sales channel for your products. As it continues to undergo rapid changes, no other country in the world will be a more fertile ground for partnerships than Japan. Exploding coffers of investment monies, growing trade tensions, and the need to access tightening overseas markets and increase exports will drive the Japanese to work with many types of foreign firms. Japanese consumer groups are growing more vocal in calling for lower prices and greater access to foreign goods. Many large companies in Japan need to diversify but lack the required technology or distribution channels. Partnering provides the solution for them, and a good opportunity for foreign firms.

There are hundreds of Japanese companies today looking for ways to secure new technology resources, expand American and European distribution, and even build new business opportunities in Japan. Many of these companies can provide worldwide capabilities and sales channels throughout Asia and can bring advanced technologies and financial resources to the party. In some ways it is easier today to secure financing for expansion in Japan than in the United States, as funds for long-term plant expansion and capital investment are running thin on Wall Street.

ADVANTAGES

- Reduced risk of failure, burden sharing
- Short term benefits
  - customer relationships
  - market exposure/access
  - customer feedback for long-term evolution
- Increased company and product acceptance—"Japanization" through local manufacturing and sales presence

DISADVANTAGES

- Significant market insulation; local partner will tend to control
  - customer interface, support
  - local organization
  - technology evolution
- Difficult to keep objectives in alignment over time
- Little opportunity for global integration of Japanese operation

There are also many opportunities to benefit from the unique skills of Japanese partners to strengthen your relative position against other competitors. Knowing the partnering resources and potential areas of new opportunity for joint activity, including financing, marketing, and co-development of new technologies and services, opens new horizons for business by expanding the customer base and improving overall capabilities. Having first-tier companies as partners and customers is a strong step forward in the beginning. The name recognition and influence gained from these associations open opportunities with other companies in the industrial group, the distribution network, and in major accounts. This association will also help attract second- and third-tier companies to your side. A pervasive mentality exists throughout Japan that "if Hitachi or C. Itoh is doing it, it must be the way to go." As well, large partners provide easy access to massive financial resources.

American companies must directly participate in the organization and management of the joint venture. A joint venture is usually a fifty-fifty partnership, yet still most U.S. companies hooking up with Japanese tend to let the local half run the entire show. Participation by the American side continues to be limited by personnel policies, geographic distance, fear, and lack of understanding of Japanese business practices. Joint planning of projects requires that each side be closely integrated in communications and acclimated to the other in culture and style—especially in Japan, where time horizons and decision processes differ dramatically. Japanese companies are usually willing to provide 100 percent of the personnel, and a large part of the financing in exchange for critical technology and marketing rights. But what should be understood is that the first loyalty of transferred managers will be to their original employers. Hooking up with a first-tier corporation in Japan with its own competitive products can seriously endanger long-term success, and its size will limit a smaller foreign company's bargaining power.

Organization has proved critical in working with Japanese companies, which often require a great deal more periodic and issue-by-issue contact for problem resolution. Most projects should have both a management committee and an operations committee, which meet quarterly in the initial stages, with each supported by working groups in functional areas—technical, quality, and purchasing—to resolve lower level issues before they escalate to the upper management committees. It may be advisable to transfer key personnel to Japan to support these committees. Partners should insist on quarterly or monthly financial reports and six-month rolling forecasts and product plans to monitor progress. Face-to-face meetings and time together socially are equally important to developing a healthy long-term relationship.

SELECTING A PARTNER

The first step to finding a suitable partner is to know what is to be gained. Each partner should be absolutely clear from the outset as to what the expectations and objectives are. Also, it is important to know the limitations and capabilities of your partner after realistically evaluating what is possible and what is not. During this "courting" stage, it is advisable to have an intermediary, known by both partners, to serve as the go-between in defining goals and expectations. An ideal partnership balances and complements both parties, and an ill-conceived or ill-fitting joining can be a drain on resources, manpower, and long-term effectiveness in Japan. Success in partnerships depends a great deal on how much mutual benefit both parties gain beyond what they could accomplish alone. *Consider the simple mathematical rule of* $(a+b)^2 > a^2 + b^2$. Potential partners in Japan should be evaluated on the basis of:

- Distribution channels and large customer associations
- Recognized technical leadership in the field

- Support and service capabilities
- Geographic coverage
- Market image and reputation
- Complementary/competitive product fit
- Industrial ranking—first-, second-, or third-tier
- Willingness for nonexclusivity
- Industrial or banking group association—and the "*exclusivity negative,*" or how much one's relations with a certain partner excludes one from doing business in other industrial groups
- Philosophical fit and possible long-term synergies
- Personal relations between management

Picking the right partners from the start, entering the right market, and making key decisions on investment of precious resources are all critical concerns. Not only will selecting a wrong partner cost effort and resources for little likely gain, it will take a good deal of time to extract your company from such an agreement. Simply pulling out of a partnership or other agreement because it is convenient or pragmatic will result in injured feelings, a poor reputation, and a possible "blacklisting" by other potential partners in Japan. The best advice is to plan thoroughly beforehand (perhaps using a Japanese consultant), and once the decision is made, expect to stick it out for a while.

Who are the most likely candidates for partners? In most cases, as we have seen, your first contacts will be with one of the major trading companies, or possibly a large manufacturer. There is an upside and a downside to this situation. Partnering with a *sogo sosha* can reduce the initial resistance to your product, provides name recognition and some legitimacy to your company, introduces you to potential customers and other partners, helps to reduce risk and start-up costs, and can result in the building of consortia to handle your products or services. But, while the *sogo shosha* companies are good at establishing initial contacts and providing baseline market expertise, they usually have limited technical product and support capabilities. And, due to their size, rarely can they invest the required resources to build product-specific sales and marketing teams just for your product. The foreign venturer should approach a number of *dai-ichi ryu,* or first-tier companies, as OEMs or major end-user customers upon first entering Japan.

A quick way to become a direct company, with access to Japan's business circles, is to enter into strategic partnerships with companies who are already well connected. By tying up with a Diamond 300 company (Japan's version of the Fortune 500) and by building interdependencies between your companies—in purchasing, sales, service, or technology development—a relatively small company can have a disproportionate influence on the Japanese market, and rapidly build an image of being a leader. Unlike smaller markets in Europe, Taiwan, or Korea where there may only be a few potential leaders, Japan has many giant companies in each industrial sector from which to choose (see Appendix E).

THE POWER OF COOPERATION

Imagine if all your products could be designed to meet actual needs—present and future—in real-time partnership with your customers. Research and development could be precisely targeted and better incorporated by both parties. Design times would be reduced and production-worthy applications could be unearthed immediately, slashing time to market. We believe this is not only a compelling idea, but a practical key to survival in the world today.

A cooperative strategy begins by viewing the customer/supplier process not as a transactional relationship, but as a true merging of interests—a partnership. This is very different from a supplier with whom you engage in only short-term relationships and who meets your immediate needs at the best price the market offers. You have no loyalty to such a supplier, and buy his products as long as the price is right and quality good. Communication is limited to the point of purchase. The supplier has only a limited commitment to you, and the only telephone number in your company he is likely to remember is the accounts payable department.

This is in direct contrast to a world class customer who is a partner with his suppliers. With a sense of joint commitment, the relationship is naturally aimed at the long term, not pegged to singular transactions, but an ongoing joint effort to solve joint problems and maximize mutual opportunities. The partner realizes that his interests are intertwined. There is extensive communication and a more intimate interplay between you and your partner, with products developed to more closely fit your needs because your input was a critical part of your supplier's development process. This is a relationship that is not at arm's length, but arm in arm.

The trend throughout the world, along with increasing competition, is toward more coordinated efforts. Today's technologies have become too complex, the world's market too globally linked, and the stakes too high to work in isolation from each other.

DEFINITION OF WORLD-CLASS CUSTOMER

Non-combative, supportive
Utilizes supplier's expertise
Reduces number of suppliers
Problem solving/mutual benefit is main goal

BENEFITS OF REAL-TIME PARTNERING

R&D and engineering focused
Design cycle times reduced
Production-worthy applications realized
Time to market shortened

NEGOTIATING FOR PARTNERSHIP

When considering a partnership with a Japanese company, there are several points to bear in mind. Like all things Japanese, there is a right way, a wrong way, and a Japanese Way to negotiate the arrangement. Failure to follow the tacit rules of etiquette—attention to detail and consideration for the comfort level of the potential partner—can imperil the entire deal. We have found some basic considerations which can greatly improve communications and success in almost any situation with the Japanese.

- Don't try to overcontrol the partnership.
- Show an interest in understanding Japanese culture.
- Understand how the Japanese are defining a "successful outcome" to the negotiations.
- Be prepared and have detailed facts and technical information readily available.
- Neatness, attention to detail, and follow-through are critical.
- Be sensitive and hospitable, follow basic rules of etiquette and language. Demonstrate a knowledge of customs, gift giving, etc.

- Respect hierarchy. Ensure representatives of correct stature at meetings.
- Don't take anything for granted; ask if you are unclear.
- Show interest in your partners' activities, not just in promoting your own.
- Take the time to listen to what they are doing.
- Spend time informally outside the business setting. Get to know your counterpart more personally and build a web of trust at all levels of the organization. Make binding obligations by taking trips, playing golf, giving gifts, and doing favors.
- Show humility—never boast, insult, or display uncontrolled emotion.
- Work at all levels of the *ringi-sho* process, including lower level managers and technical personnel. Top-down decisions in Japan usually fail without support from the managers responsible for implementation.
- Write an "air-tight" contract and business plan setting expectations for performance.
- Celebrate victory and success together.
- Have a "marathon" mentality; make a long-term commitment.
- Commit upper management's time upfront—If you can't afford it, don't do it.

In negotiations, and in all mid- to high-level contacts with major Japanese companies, it is good to augment your team with older veterans of the company. Avoid sending only "young Turks," even if they are more technically knowledgeable and better informed. Age and rank are very important in Japan, and it is wise to be sure you have the proper people to match the position of your counterparts across the table. If you are involved in a negotiation, and even if you are not the lead negotiator, expect to remain with the process for the long haul. In a meeting setting, expect to remain even after your input is completed; nothing disturbs the Japanese more than an executive who continuously enters and exits a negotiation; to them he displays inattention and a lack of serious regard for the business at hand. A caveat: In the early stages of meetings in Japan, when no terms have been agreed to and several partners are under consideration, watch out for lengthy meetings and excessive time commitments to any one company. Less scrupulous companies have been known to keep meetings going on interminably, or to go out for long dinners and drinking sessions with foreign negotiating teams night after night, in order to keep them too busy to meet with other potential partners while they are in town. Be sociable, but keep your eyes on the prize.

A WORD ABOUT MERGERS AND ACQUISITIONS

While M&A has become the rage in the United States, very few acquisitions have been successful in Japan. High stock share prices and the overvalued yen are major discouraging factors for foreign firms today. In Japan, for the most part, only companies that have been labeled "beyond hope" are up for sale. But more importantly, the Japanese corporate philosophy that people are a company's main assets, not plants and equipment, greatly discourages outright purchases. Kenichi Ohmae, managing director of McKinsey & Co.'s Tokyo office, makes a clear analogy between the Japanese company and a tree which has been nurtured over many years to bear fruit. Ripping up the tree to transplant it in the soil of another company, especially soil which has few of the nutrients required by Japanese employees, destroys its capacity to bear fruit. As Japanese organizations have more experience outside Japan, there may be an increase in the number of companies that would consider being acquired. Initially, the deals will be between existing partners, but eventually there will be compatible mergers between many unrelated organizations with common objectives. Successful foreign acquisitions have been limited in the United States with our "melting pot" acceptance of other cultures. Bridging the cultural gap and differences in management philosophies after acquiring a Japanese company will be an even greater challenge.

GLOBAL PARTNERSHIP MODEL

We find most companies have a very limited outlook regarding their potential partnering activities in Japan. These short-sighted companies see product distribution or the purchasing of components as their only opportunities in Japan, while, in fact, strategic relationships in technology and product development, joint marketing, financing, and joint venture projects in so many areas come to light when a company becomes more intimately familiar with the market, and when your own company's resources are developed and presented correctly. The Japanese are the masters of partnering, and any large company has many investors and partners, relationships and contracts, consortium activities and joint projects. Never discount Japanese flexibility and interest in new opportunities. A number of American companies find all they need to do is provide a new product idea, brand image, or marketing concept and the Japanese will do all the rest—development, manufacturing, promotion, and distribution—and provide the manpower and financing to make it a reality.

Japan's sogo shosha are famous for their ability to leverage their industry contacts, their Noren, and their powerful pool of the best college graduates into hundreds of relationships with domestic and foreign companies every year. Their versatility is renowned in arranging technology transfers, transportation, buyers, and sellers; providing financing; and leading major consortiums of diverse partners. With offices in almost every worldwide market, sogo shosha have virtually unmatched information networks and local contacts. They understand the multitudes of possibilities and the resources and areas of strength available to each of Japan's corporations. With their underlying motivations for diversification, foreign firms can use partnerships as powerful strategic weapons. This is especially true for companies carefully structuring their deals, passing on exclusivity, and picking their partners.

We have drawn a simple model for global partnerships (see Figure 9.1) as an attempt to encourage managers to take a more holistic approach toward evaluating their own internal resources and determining how they can be targeted towards global tie-ups. Beyond strict sales or purchasing relationships, companies need to leverage their technology strengths, company image, marketing and trendsetting skills, knowledge of American and European markets, relationships, own management and manpower, and domestic position to expand business through other companies.

Leverage is the essential tool today for future growth. Take advantage of people-rich organizations to sell and service your product in Japan. Every time you hire someone new, you should consider if you have leveraged external resources—partners, contractors, suppliers, distributors, sales forces. In so many areas, Americans still have the edge on Japan—the service sector, luxury markets, sporting goods, financial services, travel, entertainment, and recreation. The biggest problem is that few companies package and bring these strengths to the bargaining table, nor consider opportunities for joint partnership in geographies outside the U.S. and Japan. Also, few companies see partnerships with Japanese companies as ways to diversify, and would rather lay off thousands of employees or sell the business before finding creative ways to

Figure 9.1. The Global Partnership Model

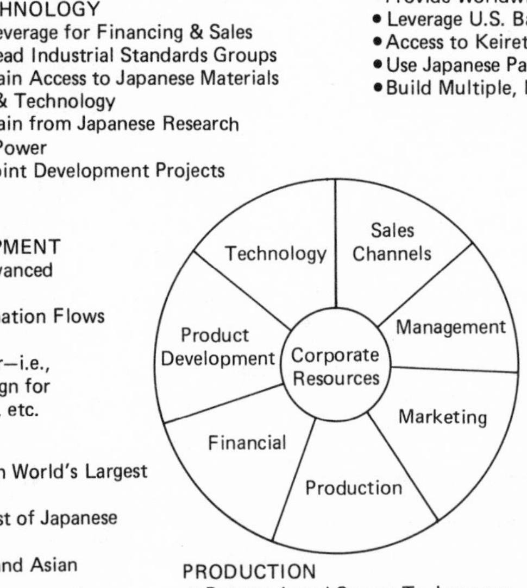

TECHNOLOGY
- Leverage for Financing & Sales
- Lead Industrial Standards Groups
- Gain Access to Japanese Materials & Technology
- Gain from Japanese Research Power
- Joint Development Projects

SALES CHANNELS
- Provide Worldwide Distribution of Japanese Products
- Leverage U.S. Base for Reciprocation of Sales in Japan
- Access to Keiretsu Industrial Groups
- Use Japanese Partner's Channels into Asia
- Build Multiple, Non-exclusive Relationships

MANAGEMENT
- Japanese Directors and Executives on Corporate Team
- Strong Joint Venture Participation in Japan
- Access to World Class Japanese Strategies and Business Philosophies
- Introduction and Inner Circle Access to Government, Banks, Industrial Leaders
- Access to Partner's Sales Channels and Suppliers

MARKETING
- Leverage American Marketing Savvy and Experience in International Markets—i.e., Europe
- Originate New Ideas for the Japanese Market
- Franchise Concepts and Distribution Technology
- Spin-off Global Products Originating in Japan
- Use Image and Design Expertise for
- Building Corporate Presence

PRODUCTION
- Become Loyal Source To Japanese Customers
- Multiple Competitive Part Sourcing in Japan
- Compatible Production Lines and Design Tools
- Joint Manufacturing-Transfer of Japanese Production Technology
- Early Access to Advanced Production Equipment

FINANCIAL
- Build Relations with World's Largest Banks
- Leverage Lower Cost of Japanese Capital
- Funding for Local and Asian Operations
- Access Regional Finance Agencies, JDB
- Public Offerings on Tokyo Stock Exchange
- Foreign Exchange Hedging-Debt-Equity Swapping

PRODUCT DEVELOPMENT
- Early Access to Advanced Technologies
- Competitive Information Flows
- Joint Development
- Knowledge Transfer—i.e., Minituration, Design for Manufacturability, etc.

enter into a new business field with eager Japanese partners. When Japan's NTT, Japan Railways, or Nippon Steel were faced with hard times and workforce reductions, they aggressively sought out partners to enter into new joint ventures and retrain their workforce to open new retail services and information service companies. American companies could do well to utilize tie-ups and financially rich, but market- and manpower-poor Japanese companies in the American market as alternatives to massive layoffs.

We have observed unique strategies utilized by a variety of companies for developing new business by tapping their entire pool of resources. Using advanced technology and facing limited financing opportunities in the United States, MIPS Computer attracted over $100 million from Kubota, a diversifying tractor maker, who is now manufacturing MIPS' hardware in Japan in a new factory built just for computer products. This source of funding, like Canon's $100 million investment in Steven Jobs' Next computer company, may enable MIPS to become a major force in the high-performance computer industry. American companies such as Avon and Levi Strauss are also using the Tokyo Stock Exchange and the newly deregulated over-the-counter market in Japan to raise large amounts of funds for worldwide expansion by making public stock offerings with favorable multiples. Applied Materials has used its banking relationships in Japan to finance its growth with low interest loans and thus gain a competitive advantage over many of its American competitors.

Japanese technology and close ties with the big players has enabled Sun Microsystems to fuel unprecedented growth. More companies are now building R&D centers in Japan to exploit the large pool of highly educated talent in electronics, biotechnology, mechatronics, advanced materials, and pharmaceuticals. Manufacturing and process technology are becoming so crucial that even Texas Instruments, one of America's largest IC manufacturers has concluded it must team up with Hitachi to jointly develop the next generation of 16-megabit DRAM memories in order to compete successfully against Toshiba.

Success in using technology leadership depends on timing and speed. Sun was fast to establish itself in Japan early, not waiting years before introducing its products. Sun was able to use its leadership in technology and close Japanese partnerships to bring almost every major computer company into its Unix International consortium to define future technical standards compatible with Sun, and with others to endorse its SPARC microprocessor technology. It used technology to its business and political advantage.

In product development, unfortunately, Japanese component suppliers have become too much a part of American product development. Japanese companies like Sony or Hitachi have a rule that all critical components must be manufactured and developed in-house. From laser printers to fax machines to video cameras, most are Japanese products and parts with an American label.

THE JAPANESE SUBSIDIARY

We have found the wholly owned, or majority-owned Japanese subsidiary to be the best long-term strategy for the Japanese market. Such a structure is the surest indicator to customers and competitors alike of a commitment to the market. A direct presence is the only way to genuinely benefit from exposure to the Japanese market, its competitors, its requirements, and its leading technologies. While many businesses can be satisfactorily managed through a distributorship or partnership, long-term opportunity can only be gained through direct operations.

A direct operation need not be grandiose. The Japanese subsidiary can be as modest or as a grand as resources and circumstances initially permit. It can be a large manufacturing or research center, or it can be a small office in Tokyo. However ambitious the nascent organizational form, the key is to back up the effort with a full, company-wide commitment. The direct subsidiary approach can ultimately give a company better access to customers, vendors, and employees. It allows for the development of Japanese managers who will, by their very presence, help the local effort succeed and add to the strength of the entire global organization. Most importantly, the direct operation in Japan permits the development and strengthening of long-term relationships with people and organizations that can help the company and its potential grow. One of the best labels a company can earn in Japan is to be called a *kakujitsu na kaisha*, a reliable company. Attaining this status demands a *direct presence.*

Advantages

- Close customer relations which improve:
  - responsiveness to the market
  - assessment of future needs, opportunities
  - feedback channels for continuous product, technology enhancements
  - avenues for cooperative development efforts, ventures
- Unified strategy and objectives across geographic markets
- Fosters corporate globalization, attainment of world-class performance

Disadvantages

- Heavy start-up costs, fixed expenses
- Few ready-to-go relationships, no track record
- Hiring challenges in Japanese market
- No off-load capability in down cycles

Like Applied Materials, many companies phase in a direct operation over time and, after participating in the market, through other avenues.

Making the transition can be difficult. For companies using an indirect channel like a distributor, OEM, or other partner for moving products, reaching the crossroads often means deciding how to manage direct sales while, at the same time, not upsetting former partners. A danger in using partners, while maintaining no direct presence, is that you can become squeezed out of the market as your product line gets replaced with internally developed products or those from a local supplier. Without direct relationships, mutually binding obligations and a strategy for support and expertise in Japan, many subsidiaries become mere trading companies without a respected engineering and manufacturing presence, or the ability to control their own destinies.

10

Growing the Japanese Business

Be not afraid of growing slowly, be afraid only of standing still.

CHINESE PROVERB

Twenty miles outside of Tokyo is a small city called Ohiso where many tourists travel each year to see the estate of Shigeru Yoshida, the former prime minister of Japan. When we visited the residence, we found it modest by Western standards. But, be assured, its historical significance aside, the house is not the attraction. The beautiful gardens surrounding it are. Exquisitely landscaped with all manner of indigenous and exotic plant life, rocks, and running water, the garden was made to be a place of peace and serenity. Landscape gardening is an ancient art form in Japan, originating during the reign of Empress Suiko (554–628 A.D.), who engaged Korean craftsmen to recreate the mystic gardens of China. Japanese tea gardens have deep religious and cultural bases, and symbolize the Japanese approach to managing their environment: nature is indomitable, man can only hope to improve its splendor. Since space is at a premium in Japan, the smallish gardens are designed to give the illusion of spaciousness and sweep. Yoshida's gardens are patterned with paths, rocks, trees, miniature *bonsai,* and flowering plants, gurgling streams traversed by arched bridges, and ponds filled with iridescent *koi,* or Japanese carp.

Tending the garden is a never-ending process. Each morning, a team of gardeners begins a ritual of pruning, shaping, cleaning, and replant-

CRITICAL ISSUES—STAGE THREE:
GROWING THE JAPANESE ORGANIZATION

- Select and entrust a Japanese leader
- Plan and invest for a long-term commitment
- Build local research, engineering, manufacturing capabilities
- Establish sales offices and new distribution channels
- Leverage complimentary channels and partners
- Integrate MIS and communication linkages
- Overcome parochialism among global operations
- Implement worldwide quality and service programs
- Globalize benefits structures and human resource organization
- Initiate worldwide joint projects and expatriate and rotational assignment programs
- Develop global corporate culture

ing. Their effort is aimed at imposing man's will and aesthetic sensibilities in a way that is not injurious to the natural essence of the flora; to work the soil's intrinsic capabilities. The day we toured the estate, the evening sun was setting beautifully in the western sky, the trees were turning golden and red, adding variety to the shades of green throughout the garden. The beauty of the scene was undeniable, yet all around us workmen toiled on the garden—making it better. Clearly, the garden represented the Japanese view that man must be ever diligent in maintaining a harmonious balance with nature.

There are many lessons to be taken from Yoshida's garden. We believe that growing the Japanese business is a similar process, for it is most important to develop a business with lasting qualities and a sense of permanence if one is to succeed in winning over the Japanese. We've outlined below some of the critical issues concerning the growth of the Japanese enterprise. They each fall into broad categories of action: people, facilities, systems, and financing.

PEOPLE

By far the most difficult challenge facing any new entrant in the Japanese market is the task of building a high-quality organization. To grow aggressively, the subsidiary in Japan must have top-caliber management to overcome inevitable obstacles and under whom a true global corporation can be built. Most American companies in Japan face difficulties in building their team because they lack experience and contacts. It is not easy for a foreign firm to hire good employees, and the competition can be fierce. Foreign companies, especially small ones, will have a tough time attracting the first-tier company professionals and top college graduates. But it can be done.

The company in Japan represents much more than a job and a salary. It is most often considered an extension of the "family" environment, a prime determinant of social status, and a sphere of relationships throughout one's life. Security and social status are top concerns in most Japanese workers' minds. Financial incentives are important, but more significant in attracting good Japanese workers is a company's stability and long-term commitment to employees (traits for which American companies are not known). The Japanese are very status conscious, and foreign firms can rarely provide the level of prestige they are seeking for their family and children. In her book *Japanese Society,* Chie Nakane summarizes the challenge in hiring Japanese employees: "Employment with a foreign firm in Japan is regarded somehow as out of the system. In spite of very high salaries, very few well-qualified men are ready to take a job in these firms. This reluctance comes first from the feeling of insecurity about the future [American firms do not generally guarantee lifetime employment]. Secondly, foreign firms are somehow beyond the pale of Japanese social recognition, so that their employees are likely to be regarded as not part of the Japanese community."[1] Overcoming this attitude requires creativity.

For a small foreign company, as Applied Materials was when it began in Japan, attracting capable Japanese in direct competition with every major electronics giant and trading company in the land was tough. Because of the nature of its business, Applied Materials found itself competing with Japan's most prestigious companies, like NEC, Fujitsu, Hitachi, and Toshiba for top engineers and technical people. As we have gradually established ourselves in the market, things have improved markedly. Yet, even after ten years, Applied Materials still has trouble competing for top graduates from first-tier universities such as Tokyo or Waseda. However, good students from second- and third-tier universities, and non-Japanese students in Japan, such as Koreans and Chinese from top schools, are joining AMJ. We have also found an untapped market for top women graduates, who are closed out in traditional Japanese companies.

Table 10.1
Ranking of Companies Most Preferred by University Graduates, 1989

1. Japan Railways Tokaido
2. Mitsui & Co., Ltd.
3. NTT
4. Sony
5. East Japan Railways
6. Mitsubishi
7. C. Itoh
8. All Nippon Airways
9. Sumitomo Bank
10. Japan Airlines
11. Dai Ichi Kangyo Bank
12. Fuji Bank
13. NEC
14. Sumitomo Corporation
15. Mitsui Real Estate
16. Matsushita Electric
17. Tokyo Fire and Marine
18. Japan Development Bank
19. Mitsubishi Bank
20. Dentsu
21. IBM Japan
22. NKK
23. Sanwa Bank
24. Nihon Life Insurance
25. Toyota Motors

SOURCE: "1989 Ninki Kigyo Ranking," *Nikkei Business* (March 27, 1989), p. 140.

Recruiting top college graduates in Japan is almost an art form. Before prospective university recruits will be impressed with a company, they first consider the regard in which it is held at the university. A very important indicator of a company's performance is its ranking as a "most preferred company" at which to work, a list published every year for college seniors (see Table 10.1). The only foreign company in the top fifty is IBM. Since college professors play the role of mentor to many students, they must be won over first if a company is to have any success in generating interest with the candidates themselves. It takes years to get professors to begin to trust you enough to recommend students to your company. Developing relationships and gaining press coverage in technical journals and career magazines is time con-

Table 10.2
Number of New Graduates Hired by Foreign Companies in Japan, 1990

1. IBM Japan	1,300
2. Nihon Unisys	520
3. Fuji Xerox	410
4. Nihon Digital Equipment	340
5. Yokogawa-Hewlett-Packard	260
6. Authur Andersen	200
7. McDonald's	200
8. Texas Instruments Japan	175
9. Yamatake-Honeywell	160
10. NCR Japan	150
11. Nippon Roche	150
12. Nippon Hoechst	150
13. Nippon Glaxo	150
14. Sandoz Pharmacueticals	150
15. Bayer Yakuhin	120
16. Bristol-Myers Japan	100
17. Olivetti of Japan	80
18. Ciba-Geigy (Japan)	80
19. Nestlé	80
20. Ajinomoto-General Foods	50

SOURCE: "Nihon Keizai Shimbun Survey of Foreign Company Recruiting," *Japan Economic Journal* (June 1989).

suming, but also critical. We routinely arrange plant tours for engineering professors, and participate in symposia and conferences. As can be seen in Table 10.2, a number of the elite major foreign companies are developing strong recruiting programs. Applied Materials is finding an increased willingness for excellent candidates to consider smaller companies and non-Japanese companies because of better opportunities. The layers of capable people in the large companies limit young people's opportunities.

Applied Materials' creative solution to the hiring crunch revolved around the Japanese fascination with leadership. It was a matter of using the environment to advantage as opposed to fighting it. Men in Japan are ranked either by the group or company to which they belong, or by the reputation of a strong, well-known individual with whom they are closely associated. We felt the strength and charisma of Tetsuo Iwasaki would be a key to hiring quality people. We were right. And since the early years, we left the strategy for staffing AMJ to Iwasaki. Even with Iwasaki as a magnet, I realize now how fortunate we were in attracting the original cadre of talented young Japanese who formed AMJ's organizational backbone. Besides AMJ's president Iwasaki, we were able to attract aggressive young turks like Yoichi Isago, Kazuyoshi Yokota, and Bunya Matsui, Yasuaki Toyouchi, Kazufumi Kuno, and Noboru Tokumasu. These men risked a great deal in joining a non-Japanese company—not to mention a virtual start-up. Yet, by joining the company, they gave us credibility and attracted others to follow. We believe it is important to focus on hiring a good core management team to start and let them build the staff.

Hiring a good manager is not easy; it is an intricate and slow-moving process. It often takes six months to a year (or more) after initial agreement with an individual before he or she actually comes on board. Hiring managers from large Japanese companies, especially when they are your customers, is a sensitive situation, far more so than in America. The employee in Japan is the company's primary resource, and hiring from a customer can be a political quagmire. There are definite rules of etiquette that must be followed. The hiring dance typically begins with one of your company's top executives meeting with the candidate's employer and even his family to request permission to negotiate with the individual and to provide assurance of his future position, security, and opportunities. From there, several meetings may take place over a long period of time. To speed up this process slightly, many foreign companies today use headhunters. This can be a good, if nontraditional approach. Often times, however, you do not get the best employees this way. You tend to look at resumes of employees who have moved around a lot. These *gairojin,* or wanderers, are like job-hoppers anywhere and may not work out in the end.

Applied Materials has done well by hiring top-quality people from outside our own industry. Our Osaka branch manager came from the steel section of Mitsui & Co. Underutilized at Mitsui, the branch manager now has stimulating and satisfying responsibilities for the entire Kansai area, with major accounts such as IBM, Seiko, and Matsushita. He has far more responsibility than he could have expected to possess after many years in a large trading company. The opportunity for more responsibility and a quicker rise through the ranks is a genuine attraction for many Japanese, and is becoming a point of advantage for foreign firms. Also, the ability to achieve a greater multinational experience is a good incentive. Applied has emphasized our international position to successfully recruit broadminded Japanese.

Retirees are another good source of solid managers. Japan's *amakudari*, literally, descent from heaven, permits retiring process managers and bureaucrats to move on with honor to new adventures. These seasoned managers often have strong connections to the ministries and/or big companies and can provide valuable contacts, ideas, and direction. Another good way to attract managers is to go after individuals who have worked for U.S. subsidiaries of major Japanese companies. But it is important to approach them immediately upon returning from America (or while they are still there) and before they have readjusted to life back in Japan and while they still miss "the states." LSI Logic, a $400 million IC manufacturer, hired K.K. Yawata, a leading executive of NEC America, as president of LSI Logic K.K. following such a stateside assignment.

While hiring employees is demanding, attracting a respected member of the Japanese business community to the board of directors of a small foreign company seems a herculean task by comparison. In 1983 Applied Materials began such a search. We felt it was important for the company to benefit from the perspective of a Japanese board member. A key criterion was to find someone who had a good reputation with our customers, but who was not tied too closely with any one customer. For this reason most of the candidates we looked at did not work out. After two years of searching we were getting very discouraged when our contacts at the Bank of Tokyo and Nikko Securities simultaneously suggested Dr. Hiroo Toyoda. President of NTT Electronic Technology, Dr. Toyoda is an eminent and well-respected technologist in Japan—one of the "fathers" of Japan's famous VLSI project. As an executive of the world's largest company and a valued member of the famous Musashino Laboratories at NTT, Dr. Toyoda seemed beyond our grasp. But it was worth a try. Through a consultant to Nikko Securities, we contacted Dr. Toyoda and began a series of discussions with him. We found he had an ideal understanding of our business, technology, and customers and, after months of courting and encouraging words from our friends and customers in Japan, Dr. Toyoda graciously agreed to join our board. Since then, Dr. Toyoda's advice and counsel have contributed handsomely to the board and the company.

People Checklist

- Hire a strong Japanese leader and top management team
- Demonstrate a long-term commitment to employees
- Develop strong relationships with university professors

- Look outside of your industry and in government for quality personnel
- Hire retiring executives from major Japanese companies and government ministries
- Seek out Japanese members for your board of directors or advisory group

FACILITIES

Applied Materials set up its first office in what is now known as Tokyo's *Yoyogi* area. To do so required the company to raise what, at that stage in the company's history, was a huge sum of money to just occupy a small space in an old, postwar building. There is routinely a large safety deposit required to occupy a space. In our case, the deposit amounted to $250,000. Iwasaki found the location and said it would be small, but adequate quarters for our then-modest needs. There was only one problem: the landlord wanted us to decide overnight whether or not we wanted the location. Since space is in high demand in Tokyo, building owners know they can pretty much call the shots. Iwasaki needed the funds wired immediately if he was to close the deal. This put us in the awkward position of not being able to gain formal approval by the board of directors to make such an expenditure. We went with our gut feelings, and decided to wire Iwasaki the funds. Since then, the board has approved of the decision many times over. As steep as the start-up costs seemed to be then, it did not take long for the decision to pay off.

That first office was nothing glamorous, but it served its purpose well. By and large, you should not look to create a glamorous environment in Japan. Location and functionality are what count. Our second office, in Osaka, was a small converted tea room that would only accommodate a small desk and some chairs. But it was near our customers, and that was what really mattered. The whole idea behind a direct presence in Japan is presence. For most companies, that entails being physically and strategically situated near customers or distribution centers. The important thing is to see as well as be seen. Applied Materials' decision to open its first office in Tokyo was primarily for visibility's sake. But as we began to make headway with customers, being nearer to them became more important. We were also very concerned about building a lasting presence. That meant locating our-

Figure 10.1. Prefecture Map of Japan

SOURCE: Population data from Ministry of Home Affairs.

selves near where employees are and want to live. Locating the Japanese operation can be tricky. Your choice can make or break your operation.

If you picture Japan in the configuration of the state of California, Tokyo is about where San Francisco is, in the middle of the country. Tokyo is also a prefecture. A prefecture is like a U.S. state, with its own regional government and laws. There are forty-seven prefectures in Japan (see Figure 10.1). Some are small and rural, others concrete jungles of commerce. Approximately eight million people live within Tokyo, with another six million just outside. Virtually every major Japanese company is either headquartered there or maintains an address. Many people prefer the cosmopolitan flavor of Tokyo, and would rather live and work nearby (nearby can be up to a two-hour drive or train ride away). But Tokyo is not the only place where the action is. Away from Tokyo are many burgeoning industrial centers, particularly in the far south of the country. Cities like Osaka, Nagoya,

Hiroshima, and Kumamoto are fast growing metropolises in their own rights. And new centers of business are sprouting up all the time. This has created a certain amount of competition among the prefectures in attracting businesses. Playing to this competition can be profitable.

While leasing an office and maintaining a local presence is a critical step, what really says "commitment" to the Japanese is buying or building a facility. By 1985, Applied Materials had clearly established its willingness to stay the course in the Japanese market. Everything we did was aimed at reaffirming our commitment to our customers and showing our staying power. But we always got the feeling that our customers remained a bit leery of our resolve until we announced the purchase of land in Narita and began to construct our technology center there. That convinced customer and competitor alike that Applied Materials had a long-term view and commitment to Japan.

FACILITIES CHECKLIST

- Expect to pay steep rents, purchase prices everywhere in Japan
- Be prepared to act quickly
- Begin with a Tokyo office for credibility; add sites closer to customers
- Explore needs and wants of prefecture governments
- Evaluate all financing options from partner companies, banks, etc.

SYSTEMS

Once a Japanese operation has been established, bringing it into harmony with the entire corporation is essential. The synergy borne of diversity is one of the principal benefits to be derived from doing business in Japan. Communications, power struggles, and politics can plague foreign subsidiaries in Japan. A conflicting culture and the inability of most Western executives to work effectively in Japan cause a great number of the problems—many conflicts which would likely not occur between similar "Western" cultures. Japanese companies have strong cultures and a paternalistic structure. In creating the Japanese subsidiary, this must be kept in mind. In Japan, managers nurture employees, establishing father-child relationships of trust over time and via informal contact. Loyalty, dedication, and hard work are directly proportionate to the level of paternalism of the companies' management system, and the example of overtime and hard work shown by one's superiors. In Japanese companies, the concept prevails that the employer is totally responsible for the livelihood of all employees. Some non-Japanese companies have done well in adopting a Japanese culture—and in exporting aspects of this culture globally. IBM Japan President Takeo Shiina wrote in the *Journal of Japanese Trade and Industry,* "Many elements of IBM's corporate culture and business style closely parallel those of Japanese business. Japan has proved fertile ground for the IBM tradition of corporate social responsibility."

Far too often, companies fail to get the best from their Japanese subsidiaries simply because they do not accord them the respect they deserve. As a result, Japanese executives may feel that headquarters is ignorant of their business strengths, is short-sighted and fails to pay enough respect for the contributions of the "locals." These resentments notwithstanding, many Japanese executives simply do not want their Western counterparts involved with customer interactions because they do not want to be embarrassed. Building a strong, worldwide team identity at Applied Materials has required the devotion of major resources in the intertransfer of U.S. and Japanese managers between countries at all levels of the operation. Based on a global model of operation, each division vice-president is responsible for the training and development of every person in his division, no matter where in the world he or she may be.

The Japanese have a very traditional view of personnel development, and it is unavoidably the employer's responsibility to develop employees throughout their tenures with the company. As a rule, companies try to find the very best "base materials" which they then can mold over time. This is in contrast to the practice employed by American companies of hiring employees to fill posts or job definitions with little emphasis on long-term employee development. In the Japanese view, American businessmen tend to underestimate the disruption caused by personnel turnover, thinking in terms of the "position" being filled by a "body" or manipulating head-count like chess pieces. When hiring an employee, usually a freshly minted college graduate, the Japanese manager looks at personality and character and makes a determination based not on present skills, but potential future ones. They are willing to invest years to train an employee in the business and, more importantly, in the ethics of group responsibility and obligation. The Japanese are accustomed to this atmosphere at work, and can be disoriented by working for an American company where individual performance is stressed and little company support exists.

The problems of culture clash can be overcome by creating a distinct and non-national corporate culture worldwide, with allowance for the uniqueness of local culture by region. Such a corporate milieu requires simple, universal philosophies as a basis. Regardless of your corporate mission, the global organization needs underlying values. At Applied Materials, we chose to make our Quality Improvement Process the global unifier. It has proven to be a mission that joins the destiny of all employees and lends language tools all its own.

The Japanese management and operation must be integrated into the overall corporation as rapidly as possible. Ultimately, the head of the Japanese subsidiary should report directly to the president and participate intimately in all executive decision making for the worldwide corporation. This will be considered a sign of commitment and a key to building trust and cooperation between the parent company and its Japanese subsidiary. The parent company must also internally promote the Japanese subsidiary, its products, marketing teams, and manufacturing divisions. As well, synchronization with the corporate organization to the local market is critical. Adapting to Japan, to such an extent that most there regard your products as inherently "Japanese," should be a major goal. Like most Americans, most Japanese do not care where a product is made; they only want to know that it is a high-quality product and that it will be fully supported if something goes wrong. Language localization and product design to satisfy the Japanese customers is simply good marketing practice. Building a quality image through local investment, advertising and product publicity, trade shows, and university recruitment is essential. For its size, Japan is a small community, and word of mouth is a very powerful medium. After years of work and much investment, American companies like IBM, Avon, Xerox, and Applied Materials are often mistaken in Japan as Japanese.

As we have stressed throughout the book, relationships are the true source of power in Japan and can mean the difference between success and failure. Many firms, such as the giant trading companies, have proven that multibillion dollar businesses can be built almost solely on the basis of trusted relationships. We have seen that it is more important to remain faithful to a trusted supplier than to buy the less costly, more advanced products from a company with which you have weaker relations. A direct linkage between supplier and customer, and an environment in which the two companies can work jointly to make incremental improvements, is a time-proven pathway to profit and growth in the Japanese market.

Sales and profit growth, however, are hollow victories compared to growing your company's relative place in the Japanese market. The performance criteria used most by Japanese companies are market share and industry ranking, in Japan and worldwide. The Japanese revere the leaders, look askance upon the also-rans. American companies must seek out market-share growth as the only real indicator of prowess and the true precursor to profit sales and growth in Japan. This will take time and sacrifice, and may be difficult for companies depending on quarterly results for their lives. Profits should be secondary to building a strong Japanese organization. Bulking up the staffing, adding capabilities, and growing market share are the only culturally acceptable goals. Once these have been achieved, the profits will follow.

It is important to support the Japanese subsidiary in other ways too. Gaining credibility for the unit among Japanese customers will not be easy. We have seen many cases where large Japanese companies prefer to deal directly with the American company, purposely sidestepping the Japanese subsidiary. This normally is a test of the strength and the respect held for the Japanese subsidiary back home. It would be advisable to allow a deal to fall through rather than to undermine the subsidiary by skirting around it. The Japanese management should always lead customer relations, supplemented at times with American managers who can abide by the rule of playing a supporting, not controlling, role. Only by making the Japanese managers the front line of attack will you empower them with the capacity needed to gain the long-term confidence and partnership of Japan's major corporations.

Do not give the Japanese market any less than your best effort. Demonstrate your commitment by investing in the marketplace. Japanese companies are showing the importance of investment in local markets and the power of having production and engineering capabilities close to the customer. NEC's $500 million investment in its Roseville, California, semiconductor complex is aimed at reinforcing its commitment to American customers and gives NEC access to the latest development efforts in the United States. Local manufacturing assures customers that they will get a rapid new product turnaround, high-quality products, and a strong technical capability to support their evolving needs. Also, taking advantage of Japan's worker discipline and engineering skills will help the company's products become more competitive not just in Japan, but all over the world. Many companies are learning valuable lessons from their Japanese operations, enabling them to defend their existing markets and enter into new ones. Not only new products can be transferred back to America, so can top Japanese managers, bringing with them a wealth of knowledge which can translate into dramatic improvements in production and company performance globally. The ability to manage a multicultural team of executives across multiple geographies and product lines is a necessary part of the future for a world-class competitor.

In striving to manage the Japanese organization, lack of communication can be one of the biggest impediments to effective performance. In a multicultural, multilingual environment, special attention must be given to the quality, not just the quantity, of communications. Applied Materials has addressed this challenge by focusing on good organizational systems and plenty of attention to detail. Some of these efforts include:

Uniform Organization Structures

Since organizational structures influence both the flow of information and the setting and meeting of objectives, all global operations should be organized similarly. That is not to say regional variations are not important, and even desired—they are. But by having parallel skeletal structures, geographically separate employees can cross-communicate with reasonable ease and certainty. This is particularly important in Japan, where employees have a genuine need to understand the relative ranking of a distant co-worker. Uniformity in structure permits good communications. At Applied Materials, all divisions and geographic operations are organized the same. Naturally, AMJ's titles and lines of reporting will tend to conform to the Japanese way of business. Yet, a *kacho,* or first line manager, at AMJ can comfortably deal as an equal with a manager in the United States or the United Kingdom. If one or the other manager was accorded a higher degree of respect, authority, or responsibility, smooth and effective communications might likely be hindered by inequities in status.

Regular Interface

Nothing brings an organization closer than frequent person-to-person contact, what AMJ President Tetsuo Iwasaki calls "face time." Applied Materials places emphasis on this basic need by encouraging regular travel between geographic locations. In 1989 alone, 200 AMJ staffers visited the United States operations; 250 American and European employees traveled to Japan. The company's Corporate Operating Committee, comprised of all top management, cycles meetings between the United States, Japan, and Europe. In addition, Applied Materials President James Bagley spends over one-third of his time in Japan to assure our successful divisionalization, globalization, and support of our Japanese customers. All the other Applied executives spend many weeks each quarter in Japan. This travel is supplemented by regular, real-time teleconferences among the geographically distant locations. In a way memorandum and electronic mail cannot duplicate, face-to-face contact can make things happen more effectively.

Cross-Cultural Training

Training employees to understand and appreciate cultural differences is absolutely critical to a global organization. Any company seeking to build its Japanese operation must work to foster better understanding of the very real cultural differences that exist in Japan. This is particularly so for a company like Applied Materials, which employs individuals with widely ranging cultural backgrounds. Some twenty-four different mother tongues are spoken at Applied Materials, ranging from English and Japanese to Korean, Chinese, Farsi, Vietnamese, and Spanish. To help reconcile these differences, Applied Materials provides a number of in-house cross-cultural training programs. Such an effort is much more than a nicety; it is a genuine business tool. As Robert Galvin, chairman of Motorola, points out, one of the most important aspects of doing business globally is effectively communicating with people who have an entirely different perspective and outlook on life than you do. "In meetings with the Japanese," Galvin notes, "you must be sensitive to the different signals and ways of articulating that are customary. If you are not, each party can walk away from a meeting thinking different things. In Japan, we try to hold meetings in Japanese—with an interpreter—and thereby minimize any miscommunications." Motorola's approach makes sense, particularly when you consider that in Japan a stated "yes" does not necessarily indicate affirmation, and a "no" many not mean no.

Personnel Exchanges

Since one of the biggest advantages of doing business in Japan, or in any global market for that matter, is the company-wide transfer and sharing of knowledge acquired in different locations, programmatic personnel exchanges are critical. Applied Materials maintains an aggressive "expatriate" program designed to build international teams, expose employees to new situations and environments, and share ideas and solutions globally. Employees are given both short- and long-term assignments to join a product development or marketing team, or to simply solve a problem. At Applied, at any point in time there are between twenty and thirty engineers and managers from Japan stationed in Santa Clara, and the same number of Americans working in Japan. Each general manager is responsible for and evaluated on his ability to integrate these people into his organization, and to push his people to develop close relationships with their counterparts and customers in Japan.

SYSTEMS CHECKLIST

- Ensure company-wide respect for your Japanese operation
- Create uniform organizational chart on a global basis
- Develop good cross-cultural training programs
- Encourage and facilitate direct interaction by employees
- Provide avenues for international work assignments, global teams

FINANCING

Providing local financing for the Japan operation can be a challenge, but the rewards are worth it. It is a long-term process, necessitating a well-reasoned strategy from the beginning. Any firm interested in attaining loans and other forms of equity participation will find numerous willing sources. Japan has been called a "bankers kingdom," owing to the power and opportunities for financial institutions to make money. But for foreign firms seeking financing for a Japanese operation, banks are just one of several sources of capital. The Japanese government, large manufacturing companies, and insurance companies also can be excellent sources of long-term capital. Choosing the form or source best suited for your organization's needs will require some research. The information below should provide a primer.

BANKS

With a massive deposit base, low asset ratios, and decreasing domestic opportunities for placement of funds, Japan's banks are becoming increasingly aggressive, international in their field of vision, and much more willing to loan to foreign firms. This is good news for foreign companies seeking local financing in Japan. (For the structure of Japa-

Figure 10.2. The Structure of Japanese Banking

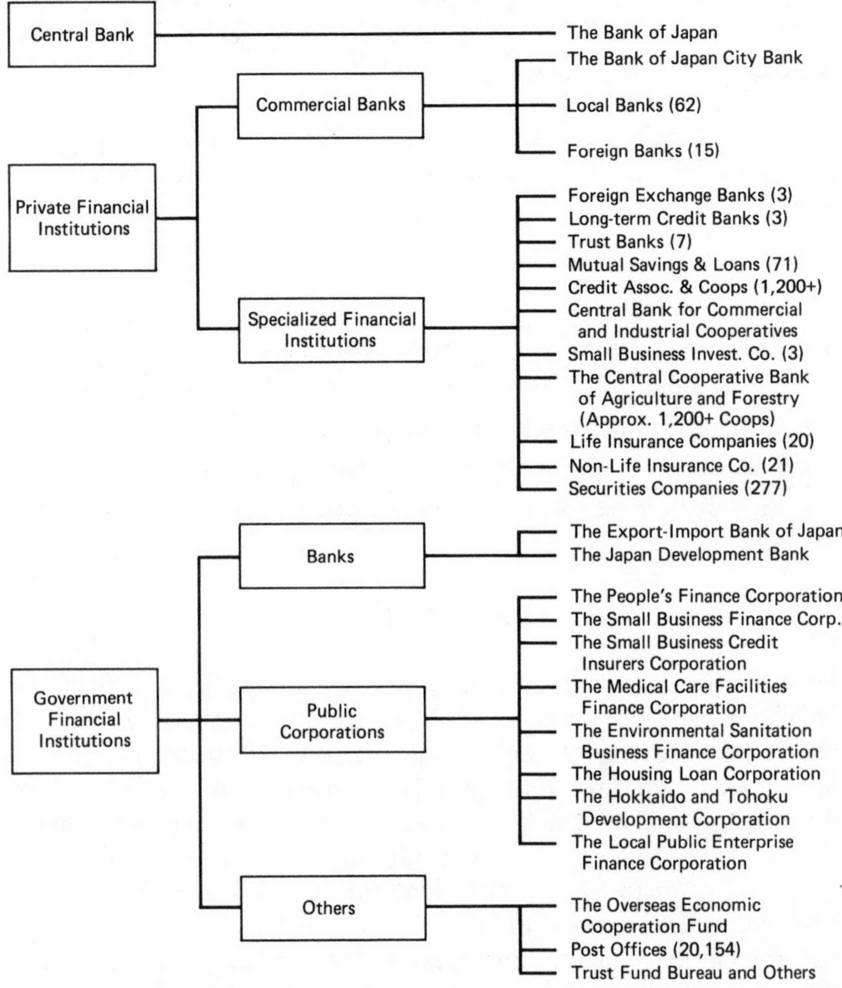

SOURCE: Adapted from "How to Succeed in Japan: A Guide for Foreign Businessmen" (Tokyo: The Mainichi Newspapers, 1974). Copyright by the Japan External Trade Organization.

nese banking, see Figure 10.2.) Beneath the umbrella of the Ministry of Finance and the Bank of Japan, there are essentially seven different kinds of "banks." These include regional banks, city banks, long-term credit banks, trust banks, sogo banks (mutual loan and savings banks), shinkin banks (credit associations), and specialized institutions for agriculture and fisheries. Each type of banking institution will have both strong and weak points depending on your businesses needs. For a review of the top banking organizations, see Appendix D.

Applied Materials initially chose the Bank of Tokyo specifically because it was not associated with any of the big trading or manufacturing concerns. Its independence and aggressiveness in attracting foreign affiliates was appealing to us. However, being a city bank, the Bank of Tokyo could not meet all of our needs throughout Japan. To accommodate payroll for nationwide operations, Applied Materials selected one of the big regional commercial banks, Mitsubishi Bank, part of the massive Mitsubishi *keiretsu*, with hundreds of locations throughout Japan.

The Japan Development Bank

Established in 1951, the Japan Development Bank (JDB) is wholly owned by the Japanese government. The bank was chartered specifically to promote industrial development nationwide. Funds for the JDB are drawn through the Trust Fund Bureau of the Ministry of Finance, which is financed principally by the postal savings system, and raised through the issuance of government guaranteed bonds in overseas capital markets. In 1989, the JDB had assets of 8,600 billion yen, or $64.5 billion. The JDB financing program forms a portion of the government's Fiscal Investment and Loan Program, with its goals set according to social needs and government policy objectives. Financing and equity participation is made available for a wide range of applications, including funding for national economic development, infrastructure, industry, and social welfare programs. When Applied Materials applied for financing, our plans fit well with the goals of the JDB at that time. Our research and development facility in Narita was in keeping with the JDB objective of seeding foreign R&D projects in the country. For information on JDB locations and contacts, see Appendix D. As well, the Industrial Bank of Japan, Export-Import Bank of Japan, insurance companies, and small business finance corporations are often sources for capital, all with growing programs for foreign companies.

Depending on your needs, your business, your size and any number of other variables, financing requirements in the Japanese market can vary widely. In some ways, the options for financing are fewer in Japan than in the United States and Europe. However, while the pipeline may be narrow, it is quite full. Once your business is into the jet stream of financing opportunities, you will find the supplies of capital plentiful. Following the banks, the next biggest suppliers of capital would be the insurance companies, pension funds, and the venture capital firms. For a list of largest firms and funds, see Appendix D.

Developing Relationships with Japanese Banks

Any banking or loan arrangement will first be predicated upon relationships. When Applied Materials first began direct operations in Japan, we immediately established a relationship with the Bank of Tokyo. We started simply enough by developing a rapport with the manager of the Shinjuku Branch, the branch closest to our Tokyo office. The manager got to know us and eventually helped us in our efforts to grow. By virtue of the relationship we developed with its managers over time, the Bank of Tokyo provided our introduction to the JDB. This introduction, and a vouching of our quality and character, made it possible for our loan process to start off on an excellent footing. Relationships, in general, will be the biggest determinant of success in attaining financing in Japan, whether with a big national bank, or with other sources of funds and financing.

While it is possible to simply walk into a Japanese bank, deposit funds and begin to work with a banker, you will normally need a facilitator to introduce your company. Facilitators can include leading businessmen, other bankers, and government officials. A good way to start a relationship before even opening a Japanese operation (and often without a proper introduction) is to begin dealings with a Japanese-owned bank in the United States or in Europe. This will provide a history and working relationship and the local people can make the necessary introductions in Japan. Often an organization like the Japan Development Bank, the Bank of Tokyo, or the Japan Export Trade Relations Organization (JETRO) can be a good source of advice and introductions.

Going Public

Japan has become the world's largest market for stocks and securities, giving ample opportunity for foreign firms seeking to go public as a means of raising capital (see Figure 10.3 for a typical timeline). Today, over a hundred foreign firms are listed on the Tokyo Stock Exchange, scores of others are traded over-the-counter. For these firms, offering stock has provided a major source of equity for Japanese and worldwide operations, as price/earnings ratios are several times those accorded stocks in the United States. A public offering in Japan also cements established business relationships and builds visibility of a worldwide trading presence in Asia. Approximately seventy American companies are listed, 80 percent of the offerings underwritten by Japan's

Figure 10.3. Typical Timeline for a Public Offering in Japan.

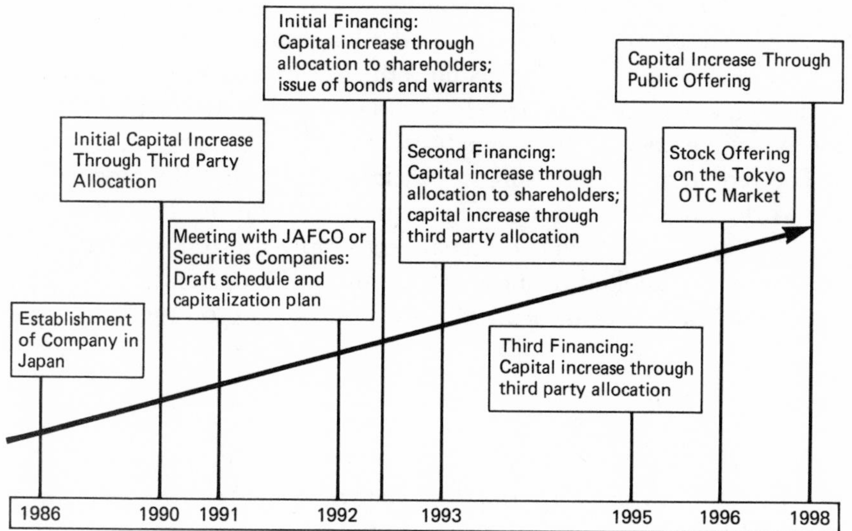

two largest securities houses, Daiwa and Nomura. A list is provided in Appendix D.

There are two basic levels to a public offering in Japan: the over-the-counter listing and the Tokyo Stock Exchange. Within the TSE are three sections: the first section for major firms, the second section for smaller companies, and the foreign section for non-Japanese companies. The requirements for the TSE are much more stringent than for the OTC. Whichever market you select, expect the initial offering process to be long.

In 1987, Avon Products, for example, raised $241.55 million in its issue in Japan on the over-the-counter market; Shaklee Japan Co. raised $92.53 million; and even Baskin Robbins' subsidiary raised $42 million. Levi Strauss, the San Francisco jean maker, raised $90 million on the TSE. "We increased our overall value as a company and, at the same time, demonstrated our commitment to Japan," explains David Schmidt, president of Levi Strauss Japan K.K. "We used the capital to buy land for a new distribution center and to help seed new projects elsewhere in the world." Offering stocks of a new issue is an ideal way to cement partnerships with Japanese companies. New shareholders include Levi's main suppliers and distributors in Japan. After a 42 percent jump in sales to 15.4 billion yen ($110 million), 1989 sales will be over $150 million, up 36 percent. "By committing some of the new shares to an employee stock ownership plan, the company is also able to offer inducements in a tight labor market," says Schmidt.[2] Being a private company, Levi Strauss did have some reservations about the offering because the TSE requires the parent company of a foreign-owned Japanese subsidiary to release often sensitive information, which can be studied closely by competitors.

The requirements for issuing stock in Japan are not the most lax in the world, but entry and reporting requirements for the TSE and OTC market have been easing in recent years. In basic terms, it requires three years of audited financial statements and a certain level of sales and capitalization to make an initial public offering on the TSE.

Financing Checklist

- Select a bank that is right for your short- and long-term needs
- Establish an early relationship (before even starting in Japan, if possible)
- Find a facilitator to introduce you to the bank
- Look to partnerships and alliances, venture capital firms, and insurance companies as other sources of capital
- Examine government-sponsored loan programs
- Consider carefully the potential for a public offering

BECOMING AN INSIDER IN JAPAN

In every local market, successful companies have become a living part of the community and the local industry structure of suppliers, customers, and trade associations. American companies have failed miserably on this score, with few even belonging to their respective industry associations, of which there are hundreds in Japan, nor to standards bodies and consortiums which are defining the markets and product specifications of the future. Few companies achieve a "non-insulated" position in Japanese society with real networks of obligations and partners, and access to the most current information and insider circles of Japanese government and industry.

An "insider" company is a non-insulated company which is considered a local player and which has control over its own destiny in direct sales to customers, product development, strategy, and manufacturing. An insider in Japan will:

- Have a management team that is close to Japan's decision makers—major banks, industrial groups, MITI and other government ministries, and other major Japanese company management
- Keep decision-making authority on deals and general operations as local and as close to the market as possible
- Maintain a direct sales force and research presence capable of tapping the pulse of both the current market and new technologies
- Maintain direct relations with major first-tier Japanese corporations
- Work with a select group of suppliers and dedicated contractors to support manufacturing
- Play an active role in industry associations and standards bodies
- Recruit from top universities and from leading Japanese companies
- Operate in local currency
- Often be mistaken for a Japanese company

Few foreign firms have attained insider status in Japan. But companies like IBM Japan, Nihon TI, Procter and Gamble, and Applied Materials have, indicating that it is possible to attain with the right approach and follow-through over time. It is useful to understand this progression and to have a strategy to move as quickly as possible to the insider stage while avoiding the pitfalls which trap so many young companies in Japan. Figure 10.4 shows the typical stages of evolution from an insulated organization to an integrated, non-insulated insider.

Insider status will not come easily. And it cannot be done from afar. It is true that some companies have been successful by merely exporting through distributors or licensing agreements. These cases of success through indirect channels are exceptions to the rule. A direct presence has proved, time and time again, to be a truer route to success in Japan. The longer you are in Japan, the more you realize that decisions are not based only on pricing and performance, but on trust, personal relations, history, and emotions. Only with a working "data base" can Americans understand the real wants and needs of the Japanese customers and consumers and the true intentions of the Japanese partner. Clearly, maintaining a direct presence in Japan is the best way to understand what is going on in the market; having direct relations with customers, suppliers, and sources of new technology, and understanding Japanese definitions of quality, service, and product performance are key.

Dr. Dan Maydan, executive vice-president of Applied Materials, and

Figure 10.4. The Insider: Stages of Evolution

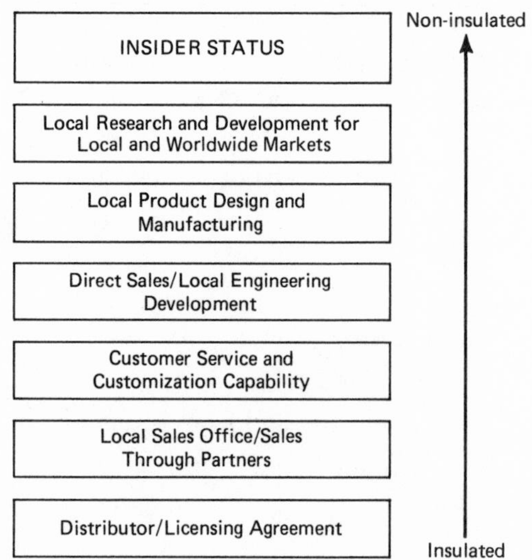

other executives have close relationships with Japanese managers and technologists extending back many years. He and others have been invaluable in continually proving our technical stature and level of commitment to Japanese industry. These relationships have assured a clear understanding of the customers' requirements and assure their support of our new products.

Clearly, growing the Japanese operation can be a source of dynamic opportunity and profit. But it is also a needed prelude to growing the global operation. As Japanese companies' influence expands globally, exposure to the Japanese market, its requirements and its benefits, prepares an organization to compete in the new world market. Only by being a successful competitor in Japan can a company truly aspire to world-class competitiveness.

11

Becoming a World-Class Competitor

Press on. Nothing in the world can take the place of persistence.

AMERICAN SAYING

The world has changed. Yet the strategies and actions of too many American companies do not reflect this change. For most, the absolute necessity of thinking and competing globally has not hit home. We believe that American businesses can only succeed by reaching out to and seizing the opportunities created by the new world economy. And further, we have argued that attacking global opportunities must begin by competing in Japan. Is your company ready for the global market?

TESTING YOUR I.Q. (INTERNATIONAL QUALITIES)

1. What percentage of total revenues come from Japan?
2. What percentage of total employees are located in Japan?
3. What is your market share and industry ranking in Japan?
4. What percentage of new products or services are developed and/or manufactured in Japan?
5. Does the head of your Japanese operation sit on the executive committee of the headquarters organization?
6. Do you have "first-tier" companies within your industry as customers or partners for sales or joint development in Japan?

7. Do you have direct sales relationships with your major customers?
8. Is your company considered a "Japanese company" in Japan?
9. Does your Japanese management have significant, independent, decision-making capability for pricing, investment, human resource count, major deals, and partnerships?
10. Are your Japanese executives world-class caliber? Could they manage global operations covering all other countries, including the United States or Europe?

For many readers these questions may prove discouraging, but it is clear that successful operations in Japan score high in each of these categories. We believe that a successful Japanese operation should be contributing at least 10 percent of total company revenues. In most product areas, 20 to 30 percent is a reasonable figure to expect. While many companies tend to leverage Japanese distributors or partners, investment in one's own operations is a must for the long run. The number of employees in Japan should correspond as much as possible to revenues generated in the country. Unlike the United States, where profits are the most important attribute of performance, in Japan the most important indicators of success are market share, ranking, and number of employees, particularly sales and service personnel as well as engineers. A direct sales and support team is the only way to build the kind of strong customer linkages needed for long-term business. Having staff dedicated to your operation, not with their hearts and minds with some other parent company, is the only way to ensure control and to develop your own identity and corporate capability.

Critical Issues—Stage Four: Becoming a World-Class Competitor

- Giving a global vision
- Developing global mindset
- Designing global operating model
- Globalizing management
- Converting local data for global use
- Girding the organization for global competition

It is important not to become dissuaded by the amount of effort required. Results will not come overnight. It will take a number of years just to build your data base in Japan and to understand true customer requirements. Time and personal effort will be required of your engineers, marketing people, and executives to absorb the cultural factors and market needs in order to best develop new products appropriate for the Japanese consumer.

THE GLOBAL VISION

Any company seeking to do business in Japan will need more than a good product or service, a local operation, and a workable strategy. It also takes a degree of vision. Since competing in Japan is a precursor to successfully competing globally, we consider the necessary viewpoint to be a global vision. When you consider the ways the world has changed today, what is most striking is the globalization of opportunity. In every corner of the world, from highly industralized nations, to newly industrialized countries, to pre-industrial regions, opportunities for economic growth are larger than they have ever been in history. Addressing this opportunity requires an expansive view, and that is the first step in becoming a truly world-class competitor.

Tools of a Global Vision

- Sales goals proportionate to global markets
- Global products appropriately tailored to local markets
- Global delivery apparatus
- Global financial management keyed to local financing
- Transnational management/project teams
- Internationalist managers
- Global operating structure

The goal of the global vision is to create an organization that can compete within its industry in any market in the world. This means an organization that can attain market share in proportion to opportunity, regardless of location. From our study in Chapter 6, few American firms were achieving a competitive market share in Japan as compared to their overall performance and as compared to the potential market size. Successfully globalized companies can approximate the same market share in Japan as they do in Europe, or the United States.

In *Competition in Global Industries,* Michael Porter asserts that a firm that "competes internationally must decide how to spread the activities of the value chain among the countries . . . and integrate their activities to capture linkages" across many geographies. The coordination of corporate tasks globally is a complex undertaking, with numerous considerations:

- Production tasks
- Transfer of production processes
- Multinational account management
- Service standards and procedures
- Development of country-specific products
- Recruiting international staff
- Managing suppliers and purchasing decisions
- Sequencing of product information
- Information networks
- Corporate image
- Product positioning
- Allocation of research tasks
- Logistics and distribution[1]

THE GLOBAL COMPANY MODEL

For almost every American company we studied, Japan is not a primary market. In all too many companies, Japan is of tertiary priority, characteristically lumped into a category like "Rest of the World," the "Pacific Operation," or "Intercontinental." Typically, Japan is approached no differently than Indonesia, Hong Kong, Singapore, or Latin America—economies less than one-twentieth the size of Japan. Where Japan organizations did exist, management reported to a director or vice-president of the overseas sales division. In only very limited cases were engineering, product development, or manufacturing management from the United States or Europe involved with their Japanese counterparts on a regular basis. The Japanese team has little access to decision making in the headquarters on issues of investment, technology direction, and research—even for products aimed at the Japanese market. In this arrangement, products are made for the American market, with Japan as merely an afterthought. Lacking adequate responsibility and authority at the local level, the Japanese operation in such cases tends to struggle, never becoming plugged into the rest of the corporation. Moreover, the parent company never comes to understand the Japanese business climate, markets, and opportunities. As a result, the Japanese organization lacks the information, motivation, and direction to become a full contributor to corporate growth and success. This, in turn, generates an organization vulnerable to Japanese competition everywhere else in the world.

We see the global corporation as something quite different. In the global company, the Japanese operation is fully integrated in all functions: engineering, marketing, operations, management, and decision making. In this structure, a Japanese division manager can run the entire operation for a product line worldwide. As you may recall, at Texas Instruments the Japanese president oversees the entire worldwide memory products group, which has factories in the United States, Taiwan, Italy, and Japan. Terms such as "headquarters," "subsidiary," or "overseas division" become meaningless in such a model. In the global company, the headquarters could conceivably be either in the United States, Japan, and Europe or rotate between geographies; and a general manager from a German factory could be running a plant in Japan; or a top Japanese technologist could be running the entire company's R&D labs. In the global company there are *worldwide product divisions* and *regional executive teams:* both the country manager and the worldwide product group manager (wherever they may be located) have responsibility for success in Japan—market share, new products, revenues, and industry position. In the global company model, all managers company-wide are judged on their performance, team-building skills, and partnerships built across various geographies, cultures, and customer markets.

The objective of the global company is to be as close to the customer as possible in every major geographic market. In this sense, the Japanese operation must become part of the cardiovascular and nervous system of the company, not merely a hand reacting to stimulus from the parent or from the heat of the market in Japan. In the global company model, the top manager from each major market area reports directly to the corporate president. Project, sales, and manufacturing managers in each region report both to their respective division executive who could be anywhere in the world, as well as to the top manager in the geographic region. Because there is minimal insulation between headquarters, the product divisions, and the geographic management, in the global model all product design and development could take place on a worldwide basis.

There are other important characteristics of the global corporation:

Local Decision Making. Once the goal of getting close to customers is established, all other priorities fall in line almost naturally. Whenever possible, decision making is brought closest to where the action is.

A certain degree of low-level autonomy reduces cycle time, enhances response time to opportunities and problems, and permits customized solutions. The goal becomes to drive requirements down the command chain—delivery, turnaround time, service, parts and repair, decision making, customization, and customer linkage are all local issues to be locally resolved.

Originate and Manufacture Products Locally. Closely related to the above, local decision making will more often than not unearth product requirements unique to the locality. For obvious reasons, these requirements should be met locally.

Integrate Intercultural Personnel Company-Wide. Promote an "internationalist" perspective within the corporate community by assigning employees to rotational tours of duties worldwide. This broadened exposure and sensitivity to alternate methodologies and approaches benefits the entire organization.

Except for a purely distribution business, the real resources of the company are at the division level. These people and the products need direct interaction with the customer. To have a separate organization through which people communicate to get to the international market is an insulated approach to doing business with Japan and other major markets. At Applied Materials, we underwent a major restructuring in order to hold the product managers responsible for their performance and success everywhere in the world. As a result, we became very careful in our selection of managers, hiring only those who we felt could operate in a global environment and could deal easily with difficult communications and different cultural extremes—from Japan to Italy. International experience became a top priority, and in parallel we implemented a training program for those not yet ready for direct responsibility on a global basis.

Applied Materials' worldwide structure functions with two major divisions of responsibility, the product divisions and the regional divisions. Regional management has responsibility for all activities in its region that are at the closest point of customer interface, sales and service, and for coordinating each functional group in the region—engineering, development, and marketing. These same groups have their own worldwide reporting strutures and work as a team under one vice-president who is responsible for maintaining our competitive position everywhere in the world. Technical and marketing management work in international teams to develop products with customers throughout the world. The company has used this organizational form to its strategic advantage by forming joint development teams in conjunction with key Japanese customers. These teams operate either at the customer site, at the Narita Technology Center, or in the United States or Europe.

Implementing an infrastructure to support global business is not easy. A fully integrated operation requires lots of travel and a dedicated international team supported by management with the vision to continually "force" team building among the geographies, especially with Japan. After ten years, Applied Materials' international integration is reaching the point today where it is conceivable that a Japanese or European could become president or chairman of the company.

In Figure 11.1, we show organization charts for two very different models of operation, the domestic-oriented company, and the global-oriented organization. The global corporate model can be difficult to implement, largely due to nationalism, entrenched power structures, ignorance, and fear, and very unique cultures, especially in Japan and Asia. New companies have a better chance to grow such an organization while young and impressionable, but at the early stages of development it is also very hard to focus limited resources on product development for remote, "overseas" markets. However, it is more difficult to change the lines of communication long after the organization has been established; a company cannot suddenly focus on Japan, but must be exposed continually to the competitive threat and the opportunity for sales. The global company model is merely meant to provide a template against which your company's progress can be measured. The following questions should be answered in studying your company's readiness and potential for the global model:

- Are divisions truly meeting the needs of major customers in Japan, Europe, and the United States?
- Are resources dedicated appropriately, relative to the opportunities in each market?
- Are organizational structures, titles, reporting, information systems, and cross-linkages identical in every operation?
- Are networks of friends and teams being built across all cultures with customers and between divisions?
- Are managers of any major geography skilled and trained enough to manage any worldwide business unit in any part of the world?

Figure 11.1. The Global Company Model

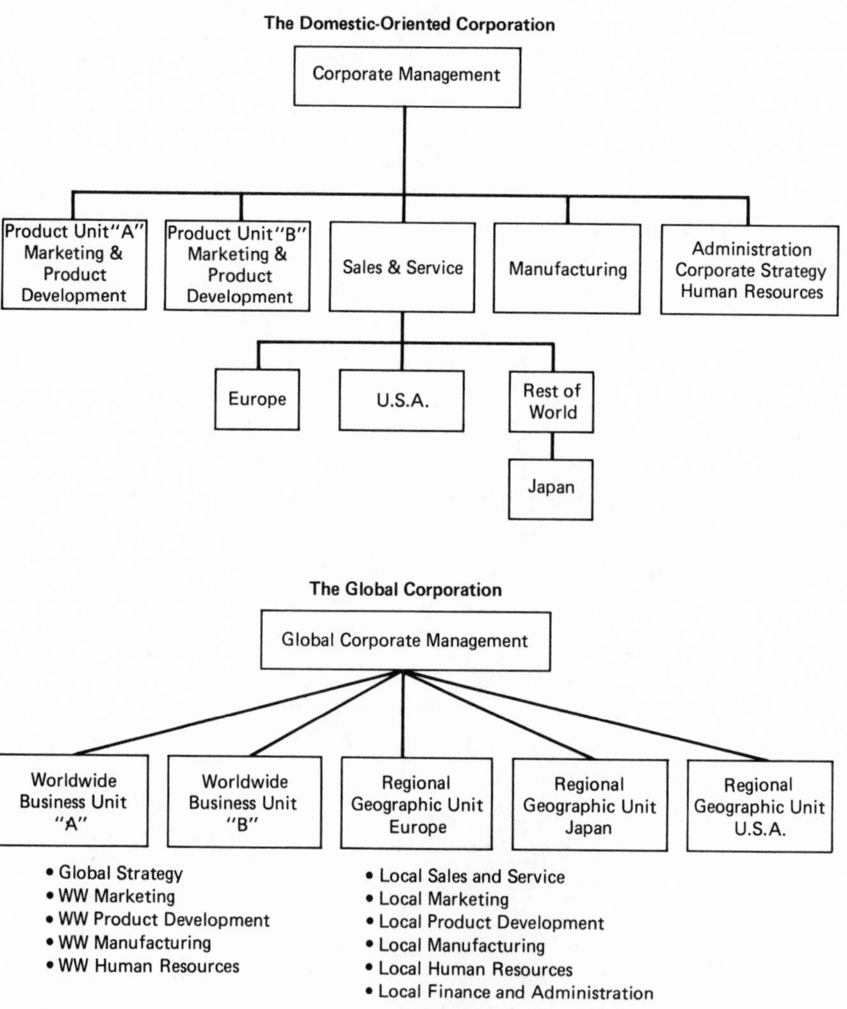

LESSONS FROM JAPAN ON WORLD-CLASS COMPETITIVENESS

What does it take to be a world-class competitor? We believe the Japanese have been showing us for two decades. Only by competing in Japan, and taking the lessons borne of that experience and exporting them worldwide to improve the entire corporation, will American firms be adequately prepared for the new global economy. Let's take a look at some of the underlying principles behind the Japanese ascendancy:

1. Reducing the cycle times for all company activities and functions
2. Pursuing continuous, incremental improvement in all company activities and functions
3. Empowering individuals throughout the workforce
4. Bridging customer linkages at both the strategic and personal level
5. Making more effective use of external resources
6. Employing a more cost-effective product design and product delivery infrastructure
7. Creating superior information systems worldwide
8. Adopting long-term thinking and commitment supported by effective short-term planning and implementation

REDUCING CYCLE TIMES

If the Japanese challenge has taught American business anything, it has taught us that the window of opportunity for any product in any market is but a brief portal. A multilayered, elephantine bureaucracy and a slow-moving decision-making process are impediments to success in a world where change moves with the speed of electronic impulses through a circuit. Cycle-time reduction is critical to the success of today's global competitor; it is a key to being responsive to the customer, which in turn is a prerequisite to the development of strategic partnerships with customers. It eliminates problems which make the move to quality performance efficient and rapid.

By improving forecasting and data collection, reducing cycle times company-wide represents the single biggest opportunity to reduce the level of investment and risk required to support a business. It improves the leverage of critical resources; you will never have as many outstanding people as you can productively use. However, if cycle times can be cut significantly, each individual can make a much greater contribution and do a much bigger job. Doing a job quicker also provides more learning cycles per unit of time, which places emphasis on making quality a part of the manufacturing process itself. *Effectively reducing cycle times keeps a world-class competitor quick of foot, able to manage variety and change and thereby respond to the niche strategy of competition, which is the most common approach used to attack the market leader.*

Reduction of cycle times is not just a goal for manufacturing and vendors only, but for all aspects of the operation such as:

- Product-development cycle times
- Spares-availability cycle times
- Sales-order-processing cycle times
- Open personnel/requisition-filing cycle times
- Problem-identification/solution cycle times
- Field-service response times
- Information-dissemination cycle times (e.g., financial reports)

These improvements will have a tremendous impact on the size of the opportunity a company can effectively manage, the level of customer satisfaction which can be attained, and the likelihood that it will be competitive and profitable.

CONTINUOUS, INCREMENTAL IMPROVEMENT

Being a world-class competitor requires achieving a balance between results and the resources required to achieve them. The issue is not always one of cost reduction. It could just as well be an issue of performance improvement (increased value to our customers, both internal and external). *The real test of excellence is the ability to sustain a leadership position. The world-class standard is constantly being elevated and changed.* American manufacturing capability was clearly world-class in the 1950s and 1960s, and just as clearly it is no longer the leader in many areas today. The requirement for sustained leadership is continuous, incremental improvement, fueled by an insatiable thirst for a better way to do things or, perhaps, to avoid doing them altogether by fundamentally rethinking the product or service itself. Whatever the method, acceptance of change as the only constant is part of accepting the challenge to be world-class, to be positioned to sustain success.

In the quest for continuous improvements, the American passion for only the "breakthrough" solution is deleterious. Genuine improvement comes from making small changes and enhancements every day, rather than ignoring a problem in the name of leapfrogging it altogether. That is why we stress "incremental" improvement in the Japanese model. This philosophical change must be ingrained in the corporate culture; its followers should be recognized and rewarded at every opportunity. Much like the blocking and tackling by an outstanding football team prepares the way for a spectacular play, continuous improvement keeps the company effectively progressing so that a big play may not be required. However, if there is an opportunity for a breakthrough, the company is well positioned to execute the breakthrough in a winning way.

EMPOWERING THE WORKFORCE

None of the above movements to reduce cycle times or to continuously improve can be driven from the top down; they must be adopted company-wide and implemented by those closest to the problems. For most American companies this will require a revolution in thinking. *In the Japanese company, every employee feels a sense of ownership and responsibility for every company activity and function.* Global competitiveness must be predicated upon an empowered workforce. By this, we mean a workforce that:

- Has a clear understanding of goals, objectives, and mission
- Has been given the responsibility and authority to decide how best to accomplish those goals
- Has the skills and has been given the training necessary to be successful
- Is supported by a chain of command which works aggressively to remove barriers that stand in the way of its success
- Takes ownership for results

The advantages of an empowered workforce include:

- Motivation, pride, and self-satisfaction.
- Leverage. Instead of being limited by the capacity of one manager to effect change, you have the benefit of the contribution of the whole organization.
- Effectiveness. No one knows more about what needs to be fixed than the person responsible for the job. Also, no one has more to benefit from problem resolution than the performer.
- A basis of continuous improvement.

There is another side to empowerment. The ability to foster pride and company loyalty will be a key determinant of success for the global company. *A sense of loyalty to the company is a major competitive asset.* People do not work for wages alone. Japanese managers have developed a corporate culture which binds the company, workers, and management into a community with a common fate and destiny. When times get tough, showing that the company truly wishes to protect the employees' interests pays off in the long term.

BUILDING CUSTOMER LINKAGES

The Japanese have mastered the partnership for mutual advantage. As they began their quest for reindustrialization after World War II, they had little in the way of technical and managerial skills to go along with even fewer natural resources. Their only hope, and a strategic dimension they have added to the world, was to build relationships—partnerships—both at home and abroad. The results have been obvious. *The American ethic to "go it alone" and to revere the "lone wolf" have hindered many companies from seizing new opportunities derived from cooperation.* This idea of "rugged individualism" runs counter to the new global realities. American companies must learn the value of establishing close relationships with key customers. The basis for customer preference is a strategic desire on the part of both parties to cooperate, often driven by the prospect of a greater value to be generated out of the sharing of proprietary technology or skills, or maximization of personal relationships that exist between the key buying influencers at the customer level and one or more individuals at the vendor level.

In order to be able to attract these types of partnerships and to deal effectively with the resulting interdependency, a company must keep technology focused on customer needs and be committed to the success of its customers' business as a prerequisite to achieving success on its own. This means, among other things, constantly striving to improve the productivity of the customers' investment in the company's products by broadening their applicability, improving their utilization, and reducing the life-cycle cost of ownership. It also means being attentive to the customers' needs through time (not just at the point of sale), working to improve customer satisfaction by orchestrating the full capability of the company that can positively impact the customers' business, and being an easy (systems and procedures) and pleasant (attitudinally) company with which to do business. As a rule of thumb, in the normal course of business, do not commit beyond your capability to achieve. This requires a clear understanding of your performance capability, whether product or organizationally related, and a clear communication of that capability to the customer, especially in areas where it falls short of the customers' perceived needs. Only by careful management of customer expectations, in combination with an absolute dedication to achieve promised results, can you expect customer satisfaction or a valid basis for strategic partnership.

It is important to constantly improve the level of committed performance to the customer. Winning requires not only that you be a reliable supplier (perform as promised), but that the level of performance promised be competitive or, better yet, world class. Since what represents world class is a moving target, so should our committed performance reflect constant improvement. Performance committed to customers will, on occasion, reflect an assumption of success in these efforts, an assumption which must be transformed to reality through focus and commitment. The Japanese have an expectation that you will never give up.

EFFECTIVELY USING EXTERNAL RESOURCES

It is a reality in today's world that no company can possibly satisfy all its needs internally. To attempt to do so is a waste of resources and talent. American companies must open up their own operations and learn to become world-class customers as a precursor to becoming world-class competitors. It means working cooperatively with others, which for most of history American companies have been loathe to do. It is no longer, however, an optional matter. As products become ever more sophisticated and incorporate an ever-widening range of characteristics, it will become necessary to sharpen the focus of corporate capabilities. *For virtually every business, there will exist another enterprise somewhere in the world that is the best at what it does, whose sole strategic mission is to be the world-class supplier in a given product, technology, or component. Competing with such an enterprise by trying to supply yourself with skills out of your area of focus is a poor use of a company's limited talents and, in fact, improves the position of competition that is willing to cooperate.* By being open to partnerships and appearing to be the most logical partner with which to do business on a cooperative basis, one can simultaneously lock up the world's top vendors and use potential competitive technology to one's advantage.

Effective implementation of this strategy requires:

- *Reduced vendor base.* As described above, the establishment of effective relationships takes a lot of effort and can be accomplished only with a small group of vendors. As we gained relationships with the world's best vendors for the technologies and components we need, Applied Materials reduced its supplier base by 75 percent over a three-year period.

- *Broadened vendor technical scope.* You can be more helpful to your customers if they allow you to participate in the solution of their problems rather than telling you what they want you to build. It follows that the value of a world-class supplier is greatest when it is given broad latitude in developing the problem solution that is the best for your company.
- *Technology-competent source selectors.* As the criteria for vendor selection becomes more heavily weighted toward the ability to make a technical contribution or value-added capability, it will be necessary to introduce into the selection process the measurement indicators of competency to make those assessments.

COST-EFFECTIVE PRODUCT DESIGN AND DELIVERY INFRASTRUCTURE

American manufacturing has been much maligned in recent years. The focus of attention has been aimed on the manufacturing process itself, and on American industry's failure to concentrate more on the process and less on new product development. Yet, fundamentally at least, American manufacturing is as good as any in the world, and still in many cases it is better. What the Japanese have taught us, however, is that the keys to manufacturing rest in the design process, in resolving issues of manufacturability before a product hits the production floor. *Product design is the major cost driver of any business because, during this process, a product's inherent characteristics are set and subsequently can be changed only with great difficulty.* Issues such as material costs, product reliability, the total number of parts, both standard and custom, the total number of vendors required, and the total number of manufacturing steps necessary are all dictated by what goes on in the design process. Each of these characteristics, either separately or in concert with others on the list, has a major impact on business complexity and/or the cost of doing business. Management of these characteristics to predetermined objectives during product design is essential to achieve cost competitiveness.

The correct product developed and introduced to the market too late is a waste of talent and money and represents a major lost opportunity for the company. Achieving world-class cycle time of product design and delivery will be a critical strategic factor in maintaining differentiation from your competitors. This leads us to contend that, from the Japanese model, a potential world-class company needs to understand the product life cycles common in its industry, the size and direction of growth (expanding or retrenching) of the customer base. The importance of achieving good performance from the start is a prerequisite is to achieving follow-on volume business from those customers, and the likelihood of one product or a product line expanding into other complementary areas.

It is clear that not only must the product design process be executed well, but that the delivery infrastructure—including marketing, manufacturing, procurement, and customer service—must also perform well, individually and as a team. Therefore, in addition to focusing on assuring you have the right product, you must work continuously on the improvement of the product delivery system. And, you must constantly test the methods by which you build the business to ensure that they are supportive of enhancing the capability levels of that infrastructure through time.

A key concept that could be of assistance in improving the performance of the product delivery process is to understand that "hand-offs" that occur throughout the entire process (which begins with design and ends with a satisfied customer) are not product responsibility transfers. Instead, they are technology or information transfers in which the overall requirements have not been met until self-sufficiency of the receiving party has been achieved. When viewed from the perspective of this requirement, the breadth and depth of support necessary to achieve the sign-off is much greater than most groups are accustomed to providing. As such, at each level in the process, there is a tendency to degrade the level of knowledge transferred. In the final analysis, the customer standing at the end of such a tenuous chain is frequently not well served.

SUPERIOR INFORMATION SYSTEMS

As we enter a period many have called the Information Age, a company's capacity to gather, process, and evaluate good information and market intelligence will be a distinct cause of competitive advantage (and the failure to do so a tremendous disadvantage). *The Japanese have succeeded in penetrating far-reaching markets, and in providing appropriate products in worlds where they have had little affinity and even less understanding, precisely because they have stressed the building of a world-class information network.* The Japanese ability to collect information about the changing tastes and wants of the American consumer, even from afar, mightily outpaced American industry's capacity to read the shifting sands—and led to Japanese domination in fields where it once played bit parts. Clearly, information is among the most valuable corporate assets today. To a great extent, the quality of the decisions each of us makes is a function of the quality of the information base we have available prior to making the decision. Among the areas where better information could make a critical difference are consumer needs, customer satisfaction levels, competitors, emerging technologies, vendor capabilities, vendor performance, product performance, and market size and composition.

Most of us probably feel there is too much information now, and perhaps this is true. But is it the right information? Is it getting to the right people in a timely manner? In order to be a leading and, therefore, a targeted player in a global business, you must look to information management as a key to creating awareness, focusing attention, measuring results, and generating continuous improvement. In this regard, it is critical that these information tools first and foremost be owned by and be useful to the performing levels of the organization, the empowered workforce, rather than be a control tool of upper management. It was Satchel Paige who said, "I never look back, something might be gaining on me." But American business will do well to look around to assure the tools are in place for the marathon ahead. If not, others will use their information system to change your competitive position.

LONG-TERM THINKING AND COMMITMENT

With all we have seen with the Japanese rise to power, patience, determination, and a long-term outlook have been possibly the most consistent traits. The Japanese place a premium on perseverance. *Ganbatte,* carry on above all else, is the word most used in the company setting. And the willingness to carry on for however long it takes to achieve a goal gives the Japanese a wide field of vision. Their long view permits them to see things like relative growth rates, a term of little short-range value but an important indicator of future business opportunity. For example, if you are growing at 5 percent per year and your competitor is growing at 8 percent per year, and if each of you were $100 million, let's look at the end of ten years. At 8 percent you would have a $215 million company, compared to $163 million growing at 5 percent. The faster growing company would have almost one-third more gross profit to provide funds for research, marketing, global distribution, and administrative infrastructure than the slower growing company. Intelligent reinvestment keeps the leader on a path that continues to increase the gap. This index can tell you whether the future market for a product will be significantly larger or smaller than that currently available, although the nature of such opportunity is subject to technical and competitive uncertainty. Looking ahead has made the Japanese fanatics for accuracy. They know that product and market development programs for global markets represent big bets which can only be justified with an accurate assessment of requirements several years into the future. The same can be said regarding the development of organizational capability. If the long haul shows the sun setting on an industry or product, the Japanese redouble their commitment to and investment in the success of the existing customer base rather than skimming the cream represented by the present opportunity and then moving on. Like spirits of past generations which haunt a Shinto shrine, the Japanese believe past misdeeds to customers of a waning product line will find their way into the future.

Most of all, a view to the future tells you that renewal is both possible and essential. If you don't raise the bar, someone else will. It's the nature of the world in which we live; there is an excess of supply in almost every business. In almost all industries, it has been clearly demonstrated that performance is susceptible to dramatic rather than marginal improvements based upon entirely new ways of doing business. One of the reasons that these changes tend to be seen as dramatic is that market leaders have not monitored competition, have not pushed the performance envelope. As a result, they are blind-sided when a more market-sensitive company can see the change coming and react much sooner.

Those companies capable of adopting a long-term view and results-based level of commitment will achieve tremendous strategic advantage over other competitors which do not—not only because the performance gap will be wide, but also because the lead time to respond in some industries is on the order of two to five years. Few companies, once upstaged, have the financial staying power to survive the reconstruction process.

From the outset, we expressed the belief that the key to global competitiveness comes from participating in Japan directly and from facing and satisfying some of the most demanding consumers and customers in the world today. Your company is forced to deliver ultimate quality, on time, and backed with superior after-sales service. Understanding Japan's fast-moving markets (and the trends and technologies which are increasingly originating there), keeping in step with your toughest potential competitors' capabilities, and meeting a new level of demand on customer service and responsiveness will have a major positive impact on your operations worldwide. In short, the experience will give you the tools to become a world-class competitor.

12

Challenge and Opportunity

The Keys to Success in Japan

The belief that there is an intrinsic symmetry to nature is deeply rooted in Eastern thought, religion, and society. As symbolized by the Taoist concept of *ying* and *yang*, the world to the Japanese mind is an organic whole comprised of opposite, but centripetal, forces. Contradictions abound in this world, but these contradictions ultimately create balance. At the beginning of this book we examined the *ying* and *yang* of opportunity and adversity that confronts and confounds many Western businesses seeking safe landing on the islands of Japan. Clearly, as the world's second largest and fastest-growing industrialized economy in an absolute sense, the Japanese market cannot be ignored. To foreign companies with the right product and the right mode of entry, the market can offer a wealth of opportunity. At the same time, Japan's market structure is obstacled by forms and forces which run counter to America's free-enterprise and free-market sensibilities. With practices steeped in history and a value system that most foreigners can never fully comprehend, many companies have opted not to participate in Japan at all. They've given up before they've even begun to fight. We believe this is a mistake. Not only are the opportunities to be found in Japan very real, not only is Japan not impregnable, but no company today can afford to abstain from the toughest market in the world and expect to be a world-class performer.

More counterproductive yet, Japan's cultural differences and market hurdles are now being amplified in the American political arena, with even more vocal politicians pointing with growing alarm to the threat of Japanese economic supremacy. This is foolhardy. The Japanese want basically the same things Americans want: fundamental needs to be met, security, and a hope of a brighter future for themselves and their children. Japanese businesses want what American businesses want: market opportunity and profits. The market is changing. Clearly more rapidly than most in the United States desire, but changing nevertheless.

A REALISTIC VIEW OF THE JAPANESE CHALLENGE

In his landmark book *Le Defi Americain* (The American Challenge) published nearly a quarter of a century ago, Jean-Jacques Servan-Schreiber warned Europeans that if they didn't wake up and look around them, American industry would soon own much of European business and be the definers of European economic destiny. Servan-Schreiber's message was clear: The Americans were coming on strong, and if Europe did not gird itself to respond, it would soon find itself at a disadvantage. He did not make use of vitriol in his argument, and he did not offer retreat or isolationism as a solution. He simply looked at the trends and said essentially, "Europe can do better for itself." That is where American business is today when compared with Japan. Fat, happy, and lethargic for too long, American industry needed a swift boot in the bottom line, and it got it. Our message is not much different from Servan-Schreiber's: "Now that Japan has got your attention, do something about it." And surely, you should begin by dealing with the Japanese on a realistic basis. As Bill Emmott pointed out in *The Sun Also Sets*, Japan today represents for America a "challenge, not a threat." There is a big difference, and understanding it will place you in the appropriate posture to take effective action.

We must begin by seeing Japan for what it is. Japan is not a free-market economy; it is a command economy controlled by a loosely defined (yet firmly entrenched) cartel of business and government interests. The government uses its revenue-generating and market-controlling influences to grow businesses and industries. This is done by providing support—from a low cost of capital to advice; and by limiting outside participants to the market—through tariffs, patent restrictions and by turning a blind eye to nontariff barriers. The private sector is no less monolithic. Competition is stiff, but the combatants cooperate to the extent that they agree to carve up market opportunities to benefit themselves. Few non-Japanese companies have been factored in this equation.

Yet, for all the resentment that has been built by the Japanese economic juggernaut, there is no mystery to its methodology. In a sense, the Japanese operate on a "hierarchy of needs" basis. First and foremost, trade is leveraged to acquire for the nation what it absolutely needs: commodities such as food and fuel. The emphasis is on attaining self-sufficiency (characteristic of an island mentality), but what it cannot produce itself it will purchase from others. Second, the Japanese seek to develop capabilities for long-term sustenance, employment for its citizenry, and domestic manufacturing capabilities. Third, the Japanese seek respect on the global stage. Their new goals of innovation and globalization are indications of a nationwide "self-actualization," and are based on a real desire to be seen as a world-class power.

The Japanese strategy, at its most fundamental level, is to seek advantage over competitors through long-term strategies and staying power. Indeed, Japanese companies would never have gained the upper hand if their competitors had not eventually conceded their positions. Moreover, they could never have gained the wherewithal to compete globally if it were not for the fact that they have faced little in the way of outside competition at home. As the worldwide market for goods and services heats up, ignoring the Japanese domestic market now could prove disastrous for any would-be player on the global stage.

These days the most successful foreign firms in Japan are doing something new and different—bringing out new products—and showing that they have a growth bias and commitment to the market. Because the Japanese constantly watch their competition, it is essential not to leave any move, announcement, or new market entry unanswered. Attack and counterattack should become a constant refrain of your business, no matter what it is, and all competitor actions need to be responded to with new concepts—a less expensive product, a new partnership, or other differentiating factors. "American companies have to be willing to go the extra mile to do business abroad, particularly in countries like Japan," says Sun Microsystems' president, Scott McNealy. McNealy believes that there is no great mystery to international marketing, that price/performance ratio, service, ease of use, and industry standards make the same compelling purchase argument abroad as they do at home.

For many companies, it is important to have both marketing and engineering capabilities in Japan, where the cutting edge of technology is, and to establish a base of operations for penetration into all of Asia, which is now a more important and a potentially larger economic unit than all of Europe. Many Southeast Asian markets, such as Taiwan and Hong Kong, are growing even faster than Japan, and while their economies are much smaller, in the aggregate they make up a huge emerging market. Eventually China will emerge as an important market. The business is there for the taking, and yet many Western manufacturers hold back. The problem with many companies is that they have 2,000 people in the United States, say, and an office of twenty in Japan run by an American, and then wonder why they are not successful.

Japan is not going to give markets away and will fight every company or government that attempts to succeed on their playing field. But what we conclude is that if you don't win in Japan over the next ten to twenty years, you will not win in Asia, and will not win in the world, for the simple reason that Japan will grow to be a yet greater part of the world economic pie and the competitive capabilities developed from these strategies will be telling in the fight for position in other global markets. The battle for survival in the fiercely competitive Japanese market is won over the long haul, not in the first initial battles. Once established in Japan, a company must continue to work ceaselessly to gain the trust of its customers, to study the markets and reassess market strategy, and even to radically alter its approach when necessary. A serious problem is the decline in new product development taking place within many companies, and the subsequent reduction of skills which goes along with this trend. If these trends continue, American human capital will be less involved in product creation, design, and engineering, and be relegated to the role of sales and manufacturing labor for products conceived and engineered in Japan.

Regardless of what industry you are in, Japan must be viewed as the center of competition. Among the trends that will be shaping the competitive environment over the next ten years are:

- Strengthening of Japanese companies as the definers of technology, global organization, and manufacturing efficiency.
- Intensifying competition in the United States from local operation of Japanese companies and in Europe from a consolidating Economic Community market along with the rapid entry of Japanese operations there.
- Development of a stronger Japanese supplier base attuned to providing for the needs of their Japanese and foreign customers worldwide—today's focus of Japanese industry is on *served market demand* as the new driver of corporate growth.
- Continued instability in oil prices exchange rates and capital mar-

kets, and intensifying trade frictions with Japan causing very mixed results for American companies operating in Japan.
- While technological differentiation serving niche markets will still have great value, it will be ever more difficult to maintain. Large global markets mean the basis of competition will increasingly be cost competitiveness, product reliability, responsive service, and support of customers' needs for specialized joint development projects and customized products—all areas in which Japanese business has demonstrated competence.

All of these dynamics should tell you that, even if your market is safe today, do not cast a blind eye to changes in the competitive climate, both as to the basis of and the quality of competition because "the lead time to change" (i.e., the time period before an effective world-class capability can be put in place) is very long. To wait until this new mode of competition is causing one to lose market share will be to have waited too long. These competitive capabilities must, therefore, be preemptively developed, and the lack of demonstrated injury must not inhibit your sense of urgency.

THE KEYS TO SUCCESS IN JAPAN

From the case studies we have examined, and from our direct experience operating in Japan, we have developed a list of keys to opening up and succeeding in the Japanese market. They have appeared in various incarnations throughout this book.

- Revering the "Customer as God"
- Controlling your own destiny
- Researching and manufacturing the right product for Japan
- Building a world-class organization and management
- Embracing cooperation and competition
- *Ningen kankei*—human relations
- Getting back to basics
- The attack/counterattack response
- Emphasizing similarities/taking advantage of differences
- Believing that success in Japan leads to global excellence

1. Revering the "Customer as God." In no other country are the requirements for customer service and support more demanding than in

Japan. American companies must mobilize their entire organizations to rise to the levels of excellence required by Japanese customers if they are to succeed worldwide. Servicing the customer is a part of the national culture and a critical part of everyone's job in Japan. Excellence in service will become one of the only differentials in the new world market, and is essential to survival in Japan.

2. *Controlling your own destiny.* While the Japanese operation can take many forms, there is no substitute for direct participation and a direct presence. Building a strong team of key people loyal to your company and then assuring and providing them full support are the key prerequisites to long-term success in the Japanese market. Customer relationships are critical; without them success can only be short-term in Japan. Distributorships, licensing agreements, and partnerships should be bolstered by a local presence aimed at growing close to the customers and end users. Any relationship which might reduce control, customer access, and future expansion opportunities in Japan must be avoided.

3. *Researching and manufacturing the right product for Japan.* An intimate understanding of the Japanese market will permit companies to provide their customers and consumers with appropriate products—distributed, advertised, and supported in the appropriate ways—which in turn will result in increased market share and profits from Japan. In the long term, this may necessitate providing development and manufacturing capabilities in Japan. Now Japan is becoming the leading center for a broad range of technologies available nowhere else in the world, for many of the primary components of the future Information Age, and in other areas of biotechnology, advanced materials, manufacturing, and electronics. Taking advantage of Japan's experienced talent and access to the latest technology offers a major strength to differentiate your company from other global competitors.

4. *Building a world-class organization and management.* With skills honed by the rigors of the toughest market in the world, Japanese managers can offer a wealth of insight and leadership capability to American firms—provided they are adequately integrated into the worldwide operation. A corporate matrix structure based on the "global company model" we outlined in the previous chapter can result in a more progressive organization, with a reporting structure appropriate to both corporate and local needs. As the company globalizes, each product division must be responsible for its performance on a worldwide basis.

5. *Embracing cooperation and competition.* In today's highly industrialized, highly specialized world, it is foolhardy for a company to attempt

to be all things to all people. By becoming a world-class customer or partner through working more closely with vendors and even competitors, technical leverage can be increased multifold in the critical areas of differentiation. In the twenty-first century, no company can support every activity or product in-house.

6. *Ningen kankei—human relations.* Trust, obligation, and respect for the human side are the foundations of business in Japan. For most American companies, a relationship with a customer begins with a deal. In Japan, the deal begins with a relationship. Loyalty, friendship, and mutual obligation between suppliers and customers have far more weight than performance considerations alone. This is because, in the long run, partners will work together to enhance performance and assure mutual benefit for maximum value (very distinct from price). The Japanese are more interested in the long-term benefits of a relationship, rather than the revenue from a specific contract or transaction, and are very attuned to the idea of reciprocity and interdependence with close partners over the long term.

7. *Getting back to basics.* Success in Japan is only possible if the company's fundamental business practices emphasize *shitsu* (quality), *kaizen* (continuous improvement), and JIT (just-in-time delivery). As we discussed in the previous chapter, only an organization that can implement and perform as expected is truly prepared to perform successfully in Japan.

8. *The attack/counterattack response.* When targeting the Japanese market, the capability to respond quickly and powerfully to a competitor's countermoves around the world is essential. Only by putting pressure on the Japanese in their home market can American companies make them divert resources from their global strategies (which are aimed at further penetrating the U.S., Asian, and European markets). Clearly, a good offense is the best defense in this case. Taking the offense requires fast-turnaround product designs, a development infrastructure in each local market, and analysis teams aimed at building a solid intelligence base. One must know what resources, partners, and technology the Japanese competitors possess and how they plan to use them. One must also have the ability to mass manufacture, with enough flexibility to meet growth in times of demand and to retool in times of product shift. Remember that information is power, and few American companies know enough about what is happening in the Japanese market.

9. *Emphasizing similarities/taking advantage of differences.* So much has been emphasized in the media and in business about the major differences between America and Japan. A non-Japanese company should

employ these differences—unhindered ideas, overseas experience, multicultural management and independence from industrial group affiliations which limit market opportunity for the competition. These qualities can also be used to recruit bright young Japanese and other managers who have been stifled in major Japanese companies.

10. Believing that success in Japan leads to global excellence. The most important reason for being in Japan is that the experience will increase your overall ability to compete in the new global economy. This argument cannot be made strongly enough. The ultimate goal of your Japan operation is to integrate the new ideas and technologies originating in Japan and to prepare your worldwide organization for the new level of performance expectation the Japanese are creating.

SHOBAI WA AKINAI—NEVER GIVE UP

In the face of long odds, the Japanese have not only survived, they have prevailed, and this may be the hardest, most important lesson from the Japanese experience: perseverance. Increasing global competition has far-reaching implications for managers, many of whom are still domestically oriented and short-term focused. If a company is to remain in a leadership position over the long term, it must operate on the premise that the world is a single marketplace of varying local needs. The global seller must listen and respond to the buyer's needs and wants. American industry must improve its posture at the microeconomic level: through individual companies improving their marketing, product design, and manufacturing strategies. Those American companies that are still focused inward must reach out to join the global economy and develop new strategies for future growth. In the final analysis, America must get back to basics and work as one nation in competition. America must work collectively as a society, not as short-term thinking, self-interested individuals. Each individual worker must put in those extra hours and gain satisfaction from making his or her company and its products the very best in the world. And most of all, never give up.

THE TIME TO WIN IN JAPAN IS NOW

We began this book by examining the very real Japanese challenge. We will close by looking at the equally real Japanese opportunity. Considered in raw form, the facts that point to major opportunities for

American firms willing to do what it takes to succeed in Japan are awe-inspiring:

- Japan is now the second-largest and fastest-growing developed industrial market in the world, an economy half the size in population, but growing twice as fast as the United States. The $3 trillion Japanese economy is adding over $150 billion of gross national product each year.
- Japan is already a leading importer of U.S. products, and our second largest foreign market. Japan buys 70 percent of its imported beef from the United States, over $5 billion in grains every year, and is America's largest overseas market for citrus fruit. In 1989, Japan bought $1.25 billion in American aircraft, $1.83 billion in fresh and processed seafoods, $819 million in MOS integrated circuits, $634 billion in office equipment and parts, $505 million in primary plastic products, $765 million in coal, and $3,036 million in wood and lumber products. As well, Japan is a major market for chemicals and pharmaceuticals. Unfortunately, imports of automobiles ($311 million versus $2.55 billion from Europe) and electronics and machinery remain quite low.[1]
- A geographically confined market of some 120 million consumers with one of the highest levels of per-capita income and education, and the highest rates of disposable income and savings in the world.
- Traditional distribution channels—one of the most troublesome "structural impediments"—are rapidly breaking down. Exclusive chains of one-brand stores are facing declining sales in favor of large discount stores bringing in imported products from all over the world. In 1989, Matsushita's 27,000-shop network of National and Panasonic dealers saw its share of its parent company's total domestic output drop from 70 percent to 60 percent in one year.
- In 1989, MITI put out a call to Japan's major corporations to double their rate of U.S. imports by 1992. In mid-1989, MITI went further, announcing it would offer tax incentives and low-interest loans to companies increasing imports of manufactured goods.
- There are over 1,200 new shopping centers proposed or under construction in Japan, all with larger stores which carry far greater numbers of imported products than smaller stores. These discount stores are expected to hit $10 billion in sales in the next five years, up from $4.2 billion in 1990.[2]

Western companies can and must look to Japan as the center of the greatest economic opportunity for this decade and beyond. Asia is a $3 trillion market growing at $3 billion per week, and Japan is providing the infrastructure to this economy. In almost every sector of the economy, Japan is growing faster and provides a single national market second only to the United States in size. The time has never been better, nor the moment more right, to make a commitment and an offensive in Japan.

Japan is changing. Owing both to Western influences and its own evolution, Japan is slowly becoming a more accessible, less alienating environment. Japanese are wealthier than at any time in their history, affording them tremendous discretionary income and spending power. The population is also aging. The "graying" of Japan means that more Japanese will draw upon savings to live and to enjoy their later years. This will result in greater consumerism and more travel by Japanese. It will also mean a lowered rate of personal savings nationwide, which will change Japanese industry's capital structures.

America is also changing. The Japanese challenge is only one of several major forces, including the democratization of Eastern Europe, the reduction of Cold War tensions with the Soviet Union, and instability in the Middle East that have ushered in new American attitudes about the world in which we live. Americans have come to see that leadership requires work—and choices. Americans have grown to understand that the world is not a mirror image of the United States; values and ambitions, hopes and dreams, differ around the world. America is learning to be more accommodating, less doctrinaire, more perceptive of the gray tones which shade the hard and fast framework that once was its reality. Change is not a negative thing. At Applied Materials we have a saying, "Change is the medium of opportunity." And so it is. The changes taking place in every corner of the globe are creating new opportunities and new markets to serve. In this world of change, everything that was no longer is.

THE GOLDEN AGE OF GLOBAL GROWTH

Unwrapping the mysteries and wonders of the Japanese market has been our central mission. Yet, the wider implications of Japan's success are equally significant, and equally part of our story. Japan's rise to power shows us, in no uncertain terms, that global trade is now the single most potent source of corporate profits and national wealth-

Figure 12.1 Booming Growth in World Trade: The Opportunity Is Now

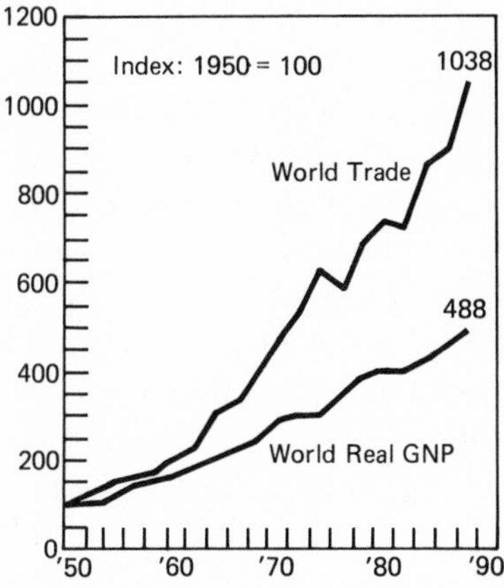

SOURCE: *Fortune* (January 15, 1990).

building. In this new era, Japanese capitalism is the model. American capitalism, to which the Western world aspired for a century, has become a relic of a quainter, gentler, less competitive time. If America can regain a competitive posture in the coming decade (and we believe it can), it will come about by emphasizing global trade in the Japanese model, not by remaining the market of last resort for goods produced elsewhere. America must wage a campaign to make and deliver "exportable" products to the world's doorstep.

As Figure 12.1 demonstrates, the world's hunger for trade has caused this area of economic activity to expand between 1960 and 1988 at a rate twice that of world output. What does this portend? We believe this gap analysis points to the major trend shaping the future of the world: the ability to trade has become even more significant than the ability to produce, per se. That point is clearly made in Japan's rise. The ramifications for American business are obvious: make products globally, make them localized, make them better than anyone else, and do not take anything for granted. The corollaries are equally obvious and far-reaching: design to manufacture, deliver to specification, shorten lines of supply, and widen lanes of communication within and outside the organization. For all of these things (and because of them) winning in Japan is essential. Japan is the quintessential proving—and improving—ground for commerce today. If you have a product that can sell in Japan, sell it. If you don't have one, get one. If you are intimidated by the Japanese market, it will not be long before you will be intimidated by any market. Because soon, all markets will become more competitive and the strength of Japan's sogo shoshas, manufacturers, electronics and automotive companies, and banks will only become greater. It's only a matter of time before your company will daily be feeling the power of an organized global trading nation.

It may be argued that we have entered into a new phase in human history, where the pulsing machinations of worldwide commerce provide as uplifting and morally significant a purpose as the pursuit of any past or present ideology. In a sense, capitalism of a global trading system has rendered other ideologies obsolete, and has provided a forum for international competition and cooperation that may one day turn the killing fields of mortal conflict fallow.

Afterword

The America That Can Compete

America is a land of wonders, in which everything is in constant motion and every change seems an improvement.

ALEXIS DE TOCQUEVILLE

In June 1989 *Time* magazine ran a feature story about the United States-Japan trade imbalance with a cover headline asking, "Does Japan Play Fair?" That question illustrates one of the keys to America's problems in the world today—as a nation we are asking ourselves the wrong questions. America's unique sense of fairness is not shared by the rest of the world. An "Americanocentric" view of right and wrong blinds us from dealing realistically with the challenges created by the new world economy. Japan's success is only symptomatic of wider changes in the world which have made Japan's way of business more relevant and effective. Indeed, many other nations now look to Japanese (not American) corporations as models, and to Japan as a model for national economic development, both because of the inherent success it has achieved and because its success tells us all something about how the world has been reshaped today. Unlike the laissez-faire, free market economy of the United States, Japan and many of the Asian countries are organized economies with proactive government involvement in the machinations of the market. Whether this is right or wrong, it just is. And if U.S. companies are to succeed in this milieu, the daily course of business must be changed relative to countries where there are very different preconceptions on what is "fair" practice.

It is part of the American heritage to be concerned with fairness. That's an admirable ideal. Yet, if you look around the world today, it is clear that America must temper its broader vision and grander ideals with practical solutions to today's problems. The United States is in the midst of a struggle for economic self-determinism. If a nation of big ideals is to survive with the wherewithal to fight the good fight; to be in possession of the financial clout to assuage the world's ills, the generosity to defend her helpless, and the might to retire the despotic, then we must have the resources generated through commerce, not continue to borrow and run deeper in debt. To this extent, America's business interests are everybody's interests. Government leadership, business cooperation, educational resources, and the endless resolve and energy of the American people must be channeled into "waging business" in the new global economy.

The most powerful "ism" in the world today is "economism." It is the ability of nation states to provide their constituents with an acceptable quality of life. You see this in every corner of the world today: peace isn't breaking out, economism is. It is a smaller world that requires bigger thinking. As Kenichi Ohmae states it, "Man's ability to create, compete and consume will not be denied by those politicians and bureaucrats who try to restrict the flows of capital, technology, and information."[1] In a world rendered borderless by the free movement of capital, technology, and information, new rules will be required for business.

WHAT AMERICA CAN DO

As part of the process of enhancing America's competitive readiness, we believe there are several areas which must be examined. Clearly the cost of capital in the United States for industries that must compete with global competitors is a major differential. This cost of capital is directly related to risk. Here, U.S. industry and government have a cooperative role to play.

There must be a clear focus on encouraging the global competitiveness of our major corporations in those industries that are relevant to the generation of future jobs and taxes. With that fundamental strategy in place, we can bring to bear our unique skills of new industry development through new ventures. The debate in the United States over which is the more effective route to regain competitiveness—supporting large corporations or start-up enterprises as mutually exclusive approaches—focuses the argument between ourselves, while our global competitors reap the rewards of our confusion.

Our ability to start new businesses is unsurpassed but if the bulk of new jobs and taxes is developed elsewhere after the high risk and cost of research and development are completed and the markets proven, we only reward a few entrepreneurs and venture capitalists, rather than society as a whole. As well, smaller companies cannot support the important infrastructure required to be competitive worldwide against major corporations like those in Japan. So, a clear understanding of the importance of a dual approach as a base line for any policy is imperative. We must be broadly competitive on a global basis and then add our unique capability for entrepreneurship as an augmentation of our national core industrial capability.

U.S. industry should adopt a cooperative approach to business by establishing more consortia for research, manufacturing, sales, and financing, by building long-term partnerships with customers and suppliers, and by bolstering a basic U.S. capability for strategic products and technologies. The U.S. government should modify its adversarial approach to economic development by:

- Establishing a strong, cabinet-level department (not unlike Japan's Ministry of International Trade and Industry) to look after industry and trade interests on a global basis.
- Establishing a policy coordinating office, reporting directly to the President, for the two major economic superpowers, Japan and West Germany. This office should provide continuous coordination of national policy among the various departments and activities of the federal government.
- Requiring "reciprocity" from America's trading partners, at least regarding market access, and possibly even in terms of the value of annual trade.
- Creating a bipartisan, multi-industry task force to implement the many good ideas that have resulted from the numerous studies of the American competitiveness crisis. As is often the case in the United States, ideas are plentiful, it's action that is missing. All concerned parties, and that includes just about everybody in America, must overcome the paralysis of analysis and move to execution with a patriotic zeal once reserved for other types of national crises.
- Encouraging local and global competition, but fostering the capability for joint research and development within U.S. (and global)

industries. This will require a relaxation of federal antitrust laws. Such laws were written to prevent monopolies among American companies but can do nothing to curtail monopolies from outside the United States, and only serve now to hamstring American industry's competitive posture on a global basis.

- Welcoming the world's best minds to live and work in America. One of the country's greatest competitive strengths is its "melting pot" character. Other nations lack this openness, and will ultimately suffer from the lack of infusion by new blood. Each year, vast numbers of foreign students come to America for an education. As Tom Peters has half-jokingly suggested, the government should staple a "green card" to every diploma received by a foreign student, thereby encouraging him or her to stay and contribute to the growth and dynamism of America.
- Developing a national educational curriculum in part designed to provide industry with an appropriate workforce to meet the challenge of global competitors. A substantial part of this curriculum should be crafted in partnership with industry, consistent with present and future needs, and be updated by industry-government coordination as needs evolve in a rapidly changing environment.

The last point addresses the wider need to better prepare America's young to be citizens of the world. The nation's youth must be brought up to worldwide standards in critical curricula like science, geography, Asian languages, and international economics. Education, including company, public, and private, needs to be revitalized to provide a broad base of capable employees. Our best international competitors, such as Japan, field a highly educated workforce dedicated to excellence and hard work. We have seen many instances in Japan where even those with only a high school education were capable of on-the-job problem analysis, making corrective recommendations and leading effective implementation. Most assuredly, they were literate. These strengths at all levels provide the workers greater control over their work environment and free up those with special training, like engineers, to bring out new equipment or new products.

Education and training is a national and business priority. Schools should be provided a broader charter which would include year-round programs for child care, skills training, physical development, and intensive education with substantially more class and study programs. Our young, multicultural citizens are clearly the greatest resource in the world if properly developed.

To compete in the global marketplace we also must learn to cooperate at home. We have clearly let our adversarial approach to solving common problems get out of hand. The unfortunate state of litigiousness we have reached illustrates how far our consensus-building skills have degenerated. In the intense competitive environment we now live in, we cannot afford to divert so much of our human and financial resources to the sort of useless wrangling, delays, and positioning that pits individuals, companies, government, employers, unions, and employees against each other. We can no longer afford to have our best and brightest minds siphoned off to engage in this costly charade. The time spent in adversarial intergroup battles leaves our global competitors unchallenged to increase their market share.

Lastly, American business must reject the quick fix and the fast buck approach which has characterized its style for the past two decades. There is no quick solution to the problems that hobble our industries: it is a fact of life that industries change—they are born, they evolve, and sometimes they die. The real answer is to stay close to the fundamentals, to stay close to the customers, and to stay close to the changes borne of competition. Similarly, a dollar quickly earned rarely stays for long. If it is a true indictment of our capital structure that it has little patience, business will get nowhere by pandering to this weakness. Think long term, act long term. Living and dying by quarterly results makes for an environment of short-term thinkers and a near-sighted perspective. If the United States continues in this self-destructive path, the massive global opportunities that will generate sales, jobs, and taxes will be defaulted to those countries with patience and the willingness to sacrifice.

WHAT JAPAN CAN DO

It should be understood, by Americans and Japanese alike, that it is not in Japan's best interests to see the American economy in trouble. Japanese industry has benefited greatly by the open markets and receptive distribution channels in the United States, and the loss of those open markets, by either legislation or economic retrenchment, will only hurt Japan. Japan can help itself in the long run by:

- Working with U.S. companies to improve their market share in Japan. This includes setting annual targets for purchase of American goods by Japanese companies and government agencies.

- Encouraging changes in existing distribution systems to make it easier for imported products to enter these channels and wend their way through to the consumers. Where appropriate, entirely new distribution systems may need to be promoted.
- Providing new technology to revitalize U.S industry through licenses, joint ventures, and other arrangements.
- Inviting U.S. employees and students to work in Japan for Japanese corporations and government agencies for periods of time.

Overall, Japan must continue to internationalize, for its own sake and for the sake of the rest of the world. By playing an increasingly proactive role in world events, Japan can help increase global opportunities. Unbounded global growth is, we believe, a very real and achievable goal. We define that as a win/win world—not a situation where one nation wins at the expense of another. Japan is presently in a position of historical consequence. It is possible for Japan now to play the role of capital exporter to the rest of the world in the fashion of the United States during most of the twentieth century and Britain throughout the nineteenth.

Japan and America's leadership should propose the striking of strategic, carefully designed alliances between U.S. and Japanese industry on the co-development of key emerging technologies: high-definition television (HDTV), fiber optics applications, space exploration, high-speed aeronautics, and superconductors, to name a few. Such a dramatic and historical embrace would provide numerous positive results for both nations. The worldwide markets created through such joint enterprise, we believe, would eclipse the lesser opportunities resulting from an adversarial approach. Research and development efforts and costs could be rationalized. Technology breakthroughs could be spectacular and the business climate created would be mutually beneficial.

A BRIGHT SHINING FUTURE

We live in an extraordinary time of world history. It is a time of hope, of unfolding dramas, of anticipation. The stifling yoke of communism is being broken in country after country. Our global economic system is becoming highly integrated, our markets interdependent. And this symbiosis is a product of how the world has changed. Political, technological, and economic power has dispersed horizontally throughout the world. What this boils down to is the difference between international trade and a global economy. International trade has existed for a millennium—since before the time of the Phoenicians. And throughout recorded history, the world has known great centers of such trade like Venice and Constantinople, and now New York and Tokyo. But a global economy is different. Peter Drucker differentiates the two this way:

> In an international economy there are no common appetites, no common demands and only a minimum of common information. Each country in an international economy is a separate unit with its own economic values and preferences, its own markets, and its own largely self-contained information. Today's world economy, however, owes almost nothing to political imagination. The demands, the appetites, and the values are preceding, by a good margin, even the creation of trading units.[2]

In other words, the common needs of our world have created a nearly unified marketplace that has superceded—temporarily—an appropriate geopolitical apparatus. Our world simply cannot afford a war of goods. Economic chaos would ruin the balance that binds neighbor to neighbor. For Japan and America together, our collective goal should be to grow the global economy. The two leading economic powers, along with an expanding Europe, must and can work in cooperation to expand global opportunities. Yes, it is an extraordinary time in history, it is a time of hope, but that hope must be liberally buttressed with courage. Each of us has a role to play, for deep down, we know that we will achieve greater ends if we each work to build more doors, not more walls.

Appendix A

Selected Foreign Subsidiary Performance in Japan, 1987–88 Estimates

Company (alphabetical listing)	Employees in Japan	Employees Worldwide	%	Revenues in Japan ($ in thousands)	Revenues Worldwide ($ in millions)	%
Ajinomoto-General Foods (AGF)	1,000	113,000	8.85	556,140	31,000	1.79
ALCOA Japan, Ltd.	21	35,700	0.05	2,000	5,487	0.03
AMD Japan, Ltd.	180	10,597	1.70	35,000	997	3.51
American Express International	3,500	100,188	3.49	800,000	22,934	3.48
AMP Japan, Ltd.	1,050	21,800	4.81	362,143	2,318	5.62
Amway Japan, Ltd.	450	7,000	6.43	533,571	1,800	29.61
Analog Devices, K.K.	230	5,400	4.24	52,521	370	14.05
Apple Computer Japan, Inc.	60	9,000	0.66	1,178	4,070	0.27
Applied Materials Japan	310	1,765	17.56	135,165	362	37.26
Austin Rover Japan, Ltd.	200	70,697	0.28	14,523	2,021	0.71
Avon Products Co., Ltd.	1,715	34,500	4.97	154,757	2,763	5.57
Banyu Pharmacuet (Merke)	2,700	31,100	8.68	554,664	5,061	10.95
BASF Japan, Ltd.	370	133,759	0.27	378,378	24,960	1.51
BMW Japan Corp.	540	54,861	0.98	667,580	11,035	6.04
Baxter, Ltd.	832	61,000	1.36	242,014	6,223	3.80
Bayer Japan, Ltd.	420	164,400	0.25	260,000	23,026	1.13
Bayer Yakuhin	1,300	164,400	0.79	234,000	40,500	0.57

Company (alphabetical listing)	Employees in Japan	Employees Worldwide	%	Revenues in Japan ($ in thousands)	Revenues Worldwide ($ in millions)	%
Beckman Instruments, Inc.	201	36,323	0.55	35,714	4,749	0.75
Bosch, K.K.	230	160,000	0.14	143,521	15,746	0.91
Bristol-Myers	1,140	34,900	3.26	380,000	5,401	7.00
Campbell Japan, Inc.	20	46,976	0.01	15,000	4,490	0.33
Ciba-Geigy Japan, Ltd.	2,088	86,109	2.42	786,300	12,059	6.52
Cincinnati Milacron International	25	9,253	0.27	20	828	2.50
Coca-Cola Japan	684	28,030	2.44	2,000,000	7,658	26.11
Corning Japan, K.K	130	25,100	0.52	37,000	2,068	1.78
Cray Research Japan, Ltd.	85	4,000	2.12	20,000	687	2.80
Dana Japan, Ltd.	7	37,500	0.01	1,240	4,142	0.02
Dow Chemical Japan, Ltd.	342	53,100	0.64	207,328	16,682	1.24
Dow Corning	170	7,000	2.43	35,078	1,303	2.69
DuPont Japan	980	140,145	0.68	575,714	32,917	1.75
DuPont Showa Denko	270	140,145	0.22	50,000	32,917	0.46
Eastman Kodak Japan, Ltd.	192	124,400	0.15	120,000	17,034	0.70
Eli Lilly Japan, K.K.	283	25,700	0.01	25,714	4,069	0.63
Emerson Japan, Ltd.	350	70,000	0.50	129,486	6,170	2.09
Esso Sekiyu, K.K.	1,300	100,000	1.30	3,691,157	84,116	4.38
Estée Lauder, K.K.	650	10,000	6.50	360,000	1,500	24.00
Flour International, Inc.	10	25,100	0.04	5,600	5,132	0.09
Ford Motor Co. Japan, Ltd.	200	350,300	0.00	40,000	82,193	0.04
Fuji Xerox	12,646	99,032	12.70	2,977,078	10,866	27.40
Grace Japan, Ltd.	300	41,400	0.72	56,328	4,515	1.25
Heinz Japan, K.K.	250	47,000	0.50	62,000	5,244	1.10
Hoechst Japan, Ltd.	1,700	167,781	1.01	589,286	23,308	2.52
IBM Japan, Ltd.	20,630	387,112	5.33	8,484,621	59,681	14.21
ICI Japan	290	127,800	0.23	—	11,123	—
Intel Japan K.K.	366	16,800	2.18	307,143	1,907	16.10
IPI Corporation (International Paper)	150	45,000	0.32	—	7,800	—
Japan Tupperware Co., Ltd.	590	113,000	0.52	—	31,113	—
Japan UpJohn (45 Sumitomo)	770	20,500	3.76	205,143	2,521	8.14
Johnson Co., Ltd.	590	12,300	4.80	211,071	1,500	14.07
Johnson & Johnson, K.K.	461	78,200	0.59	88,707	8,012	1.10
Kasei Hoescht Co., Ltd.	218	167,781	0.07	70,364	36,956	0.19
Kellogg Japan, K.K.	185	17,383	1.06	34,286	3,793	0.90
Kentucky Fried Chicken, (Japan), Ltd.,	936	225,000	0.42	311,536	13,007	2.39
Kodak Japan, Ltd.	570	124,400	0.46	500,000	17,030	2.94
Levi Strauss Japan, K.K.	102	44,000	0.23	24,286	2,820	4.40
Max Factor, K.K.	480	24,700	1.94	225,000	2,456	9.16

Company (alphabetical listing)	Employees in Japan	Employees Worldwide	%	Revenues in Japan ($ in thousands)	Revenues Worldwide ($ in millions)	%
McDonald's Co. Japan, Ltd.	2,650	169,000	1.57	1,092,590	5,566	19.60
Mead-Toppan	97	20,600	0.47	41,143	4,209	0.97
Measurex Japan, Ltd.	67	2,540	2.64	5,000	227	6.60
Mercedes-Benz Japan Co.	191	326,288	0.05	—	41,817	—
Merck Japan, Ltd.	175	8,606	2.03	61,678	6,000	102.97
Mitsubishi Monsanto	1,357	51,702	2.62	458,378	7,639	6.00
Mobil Sekiyu, K.K.	1,283	127,400	1.00	4,162,035	56,716	7.34
Molex Japan	1,030	5,900	17.46	174,635	502	34.78
Monsanto Japan, Ltd.	247	51,703	0.48	106,450	7,639	1.39
NCR Japan, Ltd.	4,332	62,000	6.98	782,264	5,641	13.86
Nestlé, K.K.	2,300	163,030	1.41	1,435,714	27,803	5.16
Nihon Data General Corp.	876	15,565	5.62	122,143	1,364	8.95
Nihon Digital Equipment	2,700	94,700	2.85	521,428	9,389	5.55
Nihon Michelin Tire Co., Ltd.	118	11,500	1.02	—	43,420	—
Nihon Philips Corp.	320	329,700	0.10	971,428	28,370	3.40
Nihon Sun Microsystems	120	8,500	1.41	20,000	1,078	11.13
Nihon Unisys	7,686	98,300	7.81	1,196,521	9,713	12.31
Nippon Coleman Co., Ltd.	10	5,400	0.18	4,300	502	0.85
Nippon Goodyear, K.K.	190	114,658	0.16	115,021	10,994	1.04
Nippon Hoescht Co., Ltd.	313	167,781	0.19	58,264	23,308	0.25
Nippon Lever, K.K.	800	298,000	0.27	428,571	30,488	1.40
Nippon Motorola, Ltd.	2,048	101,700	2.01	242,857	8,250	2.94
Nippon Otis Elevator Co.	1,800	193,500	0.93	249,093	7,700	1.40
Nippon Roche, K.K.	1,600	47,498	3.37	283,571	5,350	5.30
Olivetti Corp. of Japan	1,260	58,067	2.17	167,021	73,755	0.22
Pfizer MSP, K.K.	90	40,000	0.22	—	4,920	—
Philip Morris, K.K.	80	113,000	0.07	—	31,113	—
Prime Computer Japan, Inc.	140	8,621	1.62	30,000	961	3.12
Procter & Gamble Far East, Inc.	1,242	76,200	1.63	—	19,336	—
Rawlings Japan Co., Ltd.	2	12,500	0.00	5,814	803	0.72
Raychem, K.K.	65	10,000	0.65	22,414	1,095	2.04
Revlon	900	24,700	3.64	—	2,456	—
Rockwell International Overseas Corp.	14	116,148	0.01	—	11,946	—
Samsung Japan Co., Ltd.	210	4,300	4.88	575,000	27,386	2.09
Shin Caterpillar Mitsubish, Ltd.	6,370	53,770	11.84	1,513,814	10,423	14.52
Siemens, K.K.	375	359,000	0.10	102,221	34,129	0.29
SmithKline & Fujisawa, K.K.	609	36,323	1.67	—	4,749	—
Sony Tektronix Corp.	950	20,252	4.63	182,142	1,412	12.89

Company (alphabetical listing)	Employees in Japan	Employees Worldwide	%	Revenues in Japan ($ in thousands)	Revenues Worldwide ($ in millions)	%
Squibb Japan, Inc.	440	16,915	2.60	85,714	2,588	3.31
Storage Technology of Japan	70	8,608	0.81	17,857	673	2.65
Sumitomo 3M	2,135	82,818	2.57	729,157	10,581	6.89
Tandem Computers	106	5,700	1.86	62,493	1,036	6.03
Tandy Electronics Japan Co.	109	36,000	0.30	207,142	3,452	6.00
Teisan, K.K. (L'Air Liquide SA)	967	25,000	3.86	322,421	20,639	1.56
Teradyne, K.K.	160	4,750	3.37	30,950	377	8.20
Texas Instruments Japan, Ltd.	4,700	78,000	6.02	720,943	5,595	12.88
Thompson Japan, K.K.	65	90,000	0.07	56,542	12,566	0.45
Toray Silicone (Dow Corning)	685	7,000	9.78	181,971	1,303	13.96
Toshiba Silicon (GE, 49%)	650	300,000	0.21	142,857	38,820	0.36
Upjohn Pharmacueticals	223	20,500	1.08	—	2,521	—
Volkswagen Asia, Ltd.	20	260,458	0.01	—	33,616	—
Volvo Japan Corp.	279	77,800	0.36	17,400	5,752	0.11
Warner-Lambert, K.K.	590	53,200	1.10	235,000	3,485	6.74
Wilson Japan, Inc.	52	5,000	1.04	26,728	400	6.68
Yametake-Honeywell Co., Ltd.	3,697	78,097	4.73	683,071	6,679	10.22
Yokogawa-Hewlett-Packard, Ltd.	3,000	87,000	3.44	834,443	9,831	8.48
Yokogawa Medical (GE, 75%)	988	300,000	0.33	151,071	38,820	0.38

SOURCES: "Foreign Affiliated Companies in Japan," *Toyo Keizai Shinposha*, 1989; "You Can Make Money in Japan," *Fortune* (February 12, 1990), p. 85.

Appendix B

Japanese Corporations with the Most Potential for Growth in the 1990s

Businessman's Pick	*Consumers' Pick*
1. NEC	1. Sony
2. Sony	2. Japan Travel Bureau
3. Honda Motor	3. Bridgestone
4. Kyocera	4. Kinki Nippon Tourist
5. Asahi Chemical Industry	5. Tokyo Electric Power
6. Fujitsu	6. Mizuno
7. IBM Japan	7. Honda Motor
8. Bridgestone	8. NEC
9. Toyota Motor	9. Asahi Chemical Industry
10. Fuji Photo Film	10. IBM Japan
11. Nomura Securities	11. Toyota Motors
12. Ajinomoto	12. Asahi Breweries
13. KDD	13. Fujitsu
14. Hitachi	14. Seibu Department Stores
15. Nissan Motor	15. TDK
16. All Nippon Airways	16. Yamato Transport
17. Japan Satellite Broadcasting	17. Matsushita Electric Industrial
18. Mitsui & Co.	18. Nissan Motor
19. Takeda Chemical Industries	19. Japan Airlines
20. Kyowa Hakko Kogyo	20. Ajinomoto
21. Mitsubishi Corporation	21. Nomura Securities
	22. Japan Satellite Broadcasting

NOTE: Companies with whom you should be doing business.

SOURCE: Nikkei Research Institute of Industry and Market," NEC, Sony vie for Lead in Growth Potential," *Japan Economic Journal* (March 3, 1990), p. 12.

Appendix C

Economic Comparison between Japan and Other Industrial Countries

	Japan	*United States*	*West Germany*	*France*	*Canada*	*European Community*	*Korea*
Population (in millions)	122.6	246.3	61.2	55.87	25.9	324.7	42.8
Land area (1,000 sq. km.)	378	9,373	249	547	9,976	2,258	98
Gross National Product (in 1987 U.S. $ billions)	$2,387	$4,527	$1,124	$877	$411	$4,253	$131.3
Per Capital GNP (in 1987 $ U.S.)	$19,553	$18,570	$18,373	$15,759	$16,020	$13,690	$3,121
GNP growth rate	5.7%	4.4%	3.4%	3.5%	4.5%	3.0%	10.5%
Unemployment	3.0%	6.25%	8.0%	10.75%	9.0%	n.a.	n.a.
Inflation	1.3%	4.3%	2.6%	3.4%	5.3%	3.1%	n.a.
Total labor force (in millions)	60.3	121.6	n.a.	n.a.	n.a.	143.0	n.a.
National savings rates	18.3%	2.4%	11.4%	7.0%	n.a.	n.a.	n.a.
Fixed investment as percent of GDP (5 Year Avg. 1984–1988)	29.9%	14.8%				19.7%	26.9%
R&D expenditures (1987) (in millions of $ U.S.)	$62,353	$118,782	$31,642	$20,499	n.a.	n.a.	n.a.
R&D spending as % of GNP	3.29%	3.33%	3.13%	2.62%	n.a.	n.a.	n.a.
Technology balance of payments 1987 Receipts	$1,490	$22,281	$1,081	$1,348	$425	n.a.	n.a.
Payments	$1,958	$ 8,877	$2,443	$1,732	$541	n.a.	n.a.
International Reserves (in millions of $ U.S.)	$97,622	$47,800	$63,011	$29,219	$16,198	$267,488	$12,378
Net official development assistance (in millions of $ U.S.)	$9,134	$9,777	$4,700	$6,959	$2,340	n.a.	n.a.
Direct overseas investment Outstanding (1987) (in $ billions)	$77.0	$308.8	$100.0	n.a.	$46.1	n.a.	n.a.
Foreign Direct Investment in Japan FY 1988 (in U.S. $millions)		$1,774	$195	$27	$22	$824	n.a.
FY 1950–1988 (in U.S. $millions)		$6,268	$546	$202	$152	$9,244	n.a.
Imports of manufactured goods (% of total imports)	49.0%	81.6%	74.5%	77.9%	87.2%	n.a.	n.a.

	Japan	United States	West Germany	France	Canada	European Community	Korea
Foreign trade (1987)							
Exports (in millions of $ U.S.)	$231,332	$252,894	$294,165	$148,376	n.a.	$958,123	$60,696
Imports (in millions of $ U.S.)	$135,734	$413,174	$224,285	$157,625	n.a.	n.a.	$42,326
Balance (in millions of $ U.S.)	$96,386	-$160,280	$69,880	-$9,249	$8,759	n.a.	$7,659
Japan trade with major partners							
exports to— (in millions of $ U.S.)		$89,634	$15,793	$4,987	$6,424	$46,873	$15,441
imports from— (in millions of $ U.S.		$42,037	$8,101	$4,315	$8,308	$24,071	$11,811
Share of trade in OECD							
Exports	10.1%	11.2%	12.9%	6.5%	n.a.	n.a.	n.a.
Imports	6.4%	18.1%	9.7%	6.8%	n.a.	n.a.	n.a.
Passenger car production (1,000 units)	7,891	7,099	4,346	3,223	1,027	11,675	n.a.
Iron and steel industry (1,000 of metric tons)	105,681	90,650	41,021	19,004	n.a.	102,682	19,118
Dependence on foreign trade							
Exports as percent of GNP	9.3%	6.6%	26.8%	16.9%	24.2%	n.a.	39.9%
Imports as percent of GNP	6.6%	9.4%	20.7%	18.0%	23.0%	n.a.	34.6%
Energy consumption (in million metric tons of oil)	371.66	1,865.71	271.72	206.46	240.0	420.0	n.a.
Oil reserves (in billions of barrels)	0.1	33.4				7.6	n.a.
Natural gas reserves (in trillions of cu. ft.)	1.0	186.7				3.1	n.a.
Coal reserves (in billions of metric tons)	1.0	263.8				90.5	n.a.
Agriculture grain production (in million metric tons)	14.4	293.7	10.9	39.7	34.6	n.a.	n.a.
Military							
Active armed forces (1,000s)	245	2,163				2,483	n.a.
Ready reserves	46	1,637				4,565	n.a.
Defense expenditures as share of GNP	1.6%	6.5%				3.3%	n.a.

NOTE: All data 1988 unless otherwise indicated.
n.a. = not available.

SOURCES: *Wall Street Journal* (January 23, 1989); Asia Advisory Service; Japan 1990: An International Comparison, Keizai Koho Center (October 31, 1989).

Appendix D

Japan Database

1. LARGEST JAPANESE BANKS

Commercial Banks	*Assets (in millions of dollars)*	*Deposits (in millions of dollars)*
1. Dai-ichi Kangyo Bank	379.3	283.2
2. Sumitomo Bank	363.2	268.0
3. Fuji Bank	360.5	258.6
4. Mitsubishi Bank	349.0	251.1
5. Sanwa Bank	330.7	246.6
6. Industrial Bank of Japan	272.9	216.6
7. Norinchukin Bank	235.9	214.3
8. Tokai Bank	227.6	172.1
9. Mitsui Bank	211.4	152.7
10. Mitsubishi Trust and Banking	208.3	178.0
11. Bank of Tokyo	185.4	129.4
12. Long-Term Credit Bank of Japan	184.8	147.2
13. Sumitomo Trust and Banking	182.5	162.2
14. Taiyo Kobe Bank	175.5	131.8

NOTE: Ranking by assets, 1989 estimates.

SOURCE: Japan 1990: An International Comparison, Keizai Koho Center, October 31, 1989.

1. LARGEST JAPANESE BANKS (*continued*)

Trust Banks	*Deposits (in millions of dollars)*
1. Mitsubishi Trust	48,711
2. Sumitomo Trust	41,460
3. Mitsui Trust	27,147
4. Toyo Trust	22,468
5. Yasuda Trust	22,079
6. Chuo Trust	11,482
7. Nippon Trust	3,575

NOTE: Ranking by deposits, 1986 estimates, 140 yen/$.

SOURCE: Brian Robin, *Tokyo, A World Financial Centre* (London: Euromoney Publications, 1987); Ministry of Finance.

Regional Banks	*Deposits (in millions of dollars)*
1. Bank of Yokohama	31,540
2. Chiba Bank	26,250
3. Hokuriku Bank	25,890
4. Joyo Bank	25,810
5. Shizuoka Bank	25,320
6. Ashikaga Bank	23,920
7. Bank of Fukuoka	21,530
8. Hiroshima Bank	21,120
9. Hachijuni Bank	20,400
10. Gunma Bank	19,220

NOTE: Ranking by deposits, 1987 estimates, 140 yen/$.

SOURCE: Brian Robin, *Tokyo, A World Financial Centre* (London: Euromoney Publications, 1987); Ministry of Finance

2. LARGEST JAPANESE INSURANCE COMPANIES AND PENSION FUNDS

Insurance Companies	*Income (in millions of yen)*
1. Nippon Life Insurance	129,049
2. Dai-Ichi Mutual Life Insurance	115,252
3. Tokyo Marine & Fire Insurance	93,911
4. Sumitomo Mutual Life Insurance	69,932
5. Asahi Mutual Life Insurance	68,878
6. Yasuda Fire & Marine Insurance	48,039
7. National Mutual Insurance Federation of Agricultural Cooperatives	43,167
8. Taisho Marine & Fire Insurance	40,465
9. Mitsui Mutual Life Insurance	34,820
10. Meiji Mutual Life Insurance	34,785
11. Sumitomo Marine & Fire Insurance	31,708
12. Nichido Fire & Marine Insurance	27,971
13. Kyoei Life Insurance	27,438
14. Yasuda Mutual Life Insurance	23,539
15. Dai-Tokyo Fire & Marine Insurance	19,954
16. Chiyoda Mutual Life Insurance	17,846
17. Koa Fire & Marine Insurance	17,931
18. Zenrosai Cooperative	15,689
19. Fuji Fire & Marine Insurance	15,239
20. Chiyoda Fire & Marine Insurance	14,641

SOURCE: Top 1,500 Japanese Companies, *Japan Times* (Tokyo; 1988)

Pension Funds	*Fund Size (in millions of yen)*	*% of Total*
Daiwa Bank	27,803	12.2
Mitsubishi Trust Bank	22,771	10.0
Sumitomo Trust Bank	22,196	9.8
Nippon Life	21,235	9.4
Mitsui Trust Bank	19,740	8.7
Toyo Trust Bank	19,110	8.4
Yasida Trust Bank	18,914	8.3
Dai-Ichi Life	15,516	6.8
Sumitomo Life	11,295	5.0
Meiji Life	9,307	4.1
Chuo Trust Bank	7,795	3.4
Asahi Life	5,707	2.5

Pension Funds	*Fund Size (in millions of yen)*	*% of Total*
Yasuda Life	4,946	2.2
Chiyoda Life	3,706	1.6
Mitsui Life	3,679	1.6
Nippon Trust Bank	2.615	1.1
Daido Life	1,497	0.7
Fukoku Life	1,487	0.7
Nippon Dantai Life	1,466	0.6
Toho Life	1,326	0.6
Others	5,371	2.3
Total	227,482	100.0

NOTE: 1987 estimates.

SOURCE: Brian Robin, *Tokyo, A World Financial Centre* (London: Euromoney Publications, 1987); Daiwa Bank.

3. LARGEST PRIVATE JAPANESE VENTURE CAPITAL FINANCE COMPANIES

	Investments Outstanding (in millions of yen)
1. Japan Associated Finance (Jafco)	66,067
2. Nippon Investment Finance	19,209
3. Yamaichi Univen	10,407
4. Japan Enterprise Development	10,197
5. Tokyo Venture Capital	9,057
6. Nikko Venture Capital	9,000
7. Sanyo Finance	8,982
8. Diamond Capital	7,835
9. Kangyo Kakumaru Investment	6,407
10. New Japan Finance	6,000

SOURCE: Brian Robin, *Tokyo, A World Financial Centre* (London: Euromoney Publications, 1987).

4. RESEARCH INSTITUTES AND MARKETING RESEARCH FIRMS IN JAPAN

Access Nippon, Inc.
Yamaguchi Bldg, 2-8-5
Uchikanda Chiyoda-ku
Tokyo Japan 101
Publishers of market research for foreign companies entering the Japanese market.

Century Research Center
Comprehensive research involving contemporary urban problems, regional and local development studies, transportation issues, energy and resource management studies, industrial development and marketing surveys. Affiliated with Dai-Ichi Kangyo Bank and C. Itoh & Co.

Daiwa Institute of Research
Research into macro- and microeconomic trends, general management studies, capital market surveys, and securities analysis. Affiliated with Daiwa Securities Co.

Dataquest, Inc.
1290 Ridder Park Drive
San Jose, CA 95131-2398
408-437-8115
One of top marketing research firms in the United States, especially in high technology. Offices in Tokyo.

Dentsu Institute for Human Studies
Human behavioral analysis, consumer marketing research, and general marketing surveys. Affiliated with Dentsu, Inc.

InfoCom Research
Research focusing on trends in the information and communication industries, regional telecommunications development. Affiliated with Nippon Telegraph and Telephone Corp. and the Ministry of Posts and Telecommunications.

Keizai Koho Center
Japan Institute for Social and Economic Affairs
6-1 Ohtemachi 1-chome
Chiyoda-ku Tokyo 100
(03) 201-1415
Works in cooperation with the Keidanren (Japan Federation of Economic

Organizations). Publishers of numerous studies and Japan 1990: An International Comparison.

Kokusai Eigyo Joho Center
2-5 Toranomon 2-chome
Minato-ku Tokyo
(03) 586-1577
Publishers of Nippon 1990: Business Facts and Figures *and other data on international sales and marketing.*

Marketing Research Service, Inc.
Nagasaki Bldg. 3-9 Irifune
1-chome Chuo-ku Tokyo 104
(03) 552-5771
One of the largest marketing research companies with 100 employees and 1,200 registered fieldworkers. Research and publications primarily in packaging food stuffs, fashion, and retail.

Mitsubishi Research Institute
Comprehensive research and consulting specializing in macroeconomic forecasting, industry-specific analysis, corporate behavior and management, urban and regional economic analysis, data processing and database services, engineering, and computer software systems development. Affiliated with the Mitsubishi Group.

NeoConcepts, Inc.
Fremont, California
Sheridan Tatsuno, President
Excellent information providers and consultants on Japanese technology developments, semiconductor industry, and market entry.

Nielsen Marketing Research
1-1-71 Nakameguro Meguro-ku
Tokyo 153 Japan
(03) 710-6551
H. Kaki, Manager of Marketing & Sales
Since 1960 in Japan. Market tracking service and diagnostic/analytic services.

Nikkei Research, Inc.
Takasago Bldg. 3-1
Uchikanda 1-chome
Chiyoda-ku Tokyo 101
(03) 292-5151

Affiliated with the Nihon Keizai Shimbun. Specializes in market planning and research, consumer attitude and behaviorial surveys, product positioning, and corporate/brand image and product positioning.

Nikko Research Center
Research involving macro- and microeconomic forecasting, international and domestic money markets, and capital asset management. Affiliated with Nikko Securities Co.

Nomura Research Institute
Comprehensive research including macro- and microeconomic surveys, investment research, public policy analysis, consulting services, information systems development, and systems integration services. Affiliated with Nomura Securities Co.

Research and Development, Inc.
Najiko Bldg. 10-10 Tsukiji
3-chome Chuo-ku Tokyo 104
(03) 545-1411
Major marketing and research firm since 1968. From information gathering to strategy building, known for expertise in feasibility studies, market assessment, and distribution studies.

Toyo Keizai Shinposha
1-2-1 Hongokucho
Nihonbashi Chuo-ku Tokyo 103
(03)-246-5621

New York office:
65 East 55th St. 28th Floor
New York, NY 10022
212-418-7610
Publisher of Japan Company Handbook *and other good information.*

Yano Research Institute
3-9-19 Shibuya
Tokyo Japan 150
(03)-5485-4619
Publishers of Excellent Market Research including "Market Shares in Japan 1990."

5. U.S. COMPANIES LISTED ON THE TOKYO STOCK EXCHANGE

Daiwa	*Nomura*	*Yamaichi*	*Nikko*	*Others*
Citicorp	Dow Chemical	Bell Atlantic	Chase Manhattan	Merrill Lynch
First Chicago	BankAmerica	U.S. West	Waste Management	Brunswick
IBM	General Motors	Potomac Electric	Eli Lilly	
ITT	Disney	Bell South	Exxon	
Sears	Security Pacific	Scott Paper	AIG	
3M	American Express	GTE	Lincoln National	
Philip Morris	FPL Group			
Procter & Gamble	NCNB			
McDonald's	Georgia Pacific			
Eastman Kodak	The Limited			
Chrysler	J.P. Morgan			
DuPont	Anheuser-Busch			
Pepisco	NYNEX			
Ameritech	General Electric*			
Weyerhauser	AT&T			
Marriot	K Mart Corp.			
Abbott Laboratories	American Family			
General Electric*	Avon Products			
Rockwell International	Allied Signal			
S. Cal Edison	Archer-Daniels			
Occidental Petroleum	Dun & Bradstreet			
Transamerica	Borden			
Goodyear	Mobil			
Grumman	American Brands			
PPG	Warner-Lambert			
Hewlett-Packard	Texas Instruments			
Knight Ridder				
Ford Motor Co.				
Motorola				
Monsanto				
Greyhound				

*Jointly sponsored by Daiwa and Nomura.

6. SELECTED ORGANIZATIONS

Japan Development Bank

Head office:
9-1, Otemachi 1-Chome, Chiyoda-ku
Tokyo 100, Japan
(03) 270-3211

International department:
Direct Phone: (03) 244-1785
Facsimile: (03) 245-1938

Director: Satoshi Yamada
Deputy Director: Lazunori Kawashima

Loan division:
Managers: Mitsuru Mizuno
Yoji Inaba
Deputy
Managers: Yoshikazu Niwa
Kazuhiko Shioyama

New York representative office:
575 Fifth Avenue, 28th Floor
New York, NY 10017, U.S.A.
Phone: (212) 949-7550
Facsimile: (212) 949-7588
Chief Representative: Masashi Iwaki
Representives: Masahisa Koyama
Yoshinori Fukaya

JAFCO—Japan Associated Finance Company, Ltd.
10th Floor Toshiba Bldg.
1-1-1 Shibaura
Minato-ku Tokyo 105
03-456-5101
President: Kunio Takai

555 California St.
24 Floor Suite 2450
San Francisco, CA 94104-1785
(415) 788-0706
Manager: Tom Shiraishi

Ministry of International Trade and Industry
Overseas Public Affairs Office
3-1 Kasumigaseki 1-chome
Chiyoda-ku
Tokyo 100 Japan
(03) 501-1657
Source for data on Japanese government and industry.

Japan International Trade Organization
1221 Avenue of the Americas
New York, NY 10020
Excellent source for advice and information on Japan and trade opportunities.

American Chamber of Commerce in Japan (ACCJ)
7 Floor Fukide No. 2 Bldg.
1-21 Toranomon 4-chome
Minato-ku Tokyo 105
(03)-433-5381
Facsimile: 011-81-3-436-1446
Executive Director: Richard E. Cropp

Commercial Attaché U.S. Embassy
105 Akasaka 1-chome
Minato-ku Tokyo 107

American Electronics Association (AEA)
5201 Great American Parkway
Santa Clara, CA 95054
(408) 987-4200
Tokyo office:
Kiocho Nambu Bldg. 3F
3-3 Kioicho
Chiyoda-ku Tokyo 102
(03) 237-7195

Japan Society of Northern California
350 Sansome Street Suite 630
San Francisco CA 94104
415-986-4383
Executive Director: Thomas A. Wilkins

Japan Western Association
c/o SRI International
333 Ravenswood Ave.
Menlo Park, CA 94025
Executive Director: Ms. Karen Yorke
415-859-3602

Japan-U.S. Business Council
1-6-1 Ohtemachi Rm. 772
Chiyoda-ku Tokyo 100
(03) 216-5823

Manufactured Imports Promotion Organization
World Import Mart Bldg., 6F
P.O. Box 2129 Sunshine City

Toshima-ku Tokyo 170
U.S.-Japan Trade Association

Kinokuniya Book Stores of America Co., Ltd.
Japan Center- Kinokuniya Building
1581 Webster Street
San Francisco CA 94115-9948
Best source of books and magazines in North America.

7. RECOMMENDED PUBLICATIONS

Japan Economic Journal (Weekly)
Nihon Keizai Shimbun, Inc.
1-9-5 Ohtemachi
Chiyoda-ku Tokyo 100-66
(03) 270-0251

OCS America, Inc.
5 East 44th Street
New York, NY 10017
Best weekly information source on Japan available.

The Asian Wall Street Journal (Weekly)
200 Liberty Street, New York, NY 10281
(212) 416-2000
Good weekly 5–6 page section on Japan.

JEI Report (Weekly)
Japan Economic Institute
1000 Connecticut Avenue, Washington, DC 20036
202-296-5633
Detailed following of Japanese economy and business.

Far Eastern Economic Review (Weekly)
Occasional good articles on Japan.

The Japan Times (Weekly International Edition)
5750 Wilshire Blvd., Suite 287
Los Angeles, CA 90036
213-937-3067
800-446-0200
Compilation of all articles in Japan Times in Japan.

Journal of Japanese Trade and Industry (Bi-monthly)
Japan Economic Foundation
Journal Information Center
52 Vanderbilt Ave.
New York, NY 10017
A little dry for a magazine but has occasional good articles on Japanese companies and technologies.

Business Tokyo (Monthly)
(published by Keizaikai Co., Ltd.)
2-13-18 Minami Aoyama
Minato-ku Tokyo 107
(03) 423-8500

104 Fifth Avenue
New York, NY 10011
212-633-1880
Excellent source of market ideas and foreign success stories.

Journal of Japanese Industry and Trade (Monthly)
Tokyo Japan
Feature articles on Japanese economy and industry.

Journal of the American Chamber of Commerce of Japan (Monthly)
American Chamber of Commerce of Japan
7 Fl. Fukide No. 2 Bldg.
1-21 Toranomon 4-chome
Minato-ku Tokyo 105
03-433-5381
Magazine on business for American community in Japan.

Japan Company Handbook (Bi-annual)
Toyo Kaizai Shinposha, Ltd.
(The Oriental Economist)
1-2-1 Hongokuchu Nihonbashi
Chuo-ku Tokyo 103
03-246-5470

65 East 55th St. 28th Floor
New York, NY 10022
212-418-7610
Detailed Reports on 3,000 Japanese companies.

Japan Economic Almanac (Yearly)
The Japan Economic Journal

Nihon Keizai Shimbun, Inc.
1-9-5 Ohtemachi
Chiyoda-ku Tokyo 100-66
(03) 270-0251
Yearly overview of Japanese economy.

Market Shares in Japan (Yearly)
Yano Research Institute
3-9-19 Shibuya
Tokyo Japan 150
TEL: (03) 5485-4619
Detailed listing of marketshares in 1,400 product areas.

Japan 1990: An International Comparison
Keizai Koho Center
Japan Institute for Social Affairs
6-1 Ohtemachi 1-chome
Chiyoda-ku Tokyo 100 Japan
(03) 201-1415
Details and data on Japanese economy.

8. COMPARISON OF PATENT SYSTEMS IN JAPAN, THE UNITED STATES, AND EUROPE

Item	*Japan*	*U.S.A.*	*Europe (European Patent Treaty)*
I. Related to Application			
1. Applications	Principle of "first-to-file"	Principle of "first-to-invent"	Principle of "first-to-file"
2. Applications in foreign language	Not possible	Possible (presentation of translation within two months)	Not possible (limited to official languages of member countries)
3. Exceptions to lack of novelty	Conditions for application of exceptions: six months before application, testing, publication of findings, written presentation before academic societies, exhibition in fairs, and presentation against will	One year before application; no limitation on subject matter (sufficient to apply within one year after presentation)	Six months before application Exhibition in fairs and presentation against will
4. Inventor indicated	Cannot be waived	Cannot be waived	Cannot be waived (some countries allow rejection by domestic law; example: West Germany)
5. License based on prior use	Yes	No	Yes (in accord with domestic law)
II. Related to Review			
1. Publication of application and right of provisional protection	Application is published eighteen months from date of filing, and right of provisional protection is established.	No	Application made public eighteen months from date of application (right of provisional protection is found in laws of each nation.)
2. Request for review	Within seven years of date of filing	No	Six months after publication of search report

(*continued*)

8. COMPARISON OF PATENT SYSTEMS (*continued*)

Item	*Japan*	*U.S.A.*	*Europe (European Patent Treaty)*
3. Cause for refusal of patent	Things produced through nuclear transformation, things which may endanger public morals or health	Related to nuclear weapons	Things which are related to changing species or the matter of growth in animals or plants, and things considered to endanger public morals
4. Effect of previous technology	Exclusionary regulations do not allow extension to same applicant or same discoverer (with regard to novelty, entire detailed description is effective from date of precedence)	No exclusionary regulations (both novelty and improvements have effect from the date of application for detailed descriptions, and from the date of precedence for claims)	No exclusionary regulation (with regard to novelty, entire detailed descriptions are effective from the date of precedence
5. Protest system	Yes (within three months from date of filing notice)	No	Yes (within nine months from granting of patent)
III. Related Patent Rights			
1. Periods of patent	Fifteen years from date of notification (not to exceed twenty years from date of application)	Seventeen years from date of patent issuance	Twenty years from date of application
2. Maintenance fees	Patent maintenance fees	Patent maintenance fees	Application maintenance fees
3. Effect of patent for manufacturing processes	Extend to things manufactured in accordance with a patented manufacturing process; if novelty applies, requirement for providing proof in event of enchroachment	Extend to things manufactured in accordance with a patented manufacturing process; if novelty applies, requirement for providing proof in event of enchroachment	Extend to things manufactured in accordance with a patented manufacturing process; if novelty applies, requirement for providing proof in event of enchroachment.
4. Patent voiding	Can request adjudication for voiding	Readjudication request system; can claim that is void as means of defense from enchroachment suit	Yes (in accord with domestic law)
5. Revisions after granting of patent	Claims cannot be expanded	Claims can be expanded (within two years from date patent is granted)	Claims cannot be expanded

SOURCE: "Nippon 1990: Business Facts and Figures," ***Kokusai Eigyo Jobo Center*** (Tokyo, 1990).

Appendix E

Largest Japanese Companies by Industry

	Electrical Equipment	*1988 Profits In Millions of Yen*
1	IBM Japan	170,630
2	Matsushita Electric Industrial	137,839
3	Hitachi	88,684
4	Nippondenso	69,807
5	NEC (Nippon Electric)	44,329
6	Toshiba	40,948
7	Matsushita Electric Works	39,267
8	Sharp	37,599
9	Kyocera	35,556
10	Sony	35,063
11	TDK	31,940
12	Fanuc	31,554
13	Mitsubishi Electric	28,996
14	Fujitsu	22,824
15	Murata Manufacturing	20,317
16	Hitachi Maxell	20,217
17	Matsushita Battery Industry	16,807
18	Matsushita Communication Industrial	16,181
19	Victor Company of Japan	14,791
20	Nitto Electric Industrial	13,732

	Precision Instruments	*In Millions of Yen*
1	Canon	20,419
2	Terumo	11,105
3	Olympus Optical	9,655
4	Shimadzu Seisakusho	9,295
5	Minolta Camera	6,841
6	Yokokawa Medical System	4,803
7	Citizen Watch	3,919
8	Yuhshin	3,026
9	Mitsutoyo Mfg.	2,969
10	Mutoh Industries	2,888
11	Horiba	2,765
12	Nippon Kogaku	2,500
13	Japan Medical Supply	2,368
14	Ishida Scales Mfg.	2,336
15	Noritsu Koki	2,321
16	Tokyo Optical	2,215
17	Chinon Industries	2,152
18	Graphtec	1,841
19	Kimmon Mfg.	1,685
20	Fuji Photo Optical	1,545

	Crude Petroleum and Natural Gas Production	*In Millions of Yen*
1	Arabian Oil	65,290
2	Teikoku Oil	7,303
3	Abu Dhabi Oil	4,873
4	United Resources Industry	4,019
5	Japan Petroleum Exploration	3,450
6	Indonesia Petroleum	3,039
7	Zaire Petroleum	3,030
8	Kanto Natural Gas Development	2,301
9	Kyoei Kosan	1,821
10	Japan Petroleum Offshore	1,040
11	C. Itoh Energy Development	712
12	Toho Natural Gas	680
13	United Petroleum Development	275
14	Nihon Tennen Gas Kogyo	189
15	Hokuriku Tennen Gas Kogyo	97
16	Osadano Gas Center	66
17	Jomo Tennen Gas Kogyo	60
18	Zaiken Bussan	47
19	Kushiro Coal Kanryu	47
20	Akita-ken Gas Seizo	—

	Equipment Installation	In Millions of Yen
1	Kanto Denkikoji	24,624
2	Kinki Electrical Construction	22,975
3	Ryoden Service	18,320
4	Hitachi Elevator Engineering & Service	14,648
5	Chugoku Electrical Construction	12,915
6	Tokai Electrical Construction	10,272
7	Hitachi Electronics Service	9,801
8	Shinryo Air Conditioning	7,390
9	Kyushu Denkikoji	5,834
10	Kyowa Densetsu	4,977
11	Kanden Kogyo	4,690
12	Toshiba Engineering & Construction	4,495
13	Takasago Thermal Engineering	4,388
14	Nippon Densetsu Kogyo	4,321
15	Nippon Telecommunications Construction	4,100
16	Toyo Engineering	4,088
17	Toko Electronic Construction	4,009
18	Sanki Engineering	3,978
19	Hitachi Plant Engineering & Construction	3,836
20	Chuden Koji	3,804

	Transportation Equipment	In Millions of Yen
1	Toyota Motor	427,558
2	Nissan Motor	116,312
3	Honda Motor	77,746
4	Mitsubishi Heavy Industries	38,120
5	Suzuki Motor	21,791
6	Aisin Seiki	16,816
7	Daihatsu Motor	12,761
8	Toyoda Automatic Loom Works	11,989
9	Fuji Heavy Industries	11,061
10	Aishin-Warner	9,894
11	Futaba Industrial	6,555
12	Nihon Radiator	5,139
13	Toyoda Gosei	5,060
14	Mitsubishi Motors	5,018
15	Tokyo Seat	5,014
16	Toyota Auto Body	4,560
17	Toyoda Machine Works	4,345
18	Nissan Shatai	4,010
19	Hino Motors	3,982
20	Sanden	3,374

	Wholesalers	*In Millions of Yen*
1	Mitsubishi	58,001
2	Coca-Cola (Japan)	41,994
3	Showa Shell Sekiyu	30,469
4	Sumitomo	29,007
5	Marubeni	27,576
6	Nippon Oil	23,600
7	World	23,151
8	Mitsui & Co.	18,978
9	Hanwa	17,893
10	Matsushita Electric Trading	16,038
11	Mobil Sekiyu	15,667
12	Idemitsu Kosan	13,913
13	Kashiyama & Co.	13,474
14	Nissho Iwai	13,344
15	Toyoda Tsusho	11,980
16	Mitsubishi Oil	11,437
17	Suzuken	10,914
18	C. Itoh & Co.	10,855
19	Renown	10,787
20	Esso Sekiyu	10,600

	Retailers (General Merchandise)	*In Millions of Yen*
1	Ito-Yokado	49,861
2	Marui	33,585
3	Jusco	23,727
4	Nichii	19,663
5	Uny	16,961
6	Takashimaya	16,069
7	Daiei	15,493
8	Isetan	11,626
9	Izumiya	10,616
10	Seiyu	9,960
11	Matsuzakaya	9,610
12	Mitsukoshi	8,743
13	Yokohama Takashimaya	8,490
14	Sogo	7,455
15	Nagasakiya	7,012
16	Heiwado	6,719
17	Hankyu Department Stores	6,090
18	Chujitsuya	5,506
19	Tokyu Department Store	5,267
20	York-Benimaru3	4,871

	Securities and Others	*In Millions of Yen*
1	Nomura Securities	478,466
2	Daiwa Securities	286,363
3	Nikko Securities	241,727
4	Yamaichi Securities	220,692
5	Nippon Kangyo Kakumaru Securities	78,159
6	New Japan Securities	70,534
7	Kokusai Securities	64,698
8	Sanyo Securities	59,236
9	Wako Securities	57,187
10	Cosmo Securities	38,016
11	Okasan Securities	33,013
12	Universal Securities	29,512
13	Yamatane Securities	26,474
14	Tokyo Security	25,453
15	Marusan Securities	23,962
16	Dai-Ichi Securities	23,242
17	Maruman Securities	21,178
18	Nihon Sogo Shoken	19,597
19	Tokyo Stock Exchange	18,418
20	Pacific Securities	18,264

	Printing, Publishers	*In Millions of Yen*
1	Dai Nippon Printing	56,606
2	Toppan Printing	34,547
3	Nihon Keizai Shimbun	18,079
4	Kodansha Publishing	11,590
5	Shueisha Publishing	11,547
6	Chunichi Shimbun	9,937
7	Shogakukan Publishing	9,875
8	Fukutake Shoten	8,210
9	Gyosei	6,607
10	Toppan Moore	6,601
11	Gakken	6,184
12	Asahi Shimbun	5,666
13	Nikkei-McGraw-Hill	5,136
14	Kobunsha	4,814
15	Shingakusha	3,796
16	Daiichi Hoki Shuppan	3,682
17	Kumon Education Research Center	3,550
18	Magazine House	3,510
19	Shin Nihon Hoki Shuppan	3,300
20	Sangyo Keizai Shimbun-sha	3,166

	General Machinery	*In Millions of Yen*
1	Nintendo	46,835
2	Fuji Xerox	40,026
3	Ricoh	20,793
4	Kubota	19,870
5	NCR Japan	18,389
6	Heiwa Industrial	16,401
7	Makita Electric Works	15,630
8	Komatsu	14,510
9	Daikin Industries	14,150
10	Hitachi Koki	9,740
11	Murata Machinery	8,509
12	Shima Seiki Mfg.	8,438
13	Minebea	8,405
14	Babcock-Hitachi Tokyo	8,379
15	Amada	7,715
16	Komori Printing Machinery	7,445
17	Asahi Diamond Industrial	6,915
18	Diesel Kiki	6,817
19	Sankyo	6,784
20	Photo Composing Machine Mfg.	6,702

	Real Estate	*In Millions of Yen*
1	Mitsubishi Estate	55,931
2	Mitsui Real Estate Development	31,525
3	Daikyo Kanko	21,519
4	Mori Building	16,213
5	Sumitomo Realty & Development	16,085
6	Sugiyama Shoji	15,753
7	Recruit Cosmos	12,621
8	Nomura Real Estate Development	10,230
9	Mitsui Real Estate Sales	9,926
10	Kaneichi	9,110
11	Miyama	8,827
12	Tokyo Tatemono	8,559
13	Toyo Real Estate	7,821
14	Shuwa	7,348
15	Kowa Real Estate	6,766
16	Nichiei Construction	6,546
17	Tokyu LIVABLE	6,543
18	Jyutaku Ryutsu Center	6,290
19	Shinobu Sogyo	6,090
20	Iida Kensetsu Kogyo	6,089

	Road Transport (Freight)	In Millions of Yen
1	Nippon Express	26,576
2	Tokyo Sagawa Express	16,865
3	Fukuyama Transporting	11,164
4	Seino Transportation	9,194
5	Yamato Transport	7,205
6	Hitachi Express	6,709
7	Konoike Transportation	3,994
8	Chukyo Sagawa Express	3,166
9	Nippon Konpo Unyu Soko	2,873
10	Maruzen Showa Unyu	2,750
11	Tohoku Sagawa Express	2,478
12	Hokuriku Sagawa Express	2,392
13	Senko	2,268
14	Osaka Sagawa Express	1,770
15	Tonami Transportation	1,625
16	Kyushu Sagawa Express	1,615
17	Toyota Transportation	1,580
18	Nihon Yubin Transportation	1,466
19	Chugoku Sagawa Express	1,321
20	Oil Transportation	1,319

	General Construction	In Millions of Yen
1	Kajima	33,273
2	Taisei	33,101
3	Takenaka Komuten	31,713
4	Kumagai Gumi	28,924
5	Ohbayashi-Gumi	27,236
6	Shimizu Construction	25,648
7	Sekisui House	24,150
8	Daiwa House Industry	23,356
9	Fujita	22,677
10	Hasegawa Komuten	22,391
11	Toda Construction	16,382
12	Maeda Construction	13,857
13	Nishimatsu Construction	12,522
14	Okumura	12,226
15	Tobishima	12,164
16	Sato Kogyo	11,588
17	Aoki Construction	11,318
18	Penta-Ocean Construction	10,949
19	Hazama-Gumi	10,734
20	Konoike Construction	10,605

	Foodstuffs	In Millions of Yen
1	Kirin Brewery	81,938
2	Nestle	39,715
3	Ajinomoto	29,415
4	Yamazaki Baking	22,382
5	Nippon Meat Packers	19,547
6	Nissin Food Products	18,010
7	Nisshin Flour Milling	16,462
8	Snow Brand Milk Products	15,975
9	Yakult Honsha	15,230
10	Marudai Food	15,098
11	House Food Industrial	14,661
12	Suntory	14,527
13	Lotte	13,957
14	Takara Shuzo	13,380
15	Sapporo Breweries	12,452
16	Ito Ham Foods	12,353
17	Meiji Seika	10,773
18	Asahi Breweries	9,891
19	Ezaki Glico	8,959
20	Nisshin Oil Mills	8,901

	Pulp, Paper, Paper Products	In Millions of Yen
1	Oji Paper	27,674
2	Kokuyo	15,756
3	Jujo Paper	14,259
4	Mitsubishi Paper Mills	13,687
5	Daishowa Paper Mfg.	13,560
6	Taio Paper Mfg.	12,530
7	Sanyo-Kokusaku Pulp	10,924
8	Kanzaki Paper Mfg.	8,896
9	Settsu Paperboard Mfg.	8,718
10	Honshu Paper	7,534
11	Kishu Paper	6,223
12	Gotemba Tetra Pak	5,056
13	Hokuetsu Paper Mills	4,915
14	Chuetsu Pulp Industry	4,636
15	Seishin Tetra Park	4,075
16	Maruzumi Paper Mfg.	3,984
17	Tokan Kogyo	3,879
18	Rengo	3,718
19	Tokushu Paper Mfg.	3,223
20	Shikoku Paper Mfg.	2,869

	Chemicals	*In Millions of Yen*
1	Fuji Photo Film	124,557
2	Takeda Chemical Industries	67,257
3	Yamanouchi Pharmaceutical	53,401
4	Taisho Pharmaceutical	34,182
5	Daiichi Seiyaku	34,177
6	Shionogi & Co.	33,810
7	Sankyo (Seiyako)	32,360
8	Kao	31,125
9	Eisai	28,268
10	Mitsubishi Petrochemical	26,442
11	Ono Pharmaceutical	26,141
12	Fujisawa Pharmaceutical	26,177
13	Asahi Chemical Industry	25,825
14	Chugai Pharmaceutical	24,168
15	Otsuka Pharmaceutical	23,775
16	Sumitomo Chemical	22,239
17	Kyowa Hakko Kogyo	21,841
18	Kureha Chemical Industry	21,384
19	Taiho Pharmaceutical	21,129
20	Tanabe Seiyaku	20,776

	Electricity	*In Millions of Yen*
1	Tokyo Electric Power	519,961
2	Chubu Electric Power	319,428
3	Kansai Electric Power	318,478
4	Tohoku Electric Power	133,206
5	Kyushu Electric Power	128,318
6	Chugoku Electric Power	61,200
7	Shikoku Electric Power	53,291
8	Hokuriku Electric Power	49,326
9	Hokkaido Electric Power	36,293
10	Okinawa Electric Power	16,018
11	Electric Power Development	3,802
12	Japan Atomic Power	2,198
13	Fukui Joint Power	1,156
14	Fukuyama Joint Power	839
15	Tobata Joint Power	539
16	Tokyo Electric Generation	503
17	Mizushima Joint Power	306
18	Oita Joint Power	285
19	Wakayama Joint Power	259
20	Sakai Kyodo Power	201

SOURCE: Top 1,500 companies in Japan, *Japan Times* (Tokyo, 1988).

Appendix F

Japanese Business Meetings and Etiquette

Upon entering meetings in Japan, it is good to convey some greetings from management back home in headquarters, and to mention past meetings between your management. The start of the meeting is also a time to comment on changes in organization, relocation, or promotions, and to acknowledge mutual acquaintances and personal interests such as golf or baseball. Japanese feel it is very important to clearly understand the hierarchy and how you and your organization fit into the larger scheme of things. It is impressive also to show that you have researched the Japanese company and can mention some recent announcements in the newspaper, or new R&D accomplishments.

The Japanese side should always be given time to give an overview of the company and the activities of their particular division—sales history, number of employees, growth, and past relationship with the guest of the host company. A frequent downfall is that many American companies merely come to the meeting, hurry through introductions, rush into a long unidirectional overhead or slide presentation, answer a few questions, then go away, never getting to know the person across the table. There are so many meetings we have seen with Americans selling some project to a Japanese company where they never schedule the time for a similar presentation by the Japanese. Meetings in Japan are not just to present information and discuss contract conditions, but to build relationships, get a feeling for the people, and develop understanding and trust.

It is impressive to Japanese if you can recall details of previous meetings, and is good to take minutes during the meeting, and then compare notes to ensure each side has the same understanding. These notes can later be used to review what was said previously in future meetings and correspondence. While many of these points do seem obvious, we are continually perplexed by the lack of preparation, sensitivity, and application of basic negotiating tools by most foreign companies when dealing with large, multibillion-dollar professional Japanese companies. You can bet they are prepared and are getting the details straight.

Emphasizing human relations and working together is at the root of Japanese business; and it will be these good relations which will flavor or poison your relations over the years. Always emphasize:

- Human relations and building of understanding and trust; willingness to establish a genuine relationship both commercially and personally
- Founders and history, mutual company philosophies
- Stability of the management and persons in charge of the project
- Key personnel related to the project, and who has best contact between the organizations
- Sales records, commitment, and major activities in Japan
- Appreciation for the merits of company visited
- Stress that "you would be honored" to have the chance to meet again, visit their factory, or receive a mission from them
- Create an atmosphere of trust, adopt a humble role, avoid the hard sell, but be quietly forceful

Working toward a mutual goal with a traditional Japanese company can often end in failure—not due to any term or condition of the contract, product specification or quality, or lack of sales or production capability. Failure can occur merely because of more "soft and wet" issues like conflicts in company structures and philosophy, and distrust of personalities. Other substantive reasons often cited are differing time frames (long- versus short-term profitability), misunderstanding of the true capabilities of the partner's ability to succeed, and his ability to build consensus within his own organization and in garnering support from the many company factions. If you don't know your partner inside and out, get the advice of an insider who has past experience with the company and people you are dealing with.

Contracts, like credit cards, are still foreign to many Japanese and are usually an afterthought. Personal trust and integrity are most important as the Japanese prefer to trust people rather than paper. You must come to the realization that in the long term the real benefits will come from an enduring relationship. It is quite true that Japanese rarely read contracts after they are signed and filed.

Many Japanese who have spent their lifetimes in Japan still can not get all the nuances and verb forms correct, but there are a few simple things like politeness in introductions, customs in giving business cards, seating at meetings, gift giving, and greeting cards, that are repeated so often and which can go a long way toward increasing *anshin,* or comfort and security, with Japanese customers.

Business cards, or *meishi,* are an honored custom in Japan. To a large extent, *meishi* are used to determine a stranger's place and position in the world—something very important to Japanese who look for structure and clues on how to bow, the level of respect in language required, and other customs such as gift giving. Always have enough translated business cards before you go to Japan to meet with a number of large groups. At the very beginning of any meeting cards are exchanged before sitting down. You exchange a card with everyone you have not met before, beginning with the most senior executives, and then working down the hierarchy. Cards are exchanged in the entryway, the hall, or in the meeting room and always face to face—never across the table. It is important that there is nothing between you and the person you are meeting.

Customers always receive the card first, and the giver should present his card with a bow, holding the card in both hands, then accepting a card with the right hand. If it is not a customer-supplier relationship, being a guest or having more seniority in position and age will determine who should receive the card first. After accepting with the right hand, give another respectful bow or nod of the head to show respect, then you should read the card—taking this time to understanding the man's position, what part of the company he is in, and some understanding of his position in society. Never exchange business cards with the same person twice, unless you or they have a new title or address.

After exchanging cards and introductions, a handshake is proper. A comment at this time about a change of address, the last time you met, or a fellow friend he may be working with is also fine. Taking time in these introductions, and presenting your card the correct side up and in a respectful manner is very important. Most Japanese will then tend to arrange the cards in order on the table in front of them for reference during the meeting.

Upon entering a room for a meeting with Japanese, it is important to have the proper order in seating. In all cases, the guests should be seated on the side of the table opposite the door, with the most important person in the middle of the group but farthest from the entryway. Always motion your guests to these positions of honor, and they will then figure among themselves the seating placement in their hierarchy. Your giving to them the far side of the table shows respect for hierarchy and "correct place," and also enables any Japanese joining the meeting later to easily understand the power structure and positions of people around the table.

Whenever your company makes a visit to major customers in Japan, or those with whom you would like to do business in the future, bringing a number of gifts is a good idea to create a good feeling and some minor *on,* or obligation. A specialty from your local area or something unavailable in Japan is most appropriate. Gifts should be sensitive of rank and the interests and hobbies of the receiver. It is a good idea to keep a record so you do not give the same gift twice, or the same gift to two people of obviously disparate positions. In fact, many executives keep a simple database on their computer. In general, gifts are given by the host at the end of the visit, and by the guests in either the beginning or the end; a good time is when you walk them to their car.

In Japan one of the most important and established social customs is to send *Nenkajo* (greeting cards) to celebrate *Shogatsu,* or the coming of the new year. Each year at this time, the mailboxes and post offices are clogged with greeting cards to friends, family, and most of all business customers, suppliers, and partners. This practice of sending *Nenkajo* is often criticized as having become too commercial, with many people running address labels off large computer-generated databases and mass shipping, thus clogging the entire mail system for two weeks. However, it is a very important tradition and a *must* for any company doing business in Japan. The custom of *Nenkajo* also provides a way to keep track of your associates around the world and their promotions and relocations each year, and annually defines for many Japanese the inner and outer circles of friends and those in their business network. The same custom of card giving is used extensively for communicating news of marriages and births, and other special events like graduations.

There are a few other points to remember when working with the Japanese. While meeting with a potential partner, it is taboo to mention competitors and the names of other companies you are negotiating with. As we mentioned before, keep calm and under control—don't shout, point, walk around the room, get ahead of the interpreter, stare and such. In general, Japanese are more serious in the company setting than most foreigners, and this should not be taken as a sign of unfriendliness. Boisterous humor and show of emotions, and the American-style slap-on-the-back do not go over well in Japan. Uncontrolled displays of emotion are offensive to Japanese while control and temper are highly regarded.

Don't make negative comments about Japan, or about such things as living conditions, cramped housing, congestion, crowded trains, expensive food, or the poor status of women. Sensitive areas like the Emperor, the social system, and the trade situation might also be best avoided. As always, it is better to concentrate on the positives—clean cities, no crime, quality of products, hard-work ethic, strong education system, helpful people, excellent service, and delicious food. The old saying "If you can't say something nice, don't say it" is very applicable. Even more touchy is continually telling Japanese they must change. As a certain *bucho* at Mitsui Bussan would always say, "Don't preach! If you don't like it, get out!" There is plenty that the United States can do to get its own house in order before telling the neighbors what to do.

It is a good idea to send presentations, drafts of contracts, business plans, and meeting agendas ahead of schedule so the other side can review and thoroughly understand prior to the meeting. Even details like selection of the interpreter, and preparation to ensure electrical machinery and lighting are functioning properly, are important. In general, because Japanese like to have documents read aloud, you should plan to have hard copies of your presentations available.

While these points may seem to be trivial details, Japanese life is one of tradition, ritual, and routine which, when you follow the appropriate course of etiquette, open up whole new opportunities. Customers see your company as a secure and comfortable partner and, long-term look forward to continuing to do business.

Appendix G

Glossary of Japanese Terms

ABCD Industries. Japan's primary strategic technologies for the twenty-first century: automation, biotechnology, computers, and data processing.

Amakudari. Literally, "descent from heaven," process where Japanese ministry officials join corporations as directors and advisors.

Anshin. Security, confidence; important trait to be known for by Japanese.

Bonsai. Japanese art working with miniature trees and landscapes.

Bucho. General manager.

Bucho-dairi. Assistant general manager.

Bushido. "Way of the Samurai."

Chubu. Central part of Japan centered in Nagoya.

Chusho kigyo. Small to medium-sized industry.

Dango. The closed network of contractors and subcontractors in Japanese industry; known especially in construction industry for bid-rigging and monopolization of projects.

Diet. Japanese parliment.

Edo. Tokyo in earlier centuries, i.e., the Edo era.

Endaka. High Japanese yen.

Fugu. Blow fish used in making sashimi.

Gakubutsu. A club within a company or organization of members from the same university.

Gaijin. Foreigner or, literally, outsider.

Gairojin. A Japanese who has left his Japanese company to work in a foreign corporation.

Ganbaru. To persevere, never give up.

Ginza. "Golden street" of clubs and expensive stores in downtown Tokyo.

Giri. An obligation, a duty.

Go. A Japanese board game using the placement of small stones to immobilize your opponent.

Gurupu. Industrial group of affiliated companies, e.g., Mitsui Group.

Hanko. Personal stamp or seal with a Japanese "signature" used on official documents.

Heisei. The current Japanese era following Showa.

Hempin. The tradition of returning

goods unsold to the manufacturer or wholesaler.

Hino maru. The Japanese "Rising Sun" flag.

Hisshi. Literally, "to succeed or die"; attitude of many Japanese in business and satisfying the customer.

Hokkaido. Japan's northernmost major island; the capital is Sapporo.

Honne. Real intention, one's true colors.

Honshu. Main largest island of Japan.

Ichiryu kaisha. First-tier or major leading company.

Inaka. Countryside.

Inobesion. Innovation.

Juku. Japanese college and high school entrance exam preparatory schools.

Kakujitsu (na kaisha). Reliable and trustworthy company.

Kaisha. Japanese corporation.

Kaizen. Incremental improvement.

Kami. A god.

Kanban. Japanese manufacturing technique using billboards to show live production line status.

Kansai. Southern part of Japan centered around Osaka.

Kanto. Northern part of Honshu, the main island, centered around Tokyo.

Kasumigaseki. The famous government area of Tokyo where most government offices are centered, including those of MITI and other Ministries, the Prime Minister, and the Diet.

Keidanren. Japan Federation of Economic Organizations; Japan's most influential economic policy association.

Keiretsu. Vertically integrated bank or industrial group of affiliated companies.

Kessai. Japanese company decision-making process.

Ki ga susamanai. Literally, "My spirit is not satisfied."

Kokusaika. Internationalization.

Kokusan. Products "Made in Japan."

Kyushu. Southernmost main island of Japan.

Madogiwa minzoku. The "tribe" of Japanese workers who "sit by the window" without significant responsibilities.

Manshion. Japanese apartment.

Marugakae. The Japanese company culture of "total embrace" where the corporation becomes one's provider, community, and center of an employee's life.

Meiji Restoration. Period in the late nineteenth century when Japan broke from the old ways of fuedalism to embrace modernism and opened to the outside world.

Minsei. Home electronics products market.

MITI. Ministry of International Trade and Industry.

MPT. Ministry of Post and Telecommunications.

Natto. Japanese dish of fermented soybeans.

Nemawashi. Laying the groundwork and building support for a project or idea; literally, "cutting around the roots."

Nenkajo. End of the year card.

Nihonjinron. Theory of "Japaneseness," and how the Japanese are unique from the rest of the world.

Ningen kankei. Human relations.

Nomiya. Drinking establishment.

Noren. A company's sign or name placard, usually hung in the entrace way of a restaurant or shop.

NTT. Nippon Telephone and Telegraph, the world's largest corporation.

Ocha. Japanese green tea.

Oden. A Japanese dish of boiled meats, pressed fish paste, vegetables, and assorted other foods, served primarily in the winter.

Ohte-maker. Large manufacturing company.

Oitsuke, oikose. Literally "to catch and pass the West," a Japanese saying originating in the Meiji era.

Okyakusama. A customer; literally, "honorable customer."

On. Obligation owed to society and ancestors carried by all Japanese.

Obaasan. An elderly woman.

Ringi-seido. Process of passing a proposal throughout the corporation for approval.

Ronin. A "wanderer" who is waiting to retake university entrance examinations.

Salaryman. Japanese company salaried worker.

Sashimi. Art of eating raw fish.

Senmon shosha. Specialty trading company.

Senpai-kohai. Elder–junior relationship.

Shimoda. City south of Tokyo on the Izu peninsula; site of first U.S. consulate in Japan.

Shinto. The national "religion" of Japan tracing the descent of the imperial family back from the goddess of the sun.

Shiitake. A large capped Japanese mushroom.

Shobai wa akinai. Literally, "Never give up."

Shogatsu. New Years.

Shoshaman. Employees of Japan's sogo shosha, or major trading companies.

Sogo shosha. Japanese general trading company.

Shogun. A Japanese warlord of pre-Meiji Japan.

Showa. The era of "everlasting peace," which ended in 1989 with death of Emperor Hirohito.

Takonomon. A small home shrine or garden used to pay respects to ancestors and spirits.

Tama. A natural basin or plain in which lies the city of Tokyo.

Tatemae. Professed intension.

Tegata. Promissory note for payment of goods and services rendered.

Tohoku. Nothern region of the main island of Honshu.

TQC. Total Quality Control.

Todai. Tokyo University.

Tokugawa. Ruling warlord family of Japan for many centuries until the late 1800s.

Tsukiji. Area of Tokyo famous for its fish markets.

Typhoon note. Extended 120–240 day promissory note.

Udon. Large white Japanese noodles used in a variety of soups.

Wa. Oneness, wholeness, harmony.

Yon-kyu-pa. 498 sq. meters rule for maximum size of most stores.

Zaibatsu. The pre–World War II financial empires of such groups as Mitsui, Mitsubishi, and Sumitomo.

NOTES

Introduction

1. Robert Guenther and Michael R. Sesit, "U.S. Banks Are Losing Business to Japanese at Home and Abroad," *The Wall Street Journal,* October 12, 1989, p. A12.
2. Bruce R. Scott, "Competitiveness: Self-Help for a Worsening Problem," *Harvard Business Review,* No. 4 (July–August, 1989), p. 116.
3. *San Jose Mercury News* (December 3, 1989), p. E1.
4. *San Francisco Examiner* (June 28, 1989), p. C1.
5. Bylinsky, Gene, "Where Japan Will Strike Next," *Fortune* (September 25, 1989), p. 43.

Chapter 1
Sunrise over the Pacific: The Japanese Challenge

1. *Japan Economic Journal* (November 4, 1989), p. 8.
2. Paula Doe, "MITI report pats Japan's Technologists on the back," *Electronic Business* (May 29, 1989), p. 63.
3. Karl Schoenerger, "Education Gap May Haunt U.S. Future," *San Jose Mercury* (January 28, 1990), p. PC-1.
4. Bernard Wysocki Jr., "Harvesting the Japanese Mind," *Wall Street Journal Reports* (November 14, 1988), p. 17.
5. *New York Times,* "Foreign Push for U.S. Patents" (June 4, 1989).
6. Shintaro Ishihara and Akio Morita, "The Japan That Can Say "No" (Tokyo: Kobunsha, 1989).
7. Lester Thurrow, "Paradise Lost," *New York Times* (February 24, 1988).

Chapter 2

The Japanese Way: Origins of a Merchant Nation

1. Takeshi Uchida, "A Study on Atmospheric Pressure," a speech to EC visitors in Tokyo, September 1987.
2. Excerpt from a speech by Chairman Shinto of NTT during 1986 ceremony for new employees.

Chapter 3

The Global Farmer: Inside the Japanese Market

1. Sheridan Tatsuno, *Technopolis Strategy* (New York: Random House, 1988).
2. *Business Week,* February 12, 1990, p. 75.
3. *Keiretsu and Other Large Groups in Japan,* Japan Economic Institute (JEI) Report (January 12, 1990), pp. 1–17.
4. *Japan Economic Journal* (November 11, 1989), p. 7; also Randall S. Jones, "The Japanese Distribution System," *Journal of the American Chamber of Commerce* (December 1987), p. 47.
5. William Brooks, economic attaché to U.S. Embassy in Japan in speech to Japan Western Association (January 19, 1989).
6. "Construction and the Dango," *Business Week* (April 3, 1989), p. 74.
7. Ibid.
8. *Japan Economic Journal* (November 4, 1989), p. 6.
9. *Business Tokyo* (December, 1989), p. 66.

Chapter 4

The Customer Is God: Inside the Japanese Company

1. Edwin O. Reischauer, *The Japanese* (Cambridge: Harvard University Press, 1977), p. 213.
2. Michael Berger, "Job-Hopping Suddenly Becomes the Rage in Japan," *San Francisco Chronicle* (March 16, 1990), p. C1.

Chapter 5

Bushido: Way of the Samarai—The Japanese as Competitors

1. Michael Porter, *The Competitive Advantage of Nations* (New York: Free Press, 1990); from "*Why Nations Triumph,*" book excerpt in *Fortune* (March 12, 1990), p. 95.
2. James C. Abegglen and George Stalk, Jr., *Kaisha, The Japanese Corporation* (New York: Basic Books, 1985), p. 214.

3. "Okamoto Seeks U.S Market Penetration," *Mainichi Daily News* (February 15, 1989).
4. Andrew Tanzer, "How Do You Shut the Darn Thing Off?," *Forbes* (November 13, 1989), pp. 38–40.
5. *Japan Economic Journal* (November 4, 1989), p. 4.
6. Sony Corporation 1989 Annual Report.
7. Tanzer, "How Do You Shut The Darn Thing Off?"
8. Mitsuhiro Takahashi, "Toshiba Forges New Image with Foreign Tie-ups," *Japan Economic Journal* (June 3, 1989), p. 22.

Chapter 6
The Japan Success Quotient: American Companies in Japan

1. "Successful Foreign Affiliated Enterprises in Japan," MITI (January 1990).
2. Japan Ministry of Finance; from "Japan 1990, An International Comparison," *Keizai Koho Center* (October 1989).
3. Robert C. Christopher, *Second to None: American Companies in Japan* (New York: Fawcett Columbine, 1986).
4. "Foreign Drug Companies Go It Alone," *Wall Street Journal* (September 9, 1988), p. 26.
5. "Foreign Companies Turning Up the Heat in Japan," *Japan Economic Journal* (September 30, 1989).
6. *Japan Economic Journal* (November 4, 1989), p. 6.
7. "Kentucky Fried Chicken (Japan)," Harvard Business School Case #9-387-043 (July 1987).
8. "US Automakers Rev Up Sales in Niche Areas," *Japan Economic Journal* (August 26, 1989).
9. "Land of the Rising Sun," *Electronic Engineering Times* (January 16, 1989); and "Saavy Strategy Helps Sun Shine in Japan," *Japan Economic Journal* (May 20, 1989), p. A4.
10. *High-Tech Marketing* (March 1986), pp. 14–21.
11. Gary Jacobson and John Hillkirk, *Xerox: American Samurai* (New York: Macmillan, 1986).
12. The Rival Japan Respects," *Business Week* (November 13, 1989), pp. 108–121.
13. "Rustbelt Renaissance," *Business Tokyo* (Summer 1989), pp. 54–55.
14. *Japan Economic Journal* (July 15, 1989), p. 4.
15. Jacobson and Hillkirk, *Xerox: American Samurai.*
16. *Japan Economic Journal* (September 9, 1989), p. 4.

17. "You Can Make Money in Japan," *Fortune* (February 12, 1990), pp. 85–92.
18. "Amway Leads the Way," *Business Tokyo* (November 1989), pp. 26–30.
19. *Japan Economic Journal* (February 10, 1990), p. 1.
20. Michael Whitener, "Pursuing the Pot of Gold," *Business Tokyo* (December 1989), pp. 44–45.

Chapter 8
Kick-Starting the Global Organization

1. "Footware that won't be booted," *Business Tokyo* (Summer 1989), p. 24.

Chapter 9
Defining the Japan Strategy

1. "Japan Business: Obstacles and Opportunities," United States-Japan Trade Study Group, prepared by McKinsey & Co. Inc., 1983.

Chapter 10
Growing the Japanese Business

1. Chie Nakane, *Japanese Society* (London: Weidenfeld & Nicolson, 1970).
2. *Business Tokyo* (December 1989).

Chapter 11
Becoming a World-Class Competitor

1. Michael E. Porter, *Competition in Global Industries* (Cambridge: Harvard Business School Press, 1986).

Chapter 12
Challenge and Opportunity: The Keys to Success in Japan

1. Japan Ministry of Finance; Nippon 1990, *JETRO* (October 1989).
2. Carla Rappaport, "Ready, Set, Sell—Japan Is Buying," *Fortune* (September 11, 1989), pp. 159–164.

Afterword: The America That Can Compete

1. *Wall Street Journal* (April 27, 1990).
2. Peter Drucker, *The New Realities* (New York: Harper & Row, 1989).

Bibliography

ABEGGLEN, JAMES C., and STALK, GEORGE, JR. *Kaisha, The Japanese Corporation.* New York: Basic Books, 1985.

BENEDICT, RUTH. *The Chrysanthemum and the Sword.* Tokyo: Charles E. Tuttle, 1976.

BURNSTEIN, DANIEL. *YEN, Japan's New Financial Empire and Its Threat to America.* New York: Simon & Schuster, 1988.

CHRISTOPHER, ROBERT C. *Second to None, American Companies in Japan.* New York: Fawcett Columbine, 1986.

DERTOUZUS, LESTER, SOLOW, and the MIT Commission on Industrial Productivity. *Made in America: Regaining the Production Edge.* Cambridge: MIT Press, 1989.

DOI, TAKEO. *The Anatomy of Dependence.* Tokyo: Kodansha International, 1977.

EMMOTT, WILLIAM. *The Sun Also Sets.* New York: Times Books, 1989.

HALBERSTAM, DAVID. *The Reckoning.* New York: William Morrow, 1986.

ISHIHARA, SHINTARO, and MORITA, AKIO. *The Japan That Can Say "No."* Tokyo: Kobunsha, 1989.

ISHINOMORI, SHOTARO. *Japan Inc., Introduction to Japanese Economics (The Comic Book).* Berkeley: University of California Press, 1988.

JACOBSON, GARY, and HILLKIRK, JOHN. *Xerox: American Samurai.* New York: Macmillan, 1986.

MCKINSEY & CO. *Japan Business: Obstacles and Opportunities.* Prepared by McKinsey & Co. for the United States-Japan Trade Study Group. Tokyo: President, Inc., 1983.

NAKANE, CHIE. *Japanese Society.* London: Weidenfeld & Nicolson, 1970.

OHMAE, KENICHI. *Triad Power: The Coming Shape of Global Competition.* New York: Free Press, 1985.

OHMAE, KENICHI. *Beyond National Borders: Reflections on Japan and the World.* Homewood, Ill.: Dow Jones-Irwin, 1987.

OHMAE, KENICHI. *The Borderless World: Power and Strategy in the Interlinked Economy.* New York: Harper Business, 1990.

PORTER, MICHAEL E. *Competition in Global Industries.* Cambridge: Harvard Business School Press, 1986.

PORTER, MICHAEL E. *The Competitive Advantage of Nations.* New York: Free Press, 1990.

PRESTOWITZ, CLYDE. *Trading Places.* New York: Basic Books, 1990.

REISCHAUER, EDWIN O. *The Japanese.* Cambridge: Belknap Press, 1977.

ROBERT, JOHN G. *Mitsui: Three Centuries of Japanese Business.* New York: Weatherhill, 1974.

SUN TZU. *The Art of War.* Translated by Samuel B. Griffith. New York: Oxford University Press, 1971.

TATSUNO, SHERIDAN M. *The Technopolis Strategy: Japan, High Technology, and the Control of the Twenty-first Century.* New York: Ballinger/Harper & Row, 1988.

TATSUNO, SHERIDAN M. *Created in Japan: From Imitators to World Class Competitors.* New York: Ballinger/Harper & Row, 1990.

TAYLOR, JARED. *Shadows of the Rising Sun, A Critical View of the "Japanese Miracle."* New York: William Morrow, 1983.

TSUNODA, TADANOBU. *The Japanese Brain: Uniqueness and Universality.* Tokyo: Taishukan Publishing Co., 1985.

WOLFEREN, KAREL VON. *The Enigma of Japanese Power.* New York: Alfred A. Knopf, Inc., 1989.

ZIMMERMAN, MARK. *How to Do Business with the Japanese.* New York: Random House, 1985.

About the Authors

JAMES C. MORGAN is chairman of the board and chief executive officer of Applied Materials, Inc., the world's largest independent manufacturer of semiconductor production systems. Mr. Morgan is a member of the National Advisory Committee on Semiconductors, which advises President Bush and Congress on a national strategy to strengthen competitiveness of the U.S. semiconductor industry. He is co-chairman, with Akio Morita, of the Japan-Western U.S. Association. He is a member of the World Business Council and past member of the Young Presidents' Organization. Mr. Morgan is a director emeritus of Semiconductor Equipment and Materials International (SEMI) and a past president. He earned a B.S.M.E. degree and an M.B.A. degree at Cornell University, Ithaca, New York.

JEFF MORGAN is president of RAD Technologies, Inc., based in Palo Alto, California, a developer and international distributor of Unix desktop software applications. Prior to founding RAD Technologies, Mr. Morgan worked in international sales and marketing of advanced computer and software technologies for Sun Microsystems' Intercontinental Operation, Hewlett-Packard Company, and Mitsui & Co., Ltd. in Tokyo, Japan.

Mr. Morgan is currently writing his second book, "Global Product Design," and is a guest lecturer and speaker on international marketing and business development strategy. He holds a B.S. degree from Cornell University and is fluent in Japanese.

Index